Pilgrims in This World

A LAY SPIRITUALITY

by

Virginia Sullivan Finn

paulist press ◆ *new york* ◆ *mahwah*

ACKNOWLEDGMENTS

The publisher is grateful to Duquesne University Press, Pittsburgh, PA, for per-
mission to use selected excerpts from *The Phenomenology of Feeling* by Stephen
Strasser. Copyright © 1977; Viking Penguin, a division of Penguin Books USA
Inc., for permission to reprint excerpts from the following works: *Poetics of Space*
by Gaston Bachelard. Copyright © 1958 by Presses Universitaires de France.
Translation © 1969 by The Orion Press, Inc., and *Poetics of Reverie* by Gaston
Bachelard. Copyright © 1960 by Presses Universitaires de France. Translation ©
by Grossman Publishers, Inc.

Library of Congress Cataloging-in-Publication Data

Finn, Virginia Sullivan.
    Pilgrims in this world: a lay spirituality/by Virginia Sullivan
Finn.
        p.   cm.
    Includes bibliographical references.
    ISBN 0-8091-3144-7
    1. Spirituality—United States.   2. Spirituality—Catholic Church.
3. Laity—Catholic Church.   4. Laity—United States.   5. Spiritual
formation—Catholic Church.   6. Catholic Church—United States—
Membership.   I. Title.
BX1407.S66F56   1990
284.4′82—dc20

                                                        89-78458
                                                        CIP

Published by Paulist Press
997 Macarthur Boulevard
Mahwah, New Jersey 07430

Printed and bound in the
United States of America

CONTENTS

Introduction   1

PART ONE

1. Migrating with Vatican II   7
2. Adult Identity   24
3. The Gift of Lay Spirituality   41
4. Formation   59

PART TWO

1. Formation Through Relationships: Parental Figures   77
2. Formation Through Relationship: Friendship   93
3. Spouse: Friend or Enemy?   109
4. Call and Callings   125

PART THREE

1. Generativity and Church   141
2. Generativity and Mission   160
3. Models for Lay Mission   175
4. Disposition for Mission   192

PART FOUR

1. Places: Flavor/Texture/Mores/Ownership   209
2. Place and Spirituality   225
3. The World-Dreaming Pilgrim and Prayer   242
4. Mission Through Lay Witness and Proclamation   258

Notes   277

Study Questions for Each Chapter   286

Bibliography   298

This book is dedicated in deep affection and gratitude to Tom, my father, whose formation was intentionally indirect; to Blanche, my mother, whose formation was intentionally direct;

and to the generation forming me today

Andrew
Renee
Nicole
Leslie
Jeffrey
Katherine
Pamela
Richard
Tierney
and Mark

Ordinary Time

You will not know how long
I have been in answering this,
Or why finding the right words
Was not the problem, though God knows
I have tried to put it down to that.
What you will recognize are the old
Excuses ripening too soon, like the
Tomatoes I picked this afternoon
Before writing to you. If they had
Their way, I would have spent
The rest of the day pureeing them.
Since then, three more days
Have stopped the flow of this.

In Ordinary Time, the clothes
I hang so carefully on the line
Are seldom dry by noon. After lunch,
The mailman comes too soon, or perhaps
I have no stamps. Then I say, "My clothes
Are still damp, so why not iron them?"
But no: this one time I will forget
What is on the line and beat the mailman
At his own game. I type your name
At the top of the page, but as I do,
The doorbell rings. It is the mailman,
Wanting postage due! I think ruefully
Of my letter to you, but now the wash
Is dry. What can I do but try again
When all my chores are done? In
Ordinary Time, will that day ever come?

If I knew what Feast I should be
Celebrating, I would invite you, too.
Until I do, I am folding you into every sheet
I put away. Today, this plain white one
Must do: before my ripe tomatoes become stew,
I stamp it, seal it, and send it to you.
                    Lucretia B. Yaghjian

INTRODUCTION

One weekend last fall I found myself basking in the sun on our tiny second-floor porch. Occasionally I glanced down to the back yard where Tierney and Mark were painting a canoe. Our two-family house sits near a river in western Massachusetts, and the canoe was a gift handed down by good friends who no longer had use for it. At one point I leaned over the railing and shouted, "We should think of a name for the canoe."

"We've already named it," our daughter Tierney shouted.

"What's its name?"

"The Big C!" Mark's voice boomed.

Against the midnight blue fresh paint I visualized THE BIG C. "What's the 'C' for?" I called down.

Mark rested his brush and gazed up at me. "Contemplation." His eyes twinkled as he smiled.

Not quite knowing what to reply, I leaned back into the sun, remembering why Tierney and Mark had come from Manhattan to visit. Yesterday we had engaged in our first dialogue about the impending marriage of the two now painting the canoe. In the middle of an endless discussion of possible reception sites, my husband and I were assured by the two who are striving for careers in modern day media that they were also striving to be contemplative. The gift they identified as being handed down from our generation to theirs, before they publicly pledged the bonding of their hearts, was the gift of contemplation.

It's a new church. A few decades ago those who engaged in contemplation resided within cloisters.

The reader of this book is invited to share my attempt to contemplate the lay Christians of the Catholic Church. The lens we shall look through is a spiritual foundation for mission and formation for lay adults. The private world of friendship and family and the public world of work and of civic and social justice involvement are at the hub of the book. (Particular kinds of spiritualities and educative programs in scripture and theology are significant in formation for mission but beyond the scope of this book.)

1

People stay in the church or leave the church today for a variety of reasons. For thirty years George and Virginia, and most other lay Catholics, stayed in because they feared burning in hell and hoped for the glories of heaven. In those days my copy of *The Catholic Layman's Book of Etiquette* got regular use. As a young adult in the church, I struggled with directives like this:

> All who meet a bishop . . . may kiss the episcopal ring (worn on the right hand). The proper practice is as follows: when meeting the ordinary . . . within one's own diocese, one genuflects, touching the *left* knee to the ground while kissing the episcopal ring. While the left-knee genuflection is by custom and formal acceptance the proper manner for this salutation, it is practical for one to touch the *right* knee to the floor, lest one feel awkward and uneasy because of being off-balance.[1]

Before Vatican Council II I worried more about proper rubrics than peace on earth or the ecological survival of the planet. I saw myself as "an ordinary layman." I never gave a thought to the possible difference between God and church, faith and religion, ministry and mission. Ministry and mission were what priests and nuns did with their state in life and had little to do with what Virginia and George might do with theirs.

Mission and Ministry

This book is more about mission than ministry. In a way it steps outside the current debate being waged about when, where, and how lay Catholic adults exercise ministry. I take lay ministry dilemmas and concerns seriously. All ministry is a serious endeavor, but it is an endeavor that ultimately serves the mission of the church in the world. Ministry, whether accomplished by priests, sisters, bishops, brothers, or laity, is intended to *catalyze mission.*

Even as we worry about how to keep the vitality of the local church alive, it is essential to keep mission in the forefront. Ministry evokes connotations of service that fit the helping professions in which many lay adults engage as their life-work. Within other occupations it is not always as easy to identify ministerial dimensions. Rather than forcing the issue and skewing ministry into innovative forms, for the present I prefer to emphasize mission. A mission stance can be adopted regardless of setting.

Mission and World

Integral to the word *mission* is *world,* the world of marketplace, government, health care, educational systems, global relations, agriculture, the military, the arts, the media. Here is the primary setting for the church's mission thrust. This is not to deny that the church also needs mission efforts internally. Nor is it meant to deny that the church is in this world, both receiving the benefits and risking the temptations inherent in that placement. The church has in many ways, however, established its own *particular culture* within the world. The setting for this book is the culture most lay adults encounter daily during almost all the days and hours of any given week—the culture of modernity, of secularity, of collaboration with other adults of different beliefs and no belief. *World* has, in a sense, attached itself to lay believers as their primary setting, and there is little to be done about that even if we wanted to do something about it.

But should we want it otherwise? Should we perceive *world* as problem (and laity also as problem because of the close affiliation between lay and world)? *God so loved the world,* states the gospel of John; there should be no shame in imitating God, or in admitting that this setting is a factor *in formation as well as a place for mission.*

With Vatican II came a valorization of the world, calling for deeper reflection on the influence of our relationship to place—local and global place. When we discover how we are *spiritually related to the place we call world,* we begin to build the foundation needed for mission. My bias is that the church is called to be about God, God's people and God's good earth, bonded together.

Our formation for mission placements in this setting called world has emerged from life in family and experiences in friendship, as well as from years of participation in church and schools, the common predictors for effectiveness and for Christian witness in the world. In other words, the private realm has formed us for the public realm. The intimacy of the personal world of family and friendship and the challenge of the public world, as well as the ways in which they are linked, are considered in this book. Consequently, the text combines stories of life experience with reflective insights. It is my contention that innumerable lay adults experience within many facets of their life the integration of intimacy (love), responsibility and authority; if, when they come to the experience of church, they experience authority severed from caring, they become alienated.

At times the term commonwealth of God is found in the text to highlight the sense that the earth, as a place of peace, justice, love and harmony, comes into being through a partnership between God and women and men of good will. The sense that the kingdom or reign of God on earth is inclusive of the peoples of this earth is implied in commonwealth.

Neglect of the People Named Lay

The Notre Dame Study on Parish Life found that the lay believers who participated in their survey of thirty-six sample parishes (all non-Hispanic) defined the "true Catholic" not by faith, liturgical practice or mission, but in sexual terms:

> . . . in the perceptions of the laity, a true Catholic is defined by a range of sexual practices. In particular, a true Catholic ought not have had or supported abortion, or practiced homosexuality.[2]

Perhaps one reason for the superficial and narrow lay definition of "the true Catholic" found in the study is the scandalous lack of serious treatment dedicated to lay identity in theology, spirituality, and mission—within the church and at all levels of the church.

During the year of the Synod on the Laity, I suggested an idea for an article on the laity to a Catholic journal. The reply I received noted that the editorial board would *yawn* at the idea of an article on the laity. We have come, it seems, to tolerate with no difficulty at all a vision of church uncluttered by the people in the pews and the earthly realities of their everyday lives. We may even feel that "layness" is an impediment to mission. But without attention to the "whole people of the church" the impact of Catholic mission efforts may be more minimal than our idealistic rhetoric implies.

David O'Brien's comments are apt:

> Today it is common to avoid the word laity, on the argument that priests, religious and laity should first of all emphasize their common baptism, but almost always this is at the expense of the *lay part of lay life* and ends with an image of Christian community as detached from the messy "web" of lay life. . . . In the next decade the promise of Catholic social teaching, presented so powerfully in the recent pastoral letters, will be realized, and the American church will make a substantive contribution to the public debate about policy only if it takes with authentic seriousness the problems and possibilities of its middle class lay people.[3]

A New Model of Church

We seem to be moving toward a new, paradoxical model of church, one that may become increasingly familiar in the future. This model is a strange amalgam of populism and authoritarianism. As the shortage of priests intensifies, more and more groups of *like-minded lay people* may drift into a populistic mode, distancing themselves from leadership structures characterized by authoritarianism. This is an understandable response to clerical domination, one with which I am in sympathy. But with this trend, the church in the United States may also lose a sense *of its unity in diversity.* The church may generate less new life and leadership within the culture than earlier in the post-conciliar age when the church was less bifurcated.

I mention this at the beginning because the encouragement found in this book for bringing into the church the stories of our own lay religious experiences and mission efforts may be interpreted as populism. It is important for me to say that I believe that the best framework within the local church for these lay narratives is ministerial leadership that is diversified, collaborative, professionally educated and spiritually formed.

In order to include narratives of lay life and mission in the text, I began three years ago to search for stories in diocesan newspapers and Catholic magazines. With the exception of magazines like *Commonweal, Salt* and *U.S. Catholic,* and efforts like The Christophers, what I needed was seldom found in Catholic print media. The best source for feature stories on lay adults turned out to be the obituaries of local secular papers. Either an unusual number of remarkable lay Catholics have died in Boston within the last few years or the stories of Catholic lay women and lay men are valued more *beyond* the church than within it. My hope and dream is that these stories will someday be welcomed *within the church* and welcomed before the lay believers who live these lives are ready for burial!

During this past decade it has been my privilege to meet lay women and men in many settings throughout the United States. Their faith and perseverance keep my faith and perseverance alive. Many of them combine family and mission as has been my experience. That tone is reflected in this book.

I am also grateful to the many, many vowed religious who have been my companions and colleagues over the past twenty-five years. I wish to mention three gifts from vowed religious life that are a treasure to me, gifts that provide an irreplaceable contribution to the whole church:

    . . . the gift of understanding and valuing spirituality;

    . . . the gift of the idea of formation;

    . . . the gift of living life with a mission focus.

Any formation process that denies individual personal identity and interior freedom is destructive, but I have come to respect the *concept* of formation because I believe that *formation inevitably happens* to all of us.

Of the many lay friends and readers who have offered support I must, in particular, mention two who have stood by throughout the process of my writing this book, always ready to lift my spirits and give a helping hand—Theresa Boucher of the Weston School of Theology and Kathy Northrop of the National Association for Lay Ministry. They deserve heartfelt thanks, as do Liza Burr and Larry Boadt for their patient editorial assistance.

Lastly, I must acknowledge the depth of my love and gratitude for the one who, day and night, walked the extra mile to enable the birth of this book—my husband George. Without his faith in God and in me, there would be no book from me and far less faith within me.

PART ONE

1

MIGRATING WITH VATICAN II

Uprooting

Initially it's hard to find a good word to say about transplanting perennials. Nails and hands become encrusted with soil, knees get sore, and there's not much to show for it once the bulbs are in their new place. Last fall, for the first time, I gave it a try. The directions in the gardening book made it sound less simple than I thought it would be. There was the matter, of course, of digging up the iris and peony plants crowded by the side of the house. But there was as well the need to wash off each bulb and cut the bulbs that were bunched together in a root mass. On the first go-round I dug up a dozen irises and then found, after the washing and cutting, that I had thirty-five bulbs to carry, along with a watering can, to a corner in the back yard.

When I started the project I did not anticipate excavating thirty-five holes to house the transplanted bulbs. Toward the end of the task, feeling fatigued, I fell back onto the grass and gazed up at billowy clouds racing across a sterling sky. It was then that I had a word with God about the fecundity hidden under the ground, "You never do things halfway, do you?" I asked rhetorically.

A character in *Flight of Cranes,* contemplating refugees after World War II, exclaims, "All these uprooted people!" One of the refugees replies, "In nature everything meant to flourish has to be transplanted." Her irony comes to mind when I contemplate the people of the church and the uprooting of Vatican II.

To be sure my peony and iris plants will eventually flourish. But for a season after being transplanted they may seem to wither, to look haunted by dread. They will need special attention until the roots discover that there is as much nourishment in the new soil as in the old. Human beings, like uprooted plants, discover that every "upsetting or uprooting experience brings about a partial regression of identity." Transplanting endangers "the resiliency of maintaining essential patterns in the process of change."[1]

Vatican II was an uprooting event. Vatican II was an uprooting experience for the individual believer and for the universal body of the church. How could it be otherwise? Not to acknowledge the irony in Vatican II is naive at best or cruel at worst. The wise ones in the midst of this uprooting have held back judgments and have tried to understand the meaning of the interior uprootings experienced by the church, the pilgrim people of God. Reflecting on these uprootings can lead to better approaches toward formation for mission, approaches with a foundation based on the reality of lay life. Through this process we may learn how to "bring . . . a well-integrated self-image and group identity"[2] to the mission enterprise. In other words, we may learn how to develop the needed spiritual foundation for mission.

After the uprooting of a plant, wilting is often followed by a new spurt of growth and a stronger plant if the soil is right, and if attention and care, water and fertilizer, are generous. Was this generosity what the grassroots laity, uprooted by Vatican II, experienced in the years following Vatican II? The Synod on the Laity provided an opportunity to reflect on this question, on the post-conciliar journey of the laity, *our uprooting, our migrations.* My hope was that the synod would reveal the fecundity under the ground in the pre-conciliar church, the fecundity that through the transplanting process has begun to flourish above the ground in the last decade and a half, *the fecundity that is the lay people of the church.*

Because discussion about the Synod on the Laity started when we in the United States were celebrating the refurbished Statue of Liberty, I was reminded of others who have migrated and how they handled their uprooting.

For those of us who are cradle citizens of the United States, knowing "who I am" is often reinforced by knowing I am North American. The dilemma of those new to our land yesterday may seldom come to mind. Ancestors who enabled us to *be* cradle citizens may seem part of ancient history. Nonetheless, the transforming journey of being born in one culture and being transplanted to another has a lesson pertinent to Catholic Christians today.

Uprooted Ones

When Mauro Rio came to this country from Sicily he brought in his trunk a hand-painted glass hurricane lamp, a pearl-inlaid mandolin, and a triptych picture of three Italian leaders—Garibaldi, Cavour, and Vittorio Emmanuel II. Sixty-five years later these mementos were still displayed in the spare room of the apartment he shared with his wife Angela. Earlier in the century they may have helped Mr. Rio hold onto a sense of *personal* identity while his *national* identity was being shaped anew.[3]

Some immigrants came in the nineteenth century and some come to our shores today with little more than their names to help them remember who they are, but in 1923 one young Irish woman lacked even that assurance. At Ellis Island an immigration official couldn't pronounce Bridget McGeoghegan's last name so he changed it to Bridget McGaffigan. Later,

> Her aunts and cousins who had preceded her to this country persuaded her that the name Bridget was simply too old-fashioned to use in America, and they talked her into changing her first name to Bertha.[4]

In 1924 she married. Within one year Bridget McGeoghegan became Bridget McGaffigan who became Bertha McGaffigan who became Bertha Devlin.

Over a decade ago I helped two recent immigrants from the Soviet Union improve their facility with English. One evening when Irena and Natasha arrived for their tutoring session, Natasha presented me with a blank envelope and said, "How do I write my name? What do I put before Natasha?"

Carefully, I explained the titles Miss, Mrs., and Ms., emphasizing that Ms. was my preference. I pointed out how it avoided discriminating between married and single women.

Natasha frowned. "No! I will never be Ms."

Thinking she did not understand, I labored once more for

clarity regarding the titles. But Natasha broke in before I could finish. "No! I don't want Ms. on my name! All my life I was Comrade this and Comrade that and my husband was Comrade this and Comrade that. It made no difference what you did with your life, you were never more or less than Comrade."

Irena picked up the theme, saying, "Here in the United States women have three choices for their titles and men none."

"Yes!" exclaimed Natasha. "And I chose Mrs. What about you, Irena?"

Irena closed her eyes momentarily then smiled a bit smugly. "I don't . . . I don't know yet. To really choose you have to take time to decide, Natasha."

Vatican II Uprooting

Many of us have lived for twenty-five years in the new place called Vatican II. By now, some of us realize we have had sufficient time to decide how we name that event. We are now struggling with how, through that event and the process that followed, we are now naming *ourselves.* Women in the church are doing that with a vibrancy not seen or felt in the church before. Both women and men are also asking, "What does it mean to be an American Catholic?"

"What does priest mean now?" is being asked by lay people and by priests alike. At the same time, we are struggling with what *lay* as a designation for most of us means. One reason for this concern with identity is that people don't experience change without reacting interiorly whether or not they reveal those reactions to themselves or to others.

All of us are members of a church that is rooted in traditions of the past, one that is struggling with uprooting in the present, and one that is rooted in a world characterized by the phenomena of enormous change during the same time span that the church was changing. Some of that secular change related to naming. Minority groups began in the 1960s to name themselves with an integrity and pride non-existent when they took their naming from what others called them.

Some lay people experienced these church and secular changes within settings that were traditional, with leadership that minimized the value of Vatican II and stuck to traditional "naming." Other lay people experienced these changes within settings where leadership maximized the value of the changes and neglected those who felt resistant toward the changes or who were struggling to internalize them.

As a communal people, we have a responsibility, individually and corporately, to understand the effect of these uprootings on ourselves as persons of faith and their effect on our community of faith. Digging into what we honestly experienced can create firm footing, what gives leverage for stepping into the future.

Some lay believers, like some immigrants to the United States, seem able to negotiate their voyage in the present church and culture only by bringing along rituals unchanged from the past, just as Mauro Rio brought mementos from his heritage to his new land. These rituals and these alone confer an identity. For example, only what is identical with what has been—the Latin mass or hierarchical authority—tells me that I am still a Catholic believer.

Migratory Catholics

At the other end of the spectrum are the highly mobile lay believers who may be kin to Bridget/Bertha McGeoghegan/McGaffigan/Devlin. How mobile lay Catholics have experienced being known and named was nuanced in remarkably different ways as they, in serial fashion, experienced various church settings. For example, when Dick and Barbara Summers left their parish in Pennsylvania the altar was turned around, but folk music was still frowned upon, the nuns who taught their children still wore veils and modified habits, and the idea of a parish council had been mentioned but never implemented.

A job transfer brought the Summers family to the midwest. At first Dick and Barbara found it startling to hear themselves calling the parish priests Fr. Mike and Fr. Al. They felt strange finding themselves at a cookout in the back yard of the convent. Shortly before Easter, a fellow engineer asked Dick to help him construct a rainbow over the indoor entrance to the church to highlight a biblical passage for the vigil. Barbara found more personal support and welcome in the women's group than she had experienced in a sodality back home. The vitality Dick and Barbara soon felt in their faith surprised them. As Dick put it, "God and neighbor are so *real* to us these days."

After six years Dick was transferred back to Pennsylvania. The weekend Dick and Barbara went back to look for a house in their old neighborhood, they attended both the nine o'clock and twelve o'clock Mass in their former parish. Sunday night in the motel, Barbara cried and Dick stared stone-faced at the wall. Dick and Barbara had discovered *an adult identity* in the midwest; on their return they would be told to be children again.

More than any other group within the church, according to the Office of Evangelization, highly mobile lay Catholics have been the ones to walk away from the church, and often they have walked away feeling mauled, victims within a church that was just beginning to be mobile itself.

Natives in one culture, many of us boarded the vessel called Vatican II and found ourselves being transported to a new church culture where our efforts to reshape our identities was akin to the immigrants' struggle mentioned at the start of the book. One can imagine what Mauro Rio would have gone through had he been forced to return to live in his homeland of Sicily, Bertha Devlin to Ireland, Natasha and Irena to the Soviet Union. An analogous "return to the homeland" is what happens to innumerable post-conciliar Catholics when they migrate from place to place or when a progressive pastor in their parish or bishop in their diocese is replaced by a "traditionalist."

The story about Bridget and the story about Natasha reveal the challenge to identity that "being named" poses. These "naming" dynamics are now relevant for post-conciliar lay Catholics who are taking a closer look at what previously had been taken for granted —Catholic identity, lay identity.

How Do I Know Who I Am?

A friend who moved to an area with very few Catholics once wrote to me saying, "Imagine the church vanishing tomorrow. How would you keep your faith alive? That's what I'm facing."

Because I have always lived in regions where Catholics are the majority, I have taken for granted my religious identity. On the other hand, if I, like millions of Catholics worldwide, lived in a region where Catholics are a perceptible minority, I might have made the effort to figure out what about me is my Catholic identity. Answers to these questions are nuanced differently in Appalachia where only 3.5% of church members are Catholic than on the Gulf Coast where 82.6% of the people belong to a church and 58.4% of these church members are Catholic.[5] Then again I might understand my religious identity quite differently were I a Catholic in China where for years my only church was the house church.

On the other hand, there is no doubt that within the Catholic Church one is *named* even if one is *known* only by a small circle within one's local community, whether that be a house church or a cathedral. For example, if she wears a veil, is the principal of a parochial school, and lives with six other women in a house next door to a rectory, ten out of ten Catholics would say that she's a sister. And if he's in the pulpit preaching, at the bingo game greeting folks, and at the hospital visiting patients, most Catholics would name him a priest. Here and there across the country, one out of ten might say he's a deacon or a non-ordained pastoral administrator. They might be right. The naming process in the church also appears to be in transit. This year I've encountered a young woman whose stepfather was a former priest and a priest whose marriage, earlier in his life, had been annulled. In other words, the meanings beneath some of the namings are not as exact as they used to be.

At times one gets the idea that this name-changing process might ignite a civil war. For example, some seem ready to do battle over the audacity of those who call themselves lay ministers; ministry, they claim, is a word that should be reserved for priests.

What we still do know is that he's not likely to be named monsignor if he has three sons and two daughters, and she's not likely to be called sister if she has two sons and three daughters. He and she are named lay. Lay is the designation of identity for ninety-eight percent of the people of the church. Unfortunately, its definition, as commonly used, is often characterized by what one is not.[6]

One certainty at the present moment is that we are still named, and our name is lay. Some of us were born into one church and

have experienced twenty-five years of bringing into being a renewed church from that church. Others of us, now young adults,
were born into a church that had *already* changed; some of us
wonder what the fuss is all about. Nonetheless, we are still called
lay. Without consulting us, it might be better not to call us anything
else until we explore what lay signifies.

"Lay": Is it a valid designation? Spiritually? Communally? In
regard to ministry? To mission?

It is an adult designation. We never refer to the lay children of
the church. It does not come with baptism. Sacramentally we are
not lay. It is an ecclesiastical designation utilized before and after
the council.

Implementing Vatican II

Variations in how lay adults perceive themselves as part of the
pilgrim people of God have emerged in recent years because the
application of Vatican II was extremely uneven. In some settings
every effort seemed to be made to insure that fidelity to the council
would evoke a vibrant new life of faith for the people in that setting.
In other parish and diocesan settings a "wait and see" attitude still
prevails.

Why was there such uneven handling of such a significant
church event? In spite of being a universal church with a strong bias
toward centralized authority, enfleshing the life of Vatican II on the
local level was hierarchical yet decentralized. Implementation was
left up to the bishop responsible for each diocese, the *ordinary* of
the diocese. The ordinaries of the two dioceses in which I experienced Vatican II took quite different paths toward implementation.

In the first diocese the bishop, Ernest Primeau, seemed to
stand back and get a contemplative sense of the central thrust of the
council—collegiality, updating and mission in the world. That determined his stance for revealing the import of the council to the
diocese. The year of sermons preached on all aspects of the council,
particularly those relevant to the lay people and their mission; the
parish lecture series on the documents; the inter-parish workshops
and subsequent committees, each an outreach to the ecumenical

and civic community; the diocesan synod—all these together provided a context for the more sensitive liturgical changes and provided a rationale for these changes. In the medium-sized city surrounded by farm country where I met the council first-hand, exchanging the kiss of peace at mass went hand in hand with exchanging a new and initial gesture of friendship and reconciliation with our Protestant and Jewish neighbors which went hand in hand with extending concern to those who were in particular need. I have no memory of a discussion with folks there about whether we *liked* the kiss of peace. The conciliar experience was not a mechanism with innumerable separate components to pick apart subjectively; Vatican II was a new, or renewed, way of doing faith, of being God's people, of living church. For this I credit the wisdom of the ordinary whose careful implementation integrated insights from the documents into a process that revealed the *meaning* integral to this universal church event.

In the diocese to which we moved five years after the start of the council, Vatican II was a parish happening. The same change might be implemented in all the parishes on a particular Sunday but the lay people's expectations were geared only to their own parish because that was the initial message delivered to the diocese by the way things were done. More often than not, the Achilles heel of isolated implementation was that each change seemed to be introduced *as a separate entity,* unconnected to a greater theological and ecclesial concept of depth and meaning.

The effects of these contrasts in implementation haunt us to this day. The initial year of discovery about the council was an unrepeatable opportunity linked to the power of first impressions. Twenty-five years later, thousands of grassroots lay Catholics still think that Vatican II was mostly about liturgical changes. They have yet to internalize that the primary significance of Vatican II was updating, collegiality and mission in the world. They may have been *told* the latter, at the start or in later years, but they *experienced the liturgical changes without the opportunity to experience simultaneously collegiality and mission* because no mechanisms were established for the latter. Lacking the special attention that transplanting demands, many Catholics became confused and frustrated by the uprooting.

Reaping what is sown, the church in the United States became a church of ministries, not mission, because innumerable lay people took their cues from what they were initially taught experientially: church and liturgy are what Vatican II renewal is all about.[7]

For a time, regardless of setting, we all had fascinating stories to tell about our church, but before long the "why can't we here at St. Joseph's?" and the "why do they let the people in the next diocese?" questions began to be raised. After a time some lay Catholics began to feel resentful or bitter about the discrepancies. The stories no longer seemed humorous. They began to seem unjust.

That was a consciousness-raising moment for many lay Catholics who had never before perceived so acutely their powerlessness. What the gathered bishops had said in Rome they had said to one another. What was allowed in the parish back home came to depend not so much on what the gathered bishops had said to one another, but on what the bishop who was ordinary of that diocese had *said to himself*—then to his pastors and the people back home.

Individuating the Process of Change

If the essence of church is God and God's people, then uprooting in the church affects how God's people feel about God and about themselves. What kind of attention was given to these crucial elements in implementing Vatican II?

Vatican II introduced the need for individuation and personalism within the church.

According to the conciliar documents, the laity were called to engage in the church's mission in the world. Each believer was to hearken to his or her unique call from God; each adult voice in the church was now to be heard. The contrast between how this need was handled in the seminary setting for vowed religious where I was a faculty member in the mid-1960s and how it was handled in a typical parish within a diocese is striking. For example, each seminarian had a spiritual director. The hour of direction was an opportunity for this vowed religious to reflect on how the conciliar changes affected his relationship with God. Were the changes helping his intimacy with God or were they evoking troublesome confusion? Spiritual direction, a means for the personal appropriation and integration of faith within a swift and tumultuous transition, helped the seminarians *to name who they were before God.*

This process of individuating within community insured that the conciliar changes were no mere gloss painted over old habits and attitudes. Habits and attitudes were challenged in a personal way. The fruit of this was a conversion of faith identity. At the seminary a church event that took place thousands of distant miles away became an event that engaged each seminarian and priest in a personal way, helping him to discern his identity and trace his conversion process.

What about the lay person kneeling in the pew? Using the same lens we see a very different picture. Few parish lay women and lay men engaged in a personalized or individuating process regarding Vatican II. I know none who received a weekly hour of close attention to how his or her faith in God was being influenced by renewal. From friends and relatives in other parishes and dioceses, lay adults were hearing differing versions of Vatican II and wondering whether the version going on in their own parish was the authentic version. Because the changes and the personal faith of lay adults were seldom given significant pastoral attention in the setting of the parish, *integration of faith and self* often did not take place within the lay believer. This unfortunate situation was compounded by the fact that the "what" and the "how" of a change were often emphasized more than the "why." Because the changes and the *meaning* of the changes were not given equal treatment in the setting of parish, *integration of faith and post-conciliar church* often did not take place within the lay believer. In spite of the uprooting, his or her identity remained static.

On the other hand, some lay persons began to sense a contradiction between the message and the system that proclaimed the message. They began to sense that living out Vatican II renewal meant moving from being "a regulated people" to becoming "a participating and personalized people." And they searched for ways to make this a reality.

Conversion of Identity

A decade after the council, some lay adults began to take advantage of new, post-conciliar movements or groups. Through this process they experienced freedom in expressing themselves and trust among the persons with whom they shared. The spirit of the council more than the letter of the conciliar documents was "owned" through an experiential process that was collegial, communal, collaborative.

According to George Wilson, S.J., " 'Process' is just a word for what a group is going through or for the way members are going about it. . . . Processes that are insensitive to the rights and responsibilities of human personhood are destructive. But that is not because they are processes, it is because they are poorly chosen processes."[8]

The processes that developed within the following momentums were chosen processes, ones that meshed with the dignity and needs of an emerging adult laity. These processes, communal yet individuating, attracted many lay adherents.

Associations, separate from the parish assembly, began to flourish: cursillo, marriage encounter, charismatic renewal, nonterritorial parishes. These alternate lay communities gave more leeway to mutuality between men and women and to lay governance and participation. In addition, the focus within the association was on issues relevant to the present-day lives and faith of the people involved.

National momentums that emerged inserted an American flavor to life within the church. Call to Action, the bishops' celebration of the nation's bicentennial, encouraged lay people from some parishes to speak through town meetings and evoked a populist flavor when delegates gathered in Detroit in 1976 for the national convocation. Conferences sponsored by the National Conference of Catholic Bishops' Committee on the Laity enabled lay leaders to share their wealth of experience in the church and in the secular world.[9] *Called and Gifted* in 1980 affirmed lay participation in ministries and lay voice within the church.

Some North American lay believers assumed a stance that critiqued civic life. Affiliating with ad hoc, often ecumenical, organizations, they put their shoulders to the wheel of the civil rights movement, boycotts to aid migrant workers, resistance to the Vietnam War, and involvement in the women's movement. Through these *signs of the times momentums,* lay adults began to perceive that their evolving Catholic identity mandated a social justice mission dynamic.

Within some parishes, *small support groups* emerged. Lay adults found themselves able, within the parish setting, to articulate their own life experience without fearing judgment, significant particularly for those who had felt marginalized—the divorced, separated, widowed, and young adult. Within bereavement groups, those suffering grief ministered to one another. The *horizontal* dynamism of these small support groups, and subsequent ones like RENEW and R.C.I.A., enabled a new dignity and a closer convergence between "who I am" and my identity as a Catholic Christian. For innumerable lay Catholics "small group" spelled out the collegiality dynamic mandated at Vatican II as well as the personalization and individuation inherent in the spirit of some of the documents. At first suspect, the dynamic of "small group" proved to be prophetic and was affirmed at the 1987 Synod on the Laity.

Within these communal momentums, the care and concern of peers substituted for pastoral and spiritual attention from church leaders, providing a catalyst for *a conversion of identity.* Engagement in a new, participatory process for doing church enabled participants to know and name themselves as *individuated adult believers.* Most lay Catholics did not travel this path beyond parish or within a parish support group, but the modeling of those who did cannot be underestimated, nor can its challenge to pastors and other lay believers be overlooked.

No longer sheep among an undifferentiated flock, within associations and movements, within social justice momentums, within dynamic small group clusters in parishes, lay women and lay men did not wait to be freed and to be nurtured. In their new venture, their personal identity was enhanced, and their spiritual identity was not only informed, it was enlarged and enriched. By seeking their own path to freedom and by nurturing one another (stimulated by the risk of going beyond the known and acceptable) they discovered a sense of mission. Others may have named them rebellious but God seemed to be naming them disciples and apostles on mission. On this mission, some heard the voice of God speak with vigor. Through this, they experienced a conversion in how they perceived themselves in relation to God and in how they experienced that identity.

The community or movement or cause to which they dedicated themselves might die out, but the conversion of their identity, the freedom and nurturance they had discovered, would bear lasting fruit. Uprooted, transplanted into new soil, they now flourished. The emerging problem would be how to sustain the conversion and enable it to flourish in the mainstream of a church that was still experiencing haphazard post-conciliar renewal. But these believers had overcome the demon that must be defeated in order for conversion to adulthood in faith to occur—*the demon of dependency.*

In other settings, however, laity were still being treated as the lowest caste in a system based on aristocracy; lay adults, women and men, were still encouraged to be permission-seeking children rather than mature adults.

As the identities of others change, one's own identity is sometimes changed. This happens frequently in families. The identities of children change as they become adolescents. The identities of parents change as their offspring become adult. Bishops, diocesan priests, and vowed religious who truly wanted lay Catholics to be adults in the church made the necessary interior shifts that made room for lay adults in their vision of the church. Because so many have done that, there is hope for a vibrant church in the future. Looking to God and to one another for support and strength evokes a collaborative, communal intimacy that affirms the Christian adulthood of all. But, even as the church turned a corner with Vatican II, many lay people continued to identify themselves in ways that evoked undervaluation, a dynamic that sustained a sense of feeling owned yet feeling a sense of failure at living up to the expectations of those who did the owning.

The Call

The uprooting that was Vatican II taught some of us, however, that the new life of faith invited by Vatican II did not dovetail with this kind of dependency. As Bishop Raymond Lucker put it in addressing the bishops gathered at Collegeville in the summer of 1986:

> By our very baptism and confirmation every single member of the church is called to share in the life and mission of the church. . . . What is the teaching of the Vatican Council about

the vocation of the laity? It is that all are called. All are called to share in the life and mission of the church. All are called by their baptism and confirmation. All are called by the Lord himself. All are called to holiness. All are called within the web of their existence. All are called as instruments of God "to renew the face of the earth."[10]

"All" could no longer be just ordinary anybodies named and known by others as laity. A generic label would not renew the face of the earth, nor would a people caught in dependency renew the face of the earth. The call received in baptism and confirmation is enfleshed by those who are adults in the church, and Christian adulthood means naming and knowing one's identity, not assuming it "second-hand." To fulfill the mandate of Vatican II and answer the call to mission means affirming as equal the spiritual worth of every member of the church. Hope for the future does not lie in a particular movement or theology, nor in the development of a good parish or a good prayer style. Hope for the future of the church is in the mature adulthood of its people.

The days of hiding in a Catholic subculture are over. In the aftermath of the council all Catholics—hierarchy, clergy, vowed religious and lay people—experienced a heightened sense of *church* identity. But when the novelty of the changes began to ebb; when people began to ask "what's it all for?"; when women began to sense more meaning and transformation within women's consciousness-raising groups than from the church; when counseling provided more self-understanding than parish involvement; when we acknowledged that few of us knew how to activate mission in modern, pluralistic, first world societies—the time had come to face the facts. Regardless of naming, an entirely new *identity* for the people of the church became an absolute necessity if the central call of Vatican II—updating, collegiality and mission—was to flourish in the Roman Catholic Church. A decade or two after the council some believers realized that what was put on paper at the council eventually evoked a profound spiritual question: Would the church, both as institution and as community, let God be God, free to transform an adult people, to be ahead of them moving them forward on the mission of renewing the face of the earth?

Like Mauro Rio and Bertha Devlin, we second and third generation descendants of immigrants embarked by boat to a distant and unknown land. The younger ones among us know of the "old country" through the stories of their parents and grandparents or through the imposition of pre-conciliar styles within their local parish or diocese. All of us, in one way or another, have recapitulated the journey of our ancestors. We have done this within the hold and on the decks of the church that these ancestors revered and obeyed. We have emigrated from a land that was secure and safe in its familiarity and uniformity. Through our faith in God we have survived the storms at sea that came with the crossing. Many of us, however, are still in the vessel that brought us to where we are supposed to disembark: *mission in the terrifying, marvelously diverse cultures of our country and our world.*

We are lighter than when we shipped away from familiar shores. Many of us have left behind artifacts of an ancient culture —scapulars and novena booklets; fish on every Friday and mass on all first Fridays; days of obligation and obligatory penance; fear of pregnancy and fear of hell; blind obedience and silent voices; invisible psychic hair shirts and visible hats on more than half the congregation. It took time to loosen ourselves from what no longer, others told us, had religious meaning for us—though in truth it felt naked to be Catholic without the rigorous discipline many of us felt was the only garment one could wear if one were Catholic.

Some of us stand naked on the deck of the vessel that has sailed straight toward the horizon of reality rather than toward the clouds before the pearly gates of heaven. Placed on a vessel we did not choose, we were never told how to navigate the voyage. Some of us are stocky, some shapely, some redheads, some bald. What we share in common is our nakedness. Some of us whisper to one another that we need clothes to walk down the ramp and set our feet on mission land. Others of us prefer to stay on board, within the security of the vessel that brought us to this shore. A few of us, like Indian scouts, search for the return of those who found clothes, who disembarked, who are doing mission. They will come back and tell us how to do it. If they don't, we may slip away to other shores with other names besides mission. One thing we do know— and no one contradicts us when we say it: prying the barnacles off the side of the vessel does not by itself enable passengers to go forward to a future called mission.

But many of us are beginning to hear, with its transforming power, the voice of God through the web of our own lives. And we hear it regardless of whether the church moves right, left or center. To sense the direction of that voice we know that we need to continue to discover who we are as adult persons of faith and as a people of faith, today, in order to face tomorrow. It is this discovery that will clothe us and enable us to step forward and be the God-intended mission we are all called to be.

2

ADULT IDENTITY

Three years ago, on a visit with us over a long weekend, our just-turned-three granddaughter Nicole initiated breakfast by saying, "You already did it, Gran."

"Did what?" I replied.

"Growed up!" Then came a long sigh followed by, "I didn't do it yet."

My temptation was to say, "You're right, kid. It ain't easy."

Savoring her little folk wisdom later in the day, it dawned on me that I really hadn't done what she said I did—growed up—that I probably would never fully grow up, that, although adult, I would keep moving and growing and changing until that day when my earthly existence is no more. Over and over I would be called *to image my life and myself anew.*

The challenging migration to adulthood, as well as the ongoing task of imaging oneself anew, is part of every human person's journey. This migration and reimaging is enabled or impeded by family, friends, culture and, if one is part of a believing family, church. In the United States, Catholics are part of a secular culture where adulthood is not always exercised by those considered grown-up. We are wise, therefore, if we ask what Christian adulthood means.

Christian Tradition on Adulthood

It may seem strange to focus on what we, on an everyday level, take for granted—being an adult. The focus begins to make sense when one considers the dependency characterizing the lay status for so long combined with the fact that stress was often placed on group identity (the laity) rather than on personal identity (the lay

24

Catholic as an individuated believing person). Of like significance is the fact that perceptions about Christian adulthood have differed historically. For example, John Calvin once wrote, "So when I said that in this life we are never men, this ought not to be pressed to the other extreme, as they say, as if there were no progress beyond childhood. After being born in Christ, we ought to grow, so as not to be children in understanding . . . *although we have not arrived at man's estate, we are at any rate older boys.*"[1]

In recent years the image of Christian believer is depicted less frequently as a form of "adolescence" or as a rigid, closed model of particular attributes reached at a particular age and defined by the male model of a particular culture. (In the church the perfected models, of course, have always been the priest and the saint.)

Vatican II, *Called and Gifted,* and the Synod on the Laity revealed a new Catholic interpretation of lay adulthood, one more suited to the modern era. Consequently, as Catholic lay adults we must not be afraid to speak up when we are treated as adolescents within the church. Will lay adult identity eventually flourish to the extent that it typifies a pilgrim church engaged in mission? Only time will tell. Some lay members of the church still hanker for the days when they were told exactly what to do. But, as William Bouwsma points out:

> Christian conversion is . . . not, as in the mystery religions, an immediate entrance into a safe harbor but rather, though its direction has been established, [it is] the beginning of a voyage into the unknown. . . .[2]

In other words, Christian conversion bears the fruit of pilgrim identity—a voyage into the unknown. Pilgrim—whether we speak of each of us as a pilgrim or the church as a pilgrim people—encourages us to envision lives that move "on the road," characterized by change, by diversity.

> From this standpoint, just as the essential condition of Christian adulthood is the capacity for growth, the worst state . . . is not so much sinfulness (for sins can be forgiven) as the cessation of growth, arrested development, remaining fixed at any point in life.[3]

Women and men who have "a well-integrated self-image and group identity," who anticipate change and have the capacity to deal with growth, are most likely to model Christian pilgrim adulthood. They teach others, especially the young, how to embrace the voyage to an unknown horizon, how to be open to the stretch of faith and heart that the Spirit enables.

One never hears of a "generic pilgrim" because that would be a contradiction in terms. Pilgrim Christian adulthood affirms the unique value of one's own *personal identity* nourished by the gift of one's *spirituality* yet realized only in loving bond with others with whom one shares a like *communal identity*. These are the resources for a post-conciliar *church identity* of vibrancy, one in which *adulthood and mission are constitutive*. Security, consequently, rests on the interior assurance of God's love and not on the permanence of a particular place or office in the church. Without a process of spiritual formation that assurance may be hard to come by.

Respect for Individuation

Because mature personal identity (who I am as Susan or Mark) is integral to adult identity, and because church is a communal enterprise, it is necessary to explore adulthood from the perspective of both individuation and relationship. Two true stories illustrate dilemmas posed by this exploration.

Story One. One day during a much earlier year of my marriage, I wrote a letter to the priest columnist of a Catholic magazine, *St. Anthony's Messenger.* In the letter I poured out my heart, describing how I was trying to be a good wife, a good mother, a good neighbor, a good daughter, a good daughter-in-law, and how I was failing in each of these appointed roles. The wisdom of the priest's reply has been a touchstone for me through the years. "Stop trying to be a good wife, a good mother, a good neighbor, a good daughter, and a good daughter-in-law," he wrote. "Discover who the person Virginia is. Trust her, let others get to know her, then trust that they will love her as she is."

That afternoon my mother phoned. After a bare moment of pleasantry, she launched an attack on our cherished family cat, citing sixteen reasons why Leftover was a menace to health and a danger to her grandchildren.

I listened. I remembered the morning's letter. I said, "We'll get an elephant if we feel like it! It's our house!" I then did what I had never done before in my life. I slammed the receiver down without saying goodbye.

Perhaps the priest knew that the lesson he was trying to teach wouldn't be initiated gracefully or mastered smoothly. Perhaps he realized that I would be challenged to ratify his recommendations over and over for the rest of my life.

Being a good whatever-the-role—wife, mother, teacher, parishoner, daughter, student, girl scout—had given me an identity, I thought. *Playing adult roles* made me an adult. Today it seems odd that I was nearly thirty years old before anyone suggested to me that knowing and naming "who I am" would reveal my identity more fully than perfecting the several roles I was trying to assume in order to *have* an identity. Although I was thirty I had no sense of individuation or personhood. Although I was a mother I still gave equal weight to being a daughter.

Knowing and naming oneself is part and parcel of having self-esteem as an adult. Some of us take to doing it as if it were one of the easier challenges of life. Some of us struggle daily to come closer to an approximation of "who I might be." Some of us go through a process—therapy, conversion, crisis—that reveals to us the identity *I am.* Many of us cling to reinforcements along the way.

Story Two. Although the episcopal leadership in our country did not waver in stating in *Called and Gifted* that adulthood is the *first* call to Catholic lay women and lay men who live in the United States, the acceptance and affirmation of the adulthood of Catholic lay people continues to be a point of conflict in the American church. Feeling one's adulthood being negated can happen in the least expected places.

One summer after participating in a Catholic institute I joined my husband to visit our youngest daughter, acting in the outdoor drama TECUMSEH! in southern Ohio. As we prowled backstage and through the compound where the theater company lived, she introduced her friends to us. Sometimes she would say, "John is Blue Jacket in our production," or "Mary is Macamaloh." Other times, after we had parted from the person, she would say, "He's a generic Indian," "She's a generic settler," "He's a generic soldier."

That evening, waiting expectantly for the drama to fill the magnificent natural stage, I looked at the cast listing in the program. There were no generic Indians, settlers, or soldiers. With the whole cast listed alphabetically, each of the sixty-two young women and men acting in the production had been given a *personal* Indian, American or English name.

I wanted to show the program to a celibate back at the summer institute. He had said that he was tired of lay people who refused to live out the gospel, i.e. too many owned homes, a stance incompatible with the gospel.

Confused, I told him that after ten years of not owning a home my husband and I had just purchased a house.

"Why on earth did you do that?" he asked.

A bit rattled, I replied, "To leave an inheritance to our daughters."

He then explained to me that the desire to leave an inheritance is exactly why so many lay adults cling to the culture's false securities and turn their backs on the gospel. It was a moment of shock for me. I had never, till then, felt guilty for wanting to leave a very modest inheritance to our four daughters. For five thousand years, back to Old Testament times, leaving an inheritance had been legitimate. When had the ethical stance on what seemed to be a natural desire and responsibility, linked to the identity of parenthood, changed?

I turned my attention back to my challenger and heard him say, "You've given enough to your daughters. You've given them yourselves—your wisdom, your care."

I recognized how profound his words *sounded,* but the profundity failed to stem a sudden sense of outrage. "What do you know about what we've given our children? You didn't even know me until this week! How could you possibly know?"

I wanted to say, "Stop trying to fit me into your definition of what lay people should be! You have a name—and your name is well known. I have a name. Each and every one of the lay people has a name. We are not just named by others. Stop running roughshod over who we are as *persons.* Stop perceiving us with a generic label. There is no generic nun or brother, no generic priest or bishop, and no generic lay person—not a one—anywhere in the church anymore. The church is not sheep and goats—leaders al-

lowed to be adult persons while the rest of us remain generic instruments drafted to carry out their commands. We are all adults
and we are all persons!"

The great thing was that I didn't have to shout this. He listened
to my initial anger, and for the next two hours we shared our
personal stories. When we parted he said, "I'm glad you bought
that house! I really am."

Let's look at the approaches taken by these two priests. The
first priest was trying to be pastoral, the second was trying to be
prophetic. The first priest urged me toward an acceptance of myself
as a fully adult person. The second priest, until he heard my story,
seemed to expect me to hand over my authority as an adult lay
Christian to *his* interpretation of the gospel, a stance we usually
associate with an authoritarian pastor or bishop.

Because we are all adult persons, we have a responsibility to
listen for our own call from God through study, prayer, and reflection on life experience. We are wise to familiarize ourselves with
contemporary theological thought and the teachings of the church.
But the day is over that legitimized drafting the lay folk to be foot
soldiers for a class of officers bent on victory (accomplished by the
lay foot soldiers). Mission happens when lay people as *individuated
adults* relate in community with other adults.

Adulthood: History and Gender

Perhaps these dilemmas and confrontations emerge because
we know too little about adulthood, a recent concept, and about
the influence of gender on definitions of adulthood.

As late as 1922, the noted psychologist G. Stanley Hall characterized human "ages" as:

> adolescence—13 to 25 or 30 years of age;
> maturity—30 to 45 years of age;
> senescence (old age)—"the last half of life."[4]

According to Winthrop Jordan, the term "adulthood" first
appeared in usage about a century ago. In spite of the popularity of
articles on adulthood in magazines in the 1920s, the *International
Encyclopedia of the Social Sciences,* published in *1975,* had sec-

tions devoted to adolescence and aging, yet none on adulthood. The contemporary focus on mid-life may be what is activating an appreciation for adulthood.

Even the word *adult,* which interestingly enough comes from the word adolescent, was not commonly used until the middle of the seventeenth century.[5] Jordan relates that in the United States as late as the Jacksonian era, "distinction between women and men tended to override any perception of commonality; manhood and womanhood perceptually overrode adulthood. What room was there for adulthood when a physician could write that after menopause a woman was 'degraded to the level of a being who has no further duty to perform in this world?' "[6]

The women's movement takes on particular relevance in defining the meaning of adulthood, for without the emergence of feminism a bias in favor of masculinity characterizes all definitions of adulthood. It may be a generation before adulthood, in our own culture, is internalized as a true balance between masculinity and femininity for both sexes.

Sexism in the church is a problem that will fester until church policy, governance, theology and spirituality reflect less gender bias. As the whole meaning of womanhood is being debated we still find within the church a more rigid separation between the sexes than one finds in a secular culture like the United States. A separation between sexes that determines access to empowerment provides an increasingly striking contrast with what many lay adults experience in their work, socialization and family life. This alarms some men as well as women. For example, in preparation for a diocesan synod, at each local hearing in a southern New England diocese the issue of women was initially raised by a *layman* concerned about justice for his wife and daughters. The fact that almost thirty interventions from all over the world concerning the empowerment and participation of women in church and in secular culture were offered at the Synod on the Laity helps one to hope that this sinful church bias will eventually end. Until it does, we will have an inadequate definition and comprehension of Christian adulthood.

The quest of the women pilgrims of our age is vital. All Catholic Christians are impoverished when, within the church, adulthood is nothing more than a stale synonym for manhood. Refinements of the meanings of both adulthood and Christian adulthood are fundamental to mission. Without a conversion in meaning, both adulthood and mission will be limited to masculine models, ones that favor reason over affectivity.

Sandra Schneiders points out that what we often identify as feminine is, in many instances, what we find in Jesus:

> Jesus revealed by his preaching and his life the inadequacy of the masculine definition of humanity. Jesus repudiated competition, the exercise of coercive power, all forms of domination and control of others, aggression, and violence. He espoused . . . humility of heart, peacemaking, non-violence . . . and a nurturing concern for all, especially the sick, the oppressed, sinners, women, and children.[7]

Our discovery of a model for Christian adulthood must not bypass contemplating what Jesus revealed. As Schneiders says:

> Jesus delegitimized the stereotypically male virtues and the typically masculine approach to reality; he validated the stereotypically female virtues and lived a distinctly feminine life-style. . . . *Had Jesus been a woman there would have been nothing revelatory about this way of life;* women were expected to live and behave that way. Because he was a man Jesus' choice of life-style stood out as a contradiction . . . of humanity as defined by the dominant male culture.[8]

Male domination within Christian tradition skewed the qualities Jesus exemplified into an aberrant message that glorified suffering while tolerating an authoritarian use of male power totally alien to the way of Jesus, a power that often caused rather than alleviated suffering.

Aristocracy and Adulthood

A second reason why adulthood as a concept is a modern phenomenon is socio-economic. For centuries the fate of a man or a woman depended on which one of the "orders of society" he or she was born into—to serfdom, to knighthood or ladyship, to royalty. In eras of aristocracy, to the manor *born* was not a rhetorical saying! For innumerable centuries, regarding governance, both church and society clung to "orders of society."

In the twentieth century, alignments between the laity as the lowest caste in a class system and the will of our creator God are difficult to sustain. However, we can't avoid the fact that our church has encouraged titles, ones that have engendered authoritarian dynamics, i.e. superiors, vicars, provincials, cardinals, chancellors. (At one time certain pastors initialed I.P.P. after their names to designate that they were "irremovable parish priests.") Authoritarianism, in some settings, has lingered on after Vatican II.

We must not infer that all bishops endorse this aristocratic tone. Many have adapted the *co-discipleship* theme articulated by the episcopal delegation to the Synod on the Laity from the United States. It is as wrong to stereotype bishops as it is to stereotype lay adults. But where distinctions and titles still exist in a way that evokes a class system rather than a sense of communion, we do well to make inquiry on how this affects lay adults.

This problem is not confined to the yesteryears of the church. At the 1988 NCCB meeting in Washington Bishop Raymond Lucker suggested that the title for a special episcopal assembly to be held in California in 1990 be changed from *Priests, Prophets, and Leaders* to *Priests, Prophets, and Servant-Leaders,* citing the teaching of Jesus on leadership.

The next bishop to speak disagreed vehemently. Arguing for the title *Priests, Prophets, and Kings,* he said, "We've got to teach our people what *king* means. All our priests must be *seen and treated* like kings by their people! We must, of course, also see ourselves as kings."

The Temptation of Titles

"If there weren't all those somebodies we wouldn't feel like nobodies." This is the way Janet, born after Vatican Council II, puts it. "What does lay mean?" she asks. "If it's more than ring around the clerical collar, nobody has made that clear to me. What's *good* about being a lay person?"

Tom Smith feels that the plethora of titles in the church will lead to a scramble among lay people for titles of their own. "Already in our family we've got a secretary of the CYO, a hospitality helper, and an extraordinary eucharistic minister. Do I have to try to be a grand knight in the K. of C. to feel as though I count in the church?" Without a special appellation Tom claims he's Layman X, a close kin to Brand X in the television ads. "There are subtle put-downs, and what they say is that Tom Smith has no meaning in the church anymore."

Elsie Lonergan, feisty about the issue, wants upward mobility. At a conference for deacons' wives she asked the bishop present to speak to her parishioners. "The lay people there don't realize that since Ed was ordained a deacon we've been elevated to a place different from theirs!"

The above is not an inferred argument for democratizing the church. Designations based on gifts, talents, and call are found in scripture as well as tradition. But the above is an invitation to look at the effect that titled distinctions have on the grassroots laity and the value they attach to their own mission efforts. With fewer titles would we begin to appreciate the adulthood of all lay persons? Do titles *substitute* for adulthood in the church? How does the internalization of titles affect faith?

These issues that affect identity deserve far more attention at every level of the church if the Janets in the church are to develop a lucid understanding of what it means to be a young lay Catholic adult, if the Toms are to believe that no special role is necessary to be affirmed within the community of the church, if the Elsies and the Eds are to learn not to seek more prideful placements on the church ladder. These distinctions are not caused by the laity. Georgia Masters Keightley reminds us that ordination ". . . serves as a central symbol of the lay/clergy distinction . . . it is obvious that ordination is responsible for creating the categories clergy/laity in the first place. . . ."[9]

If the term "generic nobodies" no longer represents who the laity are, we must admit that the term "titled somebodies" hardly represents most of us either. Lay people, as they develop an awareness of the *differences* in designated roles within the church, often become more aware of their own status within the church. Not only are some "owning" a sense of empowered church identity, increasingly, as they perceive their Christian adulthood, but they also appreciate in a new way the value of personal and spiritual identity to their church identity. In other words, who they are as Janet and Tom and Elsie helps them to name who they are as Catholics.

Personal Identity

Within local church settings, deficits in pastoral attention and in the opportunity for participation may lead to passivity or feelings of frustration. With increasing frequency lay believers seem to be asking whether their local church is helping them to realize that "each adult is unique and therefore respected and loved unconditionally as an individual . . . and the process of adult learning in the church is meant to 'call forth and enable the gifts of each adult for the common good.' "[10]

In his earthly life, Jesus exemplified what it means to be a pilgrim adult on mission, yet this did not erode at all his personal identity. Jesus is Jesus as fully in Gethsemane as he was healing lepers and sharing loaves and fishes.

We are called to be wayfarers of the same sort. Making our way through the challenges and struggles, the difficulties and dangers of our human experience, we stretch and grow through these human experiences as the person each of us is. Only adults who know who they are as persons can do this. Only adults who are God-related and unique, yet united in community, can donate themselves to the mission of the church.

The post-conciliar focus on the resurrection of Jesus, his rising and appearing to others as a whole self, symbolizes for us the significance of the whole embodied self. In the pre-conciliar church, emphasis was on the "soul" part of myself. To say that spiritually we are called to be whole persons is to say that all dimensions of self need to be knit together to form the person who unites self with God. This means being *fully alive to what is happening to me* and to the other believers with whom I share faith.

What we are talking about, of course, is contemplating self in community. By that I do not mean becoming overly introspective or becoming self-absorbed, for that is the antithesis of Christian adulthood. I do mean knowing myself by contemplating my own experience of life for its meaning.

In the pre-conciliar church the role of the laity was assumed to have few rights yet many responsibilities. Sharing your life experience within a church united as a community was not perceived as valuable. In the pre-conciliar church interest in lay experience seemed to be limited to negative experience, one's sins as articulated in the confessional.

Sharing our personal experiences of life and faith in an open process, a rather new development in church settings in the United States, engenders a sense of spiritual adulthood because being adult implies *having* experience and the ability to look, with some objectivity, *on* that experience. Mature, individuated Catholic adults are called to articulate their experience, including their spiritual experience, *in the church* as well as evangelically in the world beyond the church. Small groups and movements have persisted and flourished, and they are now often defended by the institutional church, because they are the means for sharing that experience.

The Import of Experience

But what is so valuable about *experience?* One response to that question comes from a theologian, Gerald O'Collins, S.J., who says that *human life reveals itself in experience.* This crucial insight helps us to understand Christian adulthood as dynamic and active, not dependent-passive. O'Collins points out:

> . . . our life expresses itself in experience. . . . We are and will be what we experience. We identify ourselves and the course of our life through deeply lived experiences of fear, love, joy and guilt, as well as through the realities which confront us in day-to-day experience.[11]

In the past, disdain if not downright contempt for the earthly, bodily, spontaneous, and passionate dimensions of men and women for centuries characterized the church. "You're a nobody until I tell you you're a somebody" was often the message between the lines spoken by superiors, pastors, and bishops. "You're certainly a nobody to God unless I determine otherwise" was unfortunately internalized by innumerable clergy, vowed religious and lay believers. Because confession in particular symbolized that stance, it is avoided by many Catholic believers in contemporary times.

Even today that inheritance encourages some lay believers to leave their human experience on the church steps when they come to participate in the ritual which is intended to be a celebration of the faith and lives, filled with human experience, of the people of this local community. These lives are lived out in the web of workplace, friendship, family, civic and social justice commitments. If our experience of life is isolated from church, if our experience of church is isolated from the rest of our life, we may sense a gap between the human experiences within our "web of existence" and our experience of church which is also part of our human experience. We may forget that we are the church in the world.

O'Collins points out that the German verb "to experience" means literally "to be alive when something happens—to be alive to what is happening to us."[12] As believers we are called to be alive to the experience of the Holy Spirit within the web of our own lives. Consequently, we are called to be alive to what happens in our lives. By revealing our human lives to our brothers and sisters in communities of faith *as* these lives are lived out, day by day, in the ordinary and the moving experiences of life, we come to know our God of revelation more deeply in community, in the stories of scripture, and in the sacraments. In other words, a better understanding of my human experience helps me to understand my *spiritual identity*. The meaning of my human experience takes on heightened value, spiritual value.

But what characterizes our human experience as adults? According to O'Collins, all human experience has *meaning*. We are called, simply by being human beings, to discover the meaning of our human experiences. Indeed, as humans we sense within ourselves a drive to discover the meaning whatever it might be. (For example, one day in Washington, D.C. I visited an exhibit on life in the United States in the 1930s at the Smithsonian. The exhibit was interesting and I felt relaxed. Part of the exhibit was a series of glass-enclosed rooms decorated in the style of the 1930s. As I stood gazing into the kitchen, I suddenly felt myself moving through the glass into the room. The sensation ebbed and tears came into my eyes. After a few moments I moved on. Later, feeling fatigued, I sat on a bench. Immediately I sensed the 1930s kitchen. *Why* did I react so strongly? Why was I drawn into the room with the bread-box, icebox and washing machine with the old-fashioned wringers? What did the tears mean?)

We have an experience. To discover its meaning, we explore our experience and identify our feelings. We've got our religion upside down if it obfuscates the meaning of our experiences, causing us to disvalue our experiences and lust after more "heavenly" manifestations of our faith.

According to O'Collins, our human experience *takes us in some direction.* Our lives are not just chaos. There is a certain purposefulness to our human experiences that not only makes them meaningful to us but also draws us in one direction rather than another or another or another.

Our human experience is *particular.* We may consider something "in general"—falling in love perhaps. But when we actually experience falling in love it is with a particular someone—John or Martin or Sarah or Anne. Thinking about something "in general" lacks the power inherent in experiencing in particular, with particular persons, in particular places. As O'Collins remarks, "The experience of God in prayer occurs only at particular times, in particular places, and to particular persons."[13]

That's the way life is for human beings.

Within human experience there is an encounter between *expectation and novelty.* If over and over and over our expectations come to pass, we characterize such experience as "routine." The experiences that leave a mark on us as humans are those experiences which in some way surpass our anticipations, that contain within them elements of newness—like Vatican II.

Part of becoming a human adult is learning to discern between my expectations of an experience and the surprises that new experiences bring into my life.

We *react* within our experiences to our experiences. Doing this is part of being a human adult. Experiences evoke *feelings;* experiences are *evaluated and judged* negatively and positively. When we share with God those reactions and judgments we have made, rightfully or wrongly, about our experiences, God may reveal whether our evaluations are on target or whether our expectations have overwhelmed the reality we experienced.

Our human experiences evoke meanings, take us in some direction, are particular in their dynamics, sometimes reveal novelty and freshness, and are judged by our feelings—these are the "givens" of existing as human beings.

What does this mean for our *spiritual* identity?

If one's spiritual experiences are considered supernatural and set apart from ordinary experience, one still lives as a human person engaged in human experiences that have meaning, are particular, etc. If we perceive our human experiences as having the capacity to reveal spiritual dimensions, they are still human experiences to which one reacts with feelings, negotiates the expected and the novel, etc.

God created us as humans. Becoming believers, becoming believers who are adults, does not erase our humanness. If Jesus, coming from God, embraced the human condition, then part of my *adulthood* as a Christian believer is to embrace the human condition (including death and birth) by acknowledging my experiences and their spiritual value.

Our God is incarnational; thus *every human experience has the potential for being a spiritual experience.*

Spiritual Experience/Human Experience

Some readers may be saying to themselves, "But what if I don't feel 'fully alive to what is happening to me' when I am in church? Isn't that where, of all places, I'm supposed to experience God?"

Let's look at it this way. The more that the whole person I am as Susan or Mark is engaged in the human experience of my life (the more I am fully alive to what is happening to me), the more my personal identity is drawn toward realizing its capacity. This is being present to life *as* I experience it. *This is being adult.*

The same pattern is apparent in spirituality. For example, for many Catholics *religious experience* is experiencing an inner connection within myself to the reality that the symbols of the mass evoke. As I sense this inner connection, my faith deepens and I bear the fruit of that faith in mission in my everyday life because my spiritual experience now has positive meaning, takes me in some direction, is particular, etc. I also may begin to recognize the religious experiences that occur in the web of my daily life.

Religious consciousness is that part of religion which examines experience through reflection. My realizing that in this setting or that setting church "doesn't work for me anymore" may be the beginning of my *exercising my religious consciousness in relation to my religious experience.* It is possible to claim that even if it "doesn't feel spiritual," this process is a step forward in spiritual maturity, of understanding myself as a spiritual being.[14]

Reaching this juncture, so many lay people fear that they have lost their faith. They begin to drift away from church and God instead of seeking help. Finding a process that enhances both their spiritual experience and their religious consciousness often resolves the angst. A sense of healing is felt within.

Summary. For a person of faith, developing a consciousness about religious experience is not a mere option. It is a *value,* a crucial stage in achieving spiritual maturity and becoming a Christian adult. The pastoral deficits in the church may hinder recognition of this fact. On the other hand, affirmation of the validity of lay life experience, including lay spiritual experience, is not only a justice question in the church; it is an issue of significance to the spirituality and the mission of *the whole church.*

Faith is not acknowledging ideas about God. Faith is relationship with God. Relationships are rooted in experiences; experiences of one another give meaning to our relationship, take it in some direction and so on. Religious experiences and a consciousness of these experiences often determine the vibrancy of our faith. If ninety-eight percent of the church—the lay people—don't have religious experiences or don't recognize them, or aren't invited to articulate them in church, the spiritual vitality of the church is gravely diminished.

Some of us are not conscious of our own experience. Some of us are only conscious of our *own* experiences. If we are not conscious of our own experiences, we cannot understand how we function as adults who are Catholic Christians. If we are not conscious of the experiences of others, we can hardly call ourselves Christians, for there is no way we can truly *love* others unless we are conscious of them and their sufferings and trials and joys—their experiences of life. Until the lay believers of the church recognize, in a fully conscious way, their experiences and until they articulate them within church settings, the church itself can hardly be characterized as mature and adult and dedicated to mission.

Consciousness and experience are keys to adult faith, to love of God and to love of neighbor.

3

THE GIFT OF LAY SPIRITUALITY

Jesus, in the gospel accounts, warned not to be a divided self, not to have the right and left hands engaged in opposing activities. Counseling an awareness of self, he affirmed being alert to one's own experience. "Consciousness-raising" and "human experience" are terms coined in recent times but the reality they represent is found in the New Testament. When Martha, in Luke's gospel, let herself become agitated about kitchen tasks to the point of letting this disrupt her relationship with her sister and the guest in their house, Jesus cautioned her to *become aware of* her own experience, to be conscious of it, to be reflective as Mary was.

To stop and reflect on the religious experience you have had this day was the directive given by Jesus to the disciples as related in Mark 8. Jesus questions them about what they have experienced that day in the distribution of the loaves and fishes. Look inside yourself, he urges. "Are your hearts hardened? Are your minds closed? Do you not remember?"

Jesus even invites them to be aware of what their senses experienced—"Having eyes do you not see?"—and of the reality of their actions—"How many baskets full of scraps did you collect?" Jesus leads them to affirm *their religious experience* by reflecting on the events they had experienced that day at mealtime, not in the synagogue or temple.

As believers in Jesus we should not be surprised that his wisdom is as relevant today as in the past. On a spiritual as well as a psychological level, awareness and adulthood are connected. A recent study of adult men revealed that those who were able to reflect and integrate the experiences of life achieved greater balance and maturity, both essential to spirituality.

An Event in Which You Experienced God

Do lay adults affirm their religious experience?

Never allowed publicly to proclaim the gospel in church, seldom invited to articulate their religious experience in the church, lay adults played the expected silent role in the pre-conciliar church. Habits sometimes are hard to break.

In 1984 the Spirituality Task Force of the National Association for Lay Ministry made a modest effort to remedy this and to further an understanding of the spirituality of the laity by asking its members to articulate a spiritual experience. Respondents to a questionnaire sent to the membership were to answer the following three questions:

"Describe what happened in an event in which you experienced God."

"What meaning does this event have for you?"

"How has this event affected your life?"

In the effort to learn more about a particular religious experience of lay believers, each NALM member was asked to give an identical questionnaire to a lay person whose primary activity is secular rather than church centered. Interestingly, half of the persons who responded fell in each category with *no* significant differences noted in what was cited as religious experience between the two groups. To enhance the collaborative bias of the project, fifteen consultants, with particular expertise in spirituality and/or ministry, wrote commentaries on the data. Fifty-three men and women, narrating primary religious experience, returned the initial questionnaire. All but two respondents described the event they named as their experience of God in considerable detail. The staying power of the experience within the memory of respondents seemed remarkably strong even when the experience appeared elusive, e.g. a quiet moment on an evening walk. The memory of the experience of God, over time, seemed fresh enough to be called back with its original luminosity in times of difficulty, doubt, and depression.

The following is an example:

One September weekend about twelve years ago, my husband, my children and I spent the weekend with some friends who owned a Christmas tree farm. I took a walk by myself among the pine trees. In the course of that walk I began to experience a vivid sense of Presence and Love. I heard the sounds of the birds and crickets and even the silence. I saw the depth in the color and texture of the trees; I really smelled pine and earth; I felt that warmth of the air and the sun—all as if for the first time.

I had been struggling with some real "faith" questions. . . . I had felt that if there was a God, I had no awareness of God's love in my life beyond an intellectual sort of "knowing." After my walk I "knew" that not only did God exist, but God loved me in a very real and personal way. My faith came alive on that day and I came alive in a new way.

I shall never forget that experience, and even as I write about it now, I feel part of it. Even though times are few when such a powerful realization takes hold of me, I believe in God's love and presence because on that day it was so real. Several years later I entered a very dark time: my husband died and so did my parents and my husband's parents. The assurance of God's presence in my life—being with me in all that time—was what enabled me to walk through that time. It was as if God had prepared me for all of that death by giving me a taste of and profound experience of Resurrection Life.

An affective dynamic predominated in almost all of the events cited by respondents; a *felt* sense of God was experienced. According to the project's consultants, God was not "explained" or defined by the experience, yet in most cases God was known for God's Self. Some respondents perceived the presence of God incarnated in nature or the poor or friends. In the replies, forty percent of the settings cited were church located or specifically of a religious nature, i.e. cursillo weekend, charismatic gathering, sacrament of the sick, retreat experience, diocesan eucharistic liturgy, hymn singing. (A parish function was seldom mentioned as a setting.) Most intriguing was the fact that the context of sixty percent of the identified experiences of God were within existential life experiences, with twenty percent of these linked to a crisis experience (illness, death in family, interpersonal or work confrontations). Other life encounters ranged from stressful contexts like selling one's house, to simple, peaceful contexts like being with friends or waking up in the morning. Few events cited as the place for experiences of God were evoked by *routine* everydayness like driving to work or doing the dishes.

Regardless of context, the event of experiencing God happened in innumerable instances when *the person risked a deeper entry into the particular lived experience.* Whether the experience was a death experience within the family, or sensing a loss of control over one's own life, or vividly contemplating nature, or sharing bread with the homeless, becoming *absorbed in the experience* seemed to prompt the experience into becoming an experience of God for the believer. Losing self in the experience, not self-consciousness during the experience, was central.

Religious consciousness *after-the-fact* is often what brought to light the spiritual dimension of the particular experience. Because other activity (besides awareness of God) was frequently going on in the actuality of the experience, and the respondent felt caught up in this, upon *reflection* or as the experience ebbed, the respondent *noticed* the spiritual depth inherent in the experience. Many felt accepted and loved by God as the woman at the Christmas tree farm did. Naming and owning the experience through reflection *seemed to reveal more than was apparent in the immediate happening.*

Many respondents felt that this experience of God had an irreplaceable impact on their faith and lives. A savoring of God being available in an unexpected way characterized the meaning of the event. God became tangible and believable. A connection between experiencing that God *loved* the believer and that God could be *trusted* emerged. Some saw the experience as a faith conversion.

For the respondents integration with ongoing life was characterized as a *change* in ongoing life, at least to the extent of perceiving a changed self, a change in attitude, a change in actions. The *fruits* of the experience seemed to be a determinant in validating the experience as *religious.*

The new sense of self was frequently described as one characterized by:

    . . . feeling a sense of harmony within;
    . . . becoming more relaxed interiorly and exteriorly;
    . . . sensing renewed strength for the journey;
    . . . feeling a desire for a new lifestyle;
    . . . participating more actively in church.

Manifestations of these sensibilities in everyday life included a feeling of greater union with others along with an increase in charity and a desire to serve others. In addition there was a deepened awareness of God, of others, and of self, and a greater willingness to persevere in struggle.

Layness characterized many of the experiences cited by those engaged in church ministry as a life commitment and by those engaged primarily in secular activity. What do I mean by "layness"? God was experienced as the lay adult participated in the nitty-gritty of life. For one woman the experience happened as she was going home after being told by the school principal that her children had head lice. Awash in a sense of failure as a mother, she suddenly heard, "Why do you have to control everything?" That broke through her worry, and she was led to prayer and an acceptance of powerlessness in some situations. In many instances the event "happened" when the lay respondents were fully alive to an experience in the web of their existence where they are formed.

The aim of the Spirituality Task Force and its consultants was not to determine the authenticity of God's presence in the events described. The aim was to discover the *kinds* of experiences lay adults would cite as experiences of God. Interestingly, the events described evoked the characteristics of experience perceived by O'Collins: a sense of meaning, movement in some direction, particularity, revelation of newness, affect.[1]

Articulation of Religious Experience—A New Phenomenon

Among the remarkable victories of Vatican II is the development of religious consciousness within many lay believers. A fruit of this emergent consciousness is the discovery of a loving God in the midst of lived experience and a growing ability to identify and articulate particular spiritual experiences when the opportunity for this occurs. This approach may prove to be the seedbed for identifying *authentic Catholic lay spirituality.* Too little is known, on the local level, even today about the particularities of the religious experience of lay adults. Although some sociologists, i.e. Greeley, have engaged in research on religious experience, and scholars have recently studied the phenomena historically (see Joseph Chinnici's *Devotion to the Holy Spirit in American Catholicism,* Ann Taves' *The Household of Faith,* and Robert Orsi's *The Madonna of 115th*

Street), there remains a lacuna about manifestations of contemporary experience.[2]

The articulation of particular religious experience reinforces the reality of religious experience. The pastoral place for this reflection and articulation, traditionally, has been spiritual direction. Until recently spiritual direction was a pastoral service that vowed religious and some diocesan priests received, but it was not considered a pastoral need connected to the lay person. Pastoral leaders are just beginning to realize that lay adults, not able to set aside an hour or more each day for prayer, can profit from and deserve spiritual mentoring as much as clergy and vowed religious. But *lay* resistance to the articulation of religious experience may also pose a problem. Sometimes people feel that prayer and religious experience are too personal to discuss with others. It may feel strange to talk about a particular religious experience because the latter seems elusive. In addition, lay people sometimes feel insecure about the acceptable language for such articulation. Although there is no denying that prayer and sacraments are where God is encountered for many people, the emphasis in Catholic tradition on these "settings" has inhibited lay believers from looking at their own lived experience for God's presence.

In the pre-conciliar church, "state" was the perspective from which a believer perceived his or her religious and spiritual identity: our souls were either in a state of grace or in a state of sin. Confession remedied the latter, restoring us to a state of grace. Returned to the state of grace, we centered mind and heart and spirit on staying away from sin. For many lay believers *state of grace substituted for an awareness of one's personal relationship with God.*

The clarity provided by the emphasis on state of life and state of sin/grace contributed to order within the church. One result of this was that many lay believers, like myself, seemed to relate to *church* more than to God. After all it was the church who told us how to live our state in life and whether we were in a state of sin or grace.

Feelings, we were told, could be disregarded because they were irrelevant. Consequently, when I had, over a period of time, some powerful spiritual experiences during mass, it never dawned on me to share them with a priest. Perhaps there's something wrong with me, I told myself. My spiritual life was growing by leaps and bounds but I had no *consciousness* of it! It wasn't until years after Vatican II that I looked back on this period with a religious consciousness that said "Aha! That's what was going on!"

In my pre-conciliar days the church sometimes came *between* God and Virginia. That was not accidental. At times the institutional church was rigorous in its efforts to encourage that dynamic. Although I was asked regularly how long it had been since my last confession and how many times I had committed a particular sin, no one asked, "Who is God for you?" For over thirty years no one ever asked me, "How do you and God get along?" Some lay believers live their entire lives without ever hearing from a pastoral leader, "Please tell me about your relationship with God."

In the pre-conciliar church, every lay believer received the answers to those questions in the catechism, a question and answer learning device that effectively *hampered any reflection on experiences of God as well as any curiosity about God.* The theological questions that seeped into my soul such as "Why did God design so many different kinds of butterflies?" never got asked because it never seemed appropriate to ask that kind of question *in church.*

The Laity: Ordinary Compared to Others

When my mother was a child, at the end of mass as the priest left the altar, my grandmother would point to the priest each Sunday and whisper to her thirteen children, "There is God." My grandmother formed my mother's religious perception.

The above is an extreme example but it indicates a kind of putting-on-a-pedestal stance that led to a confusion within some lay believers between God and the priest. Wilfred Sheed describes this in another way in *Frank and Maisie—A Memoir with Parents:*

> For Catholics before Vatican II, the land of the free was preeminently the land of Sister Says—except, of course, for Sister, for whom it was the land of Father Says. For a layman to wedge himself into this prim hierarchy would require a more sinuous effort than getting the English to pay attention to a papist.[3]

We are talking, of course, about connections—the intricacies of inter-related realities and images. Sister was empowered to speak, putting her in a sense above the mute lay folk. But, in her servant role, the lines she spoke could seldom be her own; they were Father's, and he, in turn, seldom varied, at least doctrinally, from what he was told to say by those on the aristocratic scaffolding above him. From the 1920s to the 1950s it was not unusual in some dioceses for local clergy to receive prescribed sermon topics with sample texts, one year doctrinal, the next moral.

The lives of vowed religious and priests, lived with fidelity, are irreplaceable gifts for the whole church. Part of the distinctiveness of Catholicism, part of what enables it to be *visible* within a diverse culture like the United States, is the unique and generous life-style of vowed religious and diocesan priests. This should not, however, inhibit our asking, *when reflecting on the lay people,* how the very different criteria used in defining members of our church influence perceptions about each constituency. As lay *Catholics* within our country, we are no longer a subculture. As *lay* Catholics within our church, we must no longer be treated as a subculture. What keeps us in the subculture church placement?

Contrasting Identities

The traditional bias toward creating unity within the church through uniformity is threatened by the remarkable diversity of the laity. A compulsion to control has encouraged a tendency to make the behavior that is acceptable *within* the church the *behavior modeled by the church professional.* In an instinctive way, some lay people then feel peripheral to the internal functioning of the church. Or a tug-of-war for power becomes normative.

For the leader who is a clergyman, a vowed religious, or a professional lay minister, one's *church* identity is often what is perceived as most significant, if not to oneself, to most other church people. For professionals within the church, like me, work and church identity fuse in a way that they do not for most lay adults. In light of this, it is interesting to note that where lay people *have* been welcomed within the internal church, it is as "ministers," i.e. like priests, *identified by special functions* as priests are, functions with built-in controls. Baptismal call legitimates lay ministry, and I certainly affirm it. Nonetheless, the movement to "ministerialize" the laity has become a way to enable lay adults to participate in church leadership yet conveniently leave their lay-ness behind. Here again is an instance of not treating lay persons as *whole selves.*

In an age when the *faith identity* of many bishops, priests, and vowed religious *and* of many lay people has moved into the close kinship of *co-discipleship,* it is intriguing that *church identity* among these groups continues to provoke tensions.

Paradoxically, although it is the scandal of radical particularity and freedom that prevents a generalized meaning to attach itself to lay identity, the term ordinary has been attached to the laity. The lives of lay adults, engaged vigorously in mission, is the gift to the church of transparency to the culture in which they live. Should it be labeled ordinary?

The Message About Being Ordinary

The adjective ordinary is a two-edged sword. In spite of the affirmation of the call to holiness found in Vatican II documents, it is still not that unusual to find lay adults who think they are too ordinary to have what is called a spiritual life. It seems important to look at the term from both its negative perspective and its favorable aspect.

In her book, *Art and Ardor,* Cynthia Ozick writes about the riddle of the ordinary: "The Extraordinary is easy. And the more extraordinary the Extraordinary is, the easier it is: 'easy' in the sense that we can almost always recognize it. . . . The Extraordinary does not let you shrug your shoulders and walk away." Ozick goes on: "But the Ordinary is a much harder case. In the first place . . . it is around us all the time—the Ordinary has got itself in a bad fix with us: we hardly ever notice it."[4]

Unfortunately in the church a pejorative aura clings to the term ordinary when it is tattooed onto laity and laity alone. For example, a few years ago I received a letter that stated: "Your

audience will be ordinary lay parishioners—not at all sophisticated. . . ." The letter referred to a speaking engagement, and the
characterization of the lay audience was a familiar one. The audience in question would number over a thousand, among whom I
am sure were women and men sophisticated in many aspects of
life. They were not, however, *sophisticated about church,* evoking
the judgment on the part of a church professional that "the people"
are ordinary.

If the original intent of the link between lay and ordinary was a
reference to the fact that many adult lay believers mate, raise families, work in the marketplace, socialize with a mix of friends, and
involve themselves in local civic endeavors, then why not say *natural* or *normal* or *typical*? If the reference is its commonality with
what peoples the world over have done since time immemorial,
then natural, or normal, or typical could substitute for ordinary.
But these terms are never heard in reference to lay life. On another
level, if the term lay were eradicated, the use of "ordinary," I fear,
would increase. For that reason, among others, it seems significant
to determine what characteristics are inherent in lay, because ordinary, as it is often used by church leaders, sounds patronizing
although the term can refer to significant, positive characteristics
common to most people who walk the face of the earth. That brings
me back to Ozick's insights on the ordinary. "Ordinariness can be
defined . . . as the breathing space between getting born and dying,
perhaps, or else the breathing space between rapture and rapture. . . . Ordinariness is . . . sometimes . . . like the ride on the hour
hand of the clock; in any case the Ordinary is, above all, *what is
expected.* And what is expected is not often thought of as gift."[5]

Ordinary and Worldly

One result of efforts in the past to control the religious experience of lay adults, as well as all the answers the laity heard pastor-
ally, was that the identity the lay man or lay woman embraced was
the identity imposed externally by church leaders who gave mes-
sages *about the laity proclaimed to the laity with no response from
the laity.* Between the lines of the message there seemed to be

written "You're damned if you do, and you're damned if you don't." For example, the second term tattooed onto the lay believer, is the term *world.* Our "place is in the world." Worldly, on the other hand, has often had a negative connotation in Christian parlance.

The particular lay dilemma posed by this is the tendency at times to collapse everything within the secular culture *onto* the laity. Some church leaders going a bit further seem to transpose onto the laity all the ills they perceive in the secular culture. If the culture is materialistic, then the laity (who are identified within the church by their setting) must be materialistic. If individualism runs rampant in the United States, then it must be running rampant among the laity. Even in contemporary documents like the NCCB pastoral letter on the economy this tendency can be noted. From this perspective, working in the marketplace, mating and procreating, determining one's own future and the setting in which to live that future, the *norm* for human life somehow becomes lessened in value if not perceived as dangerous.

Collapsing *everyone "out there" beyond church* onto the laity is not uncommon. The reality of this was brought home to me in a vivid way when I was engaged in a church program in which I was the only lay person. One day, exasperated because I was bringing up the laity issue again, a priest in the program pointed to the door and said, "For heaven's sake, Virginia, if you go out that door everyone you meet on the street is lay!"

When I pointed out that in the street we might find Buddhists and Jews, agnostics and Moslems, Hindus and atheists, he smiled and said he had some homework to do on what lay Catholic means. I assured him we all have that homework to do. Part of that homework is acknowledging *the peoplehood of the Catholic laity,* their *unity* as a people of faith. Emerging from a spiritual foundation that is incarnationally embedded in the world of secular work, civic culture and family is what characterizes the people of God in spite of the fact that people of God refers to all members of the church. However, without the laity, quantitatively there would be insufficient numbers to evoke a "people" sense. Or as Cardinal Newman is said to have replied to a query about the laity, "The church would look foolish without them."

Emerging Spirituality and Sacramental Needs

Collapsing all the spirituality needs of lay people into the sacraments is a pre-conciliar attitude that still persists in many church settings. Sacramental needs must be met, and I sometimes grieve because the church, with its decline in priestly vocations, may, in the twenty-first century, be a post-eucharistic church. Ironically, some lay Catholics in years to come will be where lay Catholics were in earlier days in American history when priests were compelled to circuit ride, and innumerable lay believers received the sacraments only at sporadic times.

The post-conciliar conception of the believer as an *individuated "whole self" in community* rather than a generic "soul" has revealed a *range* of spirituality needs linked to growth in relationship to God and neighbor. This situation mandates the need for *more* rather than less pastoral leadership. Identifying particular religious experiences within lived experience, a subject treated earlier in this chapter, is an example of a spirituality need. Developing a disciplined approach to prayer might be a second need, learning to pray with scripture a third, and assistance in discerning the mission stance of one's life a fourth.

Perhaps because Vatican II was implemented in a piecemeal fashion, it was not apparent initially that the spirituality needs of lay Catholics would mandate more attentive pastoral leadership. But deficits in this regard, emphasized by the decline in clergy, are evoking reactions. Dean Hoge of Catholic University, in his remarkable book *Future of Catholic Leadership,* says:

> Robert Sherry argues that the mission of the church is vast and can use many more trained and committed full-time personnel than it has. I agree . . . I suggest, for starters, that the number of personnel be *doubled.* The church's total mission would be advanced.[6]

Hoge describes options for increasing pastoral leadership so that the spirituality needs of lay people can be met. If those spirituality needs are not met, *it is unfair to expect vitality in regard to laity and mission.*[7]

No Longer a Subculture

It's easy to forget how progressive, compared to the past, Vatican II really was. For example, Vatican II was "the first time in history that a council . . . 'introduced' . . . its doctrinal and institutional position by referring to the actual situation of the world."[8] When layman Patrick Keegan addressed the council in the name of the laity, it "was allegedly the first time a lay voice had been heard in a General Council of the Church since the days of the Emperor Constantine in A.D. 325."[9]

In the United States at the time of Vatican Council II, lay Catholics were already experiencing a change in *secular* identity. As Jay Dolan points outs, "Educationally and economically they no longer stood apart as inferior or below par . . . an important consideration in understanding the nature of contemporary American Catholicism."[10]

My immigrant ancestors, who were French-Canadian dairy farmers, Irish hod carriers, and French and Irish textile mill workers, belonged to a subculture. Later generations were "becoming more middle class . . . more like the rest of the American population in terms of income . . . they were entering graduate schools in record numbers and just as likely as other Americans 'to plan careers as scholars.' "[11]

Expertise in a variety of respected secular fields gave lay adults a new, "American" self-image.

Assimilation of a Secular Identity

Earlier in our North American Catholic history Margaret Martin, the first Catholic nurse who headed a hospital unit in the public hospital within her town, probably perceived herself and was perceived by others as "the first Catholic who . . . ." Her grand-niece, Maureen, who heads a similar unit is not distinguished by others for being Catholic. In later generations, especially the post-conciliar generation, the tables had turned. Since World War II, the Catholic nurse or doctor, the Catholic contractor or carpenter, the Catholic business executive or bookkeeper, is a nurse, doctor, contractor, carpenter, executive or bookkeeper who *happens to be a Catholic.* In other words, church identity moved from the first thing that came to mind about the person to a dimension of information about a person who is known by his or her *secular identity.* This does not necessarily mean that being a Catholic diminished in significance within the lay Catholic. But assimilation, the technical term for this phenomenon, happened to most lay believers in the latter half of this century. (It also happened to a lesser degree to church professionals.) No longer separated in identity from other Americans, Catholic lay adults, no longer a subculture, had bonded in identity with other Americans.

One reason this was so easily accomplished is that the secular culture, for later generations, affirmed and appreciated what many church settings ignored or found suspect or dangerous—the *secular lived experience* of the lay Catholic: what happened at work, what was actually going on in a marriage, what avocations were favored.

Lay Spirituality

In some instances, through a gradual process, the good cop like Jim O'Rourke no longer perceived himself as a good cop because he was a good Catholic. Rather, because Jim was a good cop, Jim began to see himself as a good Catholic. This momentous transition, I would say, marked the beginning of what is now referred to as *lay spirituality.* After being baptized and formed in faith, some post-conciliar lay adults, for the first time, began to *originate* their spiritual value as Catholic Christians by their mission in the mainstream culture.

In other words, Jim O'Rourke was not marching from the church after Sunday mass in order to sanctify "the world" as a good Catholic. Jim was discovering his sanctity *in the world* and *through that perceiving the development of his faith.* This was an important shift. It did not mean that Jim no longer had to go to church. Far from it. Things emerged in his family and on the job that Jim looked to his church to help him clarify or discern. His church community, and participation in the eucharist, more and more became a primary faith "resource" to enable Jim to engage in the mission to which he felt called by God.

How does this differ from my story of trying to discover a spiritual and personal identity by being a good mother, wife, daughter, and daughter-in-law? I was locating my worth as a Catholic Christian in *playing only a serving role.* The one responsible for *everything* connected to my relationships with husband, children, parents, and in-laws was me. It was impossible for me to perceive myself *as a whole self.* Cop Jim O'Rourke may be in the same boat. If he perceives his whole worth in being a cop, he is collapsing role and spiritual identity. On the other hand, if he perceives himself as a whole self, then those facets that comprise *his being Jim O'Rourke*—a cop, a husband and a father, a neighbor and a citizen, part of a local church that truly is a community—come together and integrate in order to *form his identity as a Catholic Christian.*

Jim O'Rourke is not absorbed in his role so much as he is absorbed in the particular work experience of each day, and the challenges in his particular civic setting, and his particular home experience of each day. He knows the values he wants to further in these settings. Consequently, he can let himself become absorbed in these daily experiences because he knows who Jim O'Rourke the *person* is. And he discovers challenges and reinforcements regarding *that* identity in the give and take of his lived experience as well as through prayer and through small group sharing in his faith community.

Because he lives out his Christian formation in the culture in a wholistic way, Jim does not rigidly separate church and culture. Instead of receiving directives from *two separate realms,* Jim O'Rourke feels that he, in a sense, receives cues from God—in church, in family, at work, enabled by his own deep faith. And he follows these intimations in dealing with his placements. In other words, Jim O'Rourke doesn't see God locked into church territory where he, Jim, must go to check things out with God. *Jim O'Rourke grants God the same freedom of setting he experiences himself.*

Sometimes spirituality, embedded by believers in the marketplace, calls for more than an extra mile of courage. Yvonne Gagnon, a single mother, described this kind of courage in the NALM survey:

> I held a management position in a firm that did government work, being responsible for the financial transactions of a major department. While in that department I discovered some

very illegal and immoral transactions which would cost our
department hundreds of thousands of dollars. The specifica-
tions had been custom designed so that only one firm could
possibly be awarded a contract with subsequent benefits going
to the one person who drew up the specs. I reported my findings
to my immediate supervisor and he chose to avoid the matter
entirely, ordering me to drop the subject. Eventually I saw that I
couldn't change things and would be fired if I tried. I did not
want to be part of illegal activities, but I couldn't leave the firm
because of my need to support my children and there being no
other employment opportunities in the area. But St. Paul says if
you can't change it, don't be part of it.

So I took one of the biggest steps in my faith and my life by
taking a voluntary demotion which meant a huge cut in salary. I
was a nervous wreck while making my decision but I finally
submitted my letter requesting a demotion. But I had decided to
live my faith, not just talk it. I sweated blood when I considered
all the repercussions which might follow. With a "gag" rule
placed on me at work, my co-workers thought I was losing my
mind. Friends and relatives thought I was having a breakdown.
It's nice to read about people choosing great sacrifice for their
moral values, but when it's you! Good Lord, who's going to pay
the bills? Who's going to explain the loss of prestige? Who's
going to respond when the kids say, "Mom, why can't you stay
in your old job?"

When I was finally demoted to a bottom rung, I began to
sleep nights peacefully. My new co-workers accepted me, and
my worst fear, being treated as an outcast, didn't happen. It
would have been so easy to look the other way. But God seemed
to keep pointing in the direction of owning up to what was going
on. In the months of struggle I thought I wouldn't make it. The
funny thing was that God seemed closer then than usual. I had
to swallow my pride and ask creditors for more time, I had to
take humiliating remarks, but throughout it all I sensed God
telling me, "I never said it would be easy, but you'll be better off
for it." In some of my darkest moments God would bring parts
of scripture to my mind like the mustard seed passage and Peter
walking on water. It takes more courage than we think we have
to step out in faith and live it, but by trusting God we discover
the provider is there keeping us from drowning. I have known
the help of my God first-hand. That keeps me reaching out to
help others.

Jim O'Rourke and Yvonne Gagnon do not believe that the *world* in which they spend their days is the territory of an enemy of God. Being realists, both would not be slow to admit that God has enemies lurking in the world, but that does not make the world itself enemy territory. God as well as God's enemies can be found in that territory. Since the council, a number of lay believers have come to see what M.-D. Chenu, O.P. pointed out at the time of the council, "Grace does not 'sacralize' nature; in making it partake of divine life, it restores it to itself, so to speak."[12]

This affirmation of our lived experience regardless of setting does not necessarily mean that being a Catholic has diminished in significance within the lay Catholic. Assimilation means that lay Catholics now see junctures between their secular and their spiritual identities. Until this happened there could be no entity called *lay spirituality* because Catholics clung to their church identity to help them know who they were in an alien land. For some Catholics today the integration of personal identity, family identity, and secular identity not only names them in some way, but also becomes the content by which they recognize, in a primary way, their *spiritual* identity. They live out internalized values of justice and mercy in the encounters they experience day after day. At times they also work to socially transform their settings in intentional and organized ways. If lay Catholics are told to leave the rest of their lives on the church steps when they come to church, then what characterizes the Catholic believer as *authentically lay and authentically spiritual* is not invited into this Catholic believer's local church.

As this error is remedied in the future, we will see a church with an appearance quite different from the one we now see. Within the church, lay people will assume not only responsibility and authority based on baptismal call to minister through a broadening of clerical authority related to *internal* church functions (like becoming chancellor of a diocese), but also responsibilities and authority within the church rooted in the responsibilities and authority these lay adults hold within their ongoing web of *lay* existence. When that happens the full gift of lay spirituality will vivify the whole church.

Incarnate Life

This chapter described gaps that must be closed:

1. the gap between the reality of lay identity and how lay identity is sometimes perceived within the church;

2. the gap between living the reality of lay life experience and articulating that experience within the church;

3. the gap between the spiritual needs of the laity and the means available for meeting those needs.

Narrowing these gaps is essential if lay Catholics are to continue to identify with the church and intensify their mission vocation within the world.

Through the transparency that characterizes lay identity shines a great diversity of lifestyles and tasks. Through it "lay men and women hear the call to holiness in the very web of their existence (L.G. #31), in and through the events of the world, the pluralism of modern living, the complex decisions and conflicting values they must struggle with, the richness and fragility of sexual relationships, the delicate balance between activity and stillness, presence and privacy, love and loss."[13]

There is no single passage in the gospels to which we can point and say, "See, there is the incarnation." It is to the whole self and the whole life of Jesus toward which we must direct our gaze to perceive the incarnation. The same is true of the incarnated life of lay women and lay men.

4

FORMATION

Spirituality and Theology

When I entered public high school, I discovered that religious education classes conflicted with the Miraculous Medal novena devotions my mother and I regularly attended. My mother did not hesitate for even a moment in making a decision about the situation. We would both continue to attend Monday night's novena, and I would skip the catechism classes. "That book learning kind of religion you can pick up later," she said. "It'll be worse for you if you never learn to pray."

My mother knew instinctively that praying to God was more important than studying about God, that spirituality was a treasure greater than theology. My mother was about the business of *formation* though she probably never used the word. That formation "stuck." Friends envied me when Vatican II came along. Knowing little, I had little to unlearn. Later in life, as my mother suggested, I spent four years immersed in "the book learning kind of religion," but I never forgot that spirituality is more valuable than theology.

Underestimating theology is a practice popular today in some Catholic circles. Despite my early formation, it is not one I wish to encourage. Theology frames significant faith and church questions. If theology about a dimension of faith or church is in short supply, that dimension may not receive attention and clarity within our vast church system. During my studies in the late 1970s, I discovered that theology about the laity is in very short supply. Two giants stood forth—Congar and Chenu. The rest of the alphabet of theologians seem to have turned their minds to greener theological fields.

I began to get feisty about this lacuna. During a church history course, I told the professor that I wanted to write my term paper on the laity. I was told there was no laity until Martin Luther. "Who were all those people occupying the pews?" I asked.

59

"They were lay people," I was told. "But there was no consciousness of their value until Martin Luther."

He went on to explain that in the middle ages some lay folk insisted on being dressed in religious habits in their coffins in the hope that such garb would guarantee entrance through the gates of heaven.

Excluding ninety-eight percent of the church from theological reflection about faith and church struck me as a curious phenomenon then, and it does now. Somehow I had reached mid-life with the erroneous notion that what seminarians and theology students studied, at least in part, was theology about the people they would spend the rest of their lives serving, teaching, leading, and motivating to serve others.

If the institutional church is serious about laity engaged in mission, then it would be wise to take notice of lay theologians as well as theology about the laity. Needed are theologians who understand the secular world first-hand and who can help other lay people interpret theologically their lives immersed in that world. The emergence of feminist theology is a valiant effort to rectify an enormous theological error. What is beginning to be done by women needs also to be done by and with lay believers.

Later in my studies I met another theological giant, one who was a flesh-and-blood *lay theologian,* one whose perspective is thoroughly lay *and* thoroughly spiritual—Friedrich von Hugel.

If some of our present day ministerial leaders do not understand what it means to be a Christian adult in the real world of pay-offs, price-fixings and legal loopholes, von Hugel, the English theologian who lived from 1852 to 1925, did. Reality is a constant theme found in von Hugel's writings. Although there is a lesser focus on what the contemporary church characterizes as social consciousness in von Hugel's writings, the openness of his spirituality to the world, the way he invites an engagement with secular realities as well as the manner in which he "looks hard at the facts and does not assume that this 'look' will be easy" makes him an appropriate theologian for lay adults in our age.

Von Hugel saw the same flaw in both secularism and pietism: *foreclosure.* Both distort the experience of reality, in its full historical drama of God-and-world, by foreclosing on *experience,* on the experience of women and men as fleshed spirits and spirited enfleshment. Secularism forecloses through cyncism or false optimism. Pietism forecloses by not plumbing spiritual experience for its full reality, by imposing facile interpretations before the believer can articulate honestly the reality of his or her own experience. Both secularism and pietism evoke living that is inauthentic, dishonest, and irrelevant.[1]

Joseph Whelen, S.J. sums up von Hugel's insights this way:

> Only the religious human person, the one who prays, can fully manage the terrors and wholly accomplish the joys of his or her destiny through secularity . . . a valid person in a robust world and not their shadows or stunted versions are the truth . . . and only those who come to prayer with a deeply worldly heart are in full adoration of God.[2]

Most lay men and women are not messianic. They meet the world on the world's terms, and from and within that place enspirit and energize for the good of humankind what they can. Von Hugel thought of it as requiring a homely and humble heroism, one that does not deny reality, yet one that lets God, and only God, be God.

To be actively engaged in mission requires that movements toward and within the crowded and busy secular world be balanced by counter-movements that involve one in solitude, prayer, and quiet contemplation, enabling one to reflect on "crowded experience." Writing to his niece, von Hugel says, "Day and night, sunshine and storm, union and aloneness . . . *both* are necessary sooner or later, Sweet."

In lay life a rhythm of engagement with secular setting and engagement with some form of solitude and prayer is essential. As Harvey Cox puts it today, ". . . this new spirituality is nurtured not by a single-minded withdrawal from the world but by a rhythm of advance and retreat, of wading into the pain and conflict of the secular realm, and repairing regularly into the sustenance of solitude and of a supporting community."[3]

This insight is echoed by Pierre Babin, speaking about Christians who work in media:

> To produce a video, get a programme together, or make a film means that there are "rush" times of total tension: no question of sleeping one's full eight hours, nor of eating at the right time.

Given these circumstances there is no solution except that of the law of swings and roundabouts; that is to say that you have to accept periods of complete involvement during which you give yourself without pause and times of deep silence and space; the studio is balanced by the monastery, the office by the weekend. Whoever wants to survive "in spirit and in truth" must give serious attention to setting up this balance.[4]

As a lay friend once put it, "I live a mission-hermit existence."

According to von Hugel, each person and every culture are initially in tension, even conflict, and are destined for tension. *Friction* is the name he gave to this. The religious person, through this friction, moves toward his or her destiny, drawing the multiplicity into harmony. When this process is blocked or concluded in a contrived way, injustice, ideology, fanaticism, idolatry and/or impoverishment result. Only by being "friends of God and prophets" can we offer a corrective. Prophetism (the spirit of protest) is necessary, says von Hugel; its task is to purify, create and reform, remembering that it is doing this in a setting with multiplicity so that no *one* protest, no *one* program, will bring perfection because reality is always "multiple." To bring harmony and justice in and through "conflict-friction-tension" is always slow and costly.

Von Hugel was one of the first theologians *to perceive the value of experience.* As Evelyn Underhill's spiritual director he tells her to visit the poor to distribute some of her blood away from her mind where he felt too much of it was lodged. Von Hugel saw the agnostic as a land animal, the religious person as an amphibian. The religious person is an amphibian because this person integrates the realities of spirit and world. Each of us is "spirit-in-a-body-in-a-world," called to love the world as God loves it, that is, *with* God's love *in* God's world-affirming Spirit. To do this we must contemplate both God and world.

To be religious means to become, in the deepest and most vibrant sense, an individuated person. At the heart of it is this fact: *God gives God's own self to us as God gives a self to each of us.* Development of what we call today "religious consciousness," of personhood, of spiritual maturity—the self God gives to us by giving God's own Self to us—is vital because it frees us engage in the mission "of seeking, of occupation with, of learning from and teaching, of being stimulated by and of leavening and transforming, in a word, of loving the actual world of time and space around us and within us."[5]

The passage from "self-entrenchment" to devotion to God's kingdom means self-surrender, asked and given. According to von Hugel, this does not mean the dissolution of personality. It is a formation by God that leads to liberation, which is an ecstatic gift creative of a truly free self, for the action of God is personal, not deterministic. For von Hugel,

> God is Reality. Reality that is near. People put God so far away, in a sort of mist somewhere. I pull their coat-tails. God is *near*. God's otherness and difference, and nearness. You *must* get that. God's nearness is straight out of the heart of Jesus . . . God infinite and other, yet working in men and women.[6]

If I were asked to give a brief explanation of *spiritual formation,* I would echo von Hugel, claiming that it is a process through which God gives a self to us by giving God's own Self to us. That sounds more simple than it usually turns out to be in the reality of our lives. True, some women and men are blessed with instant and powerful conversion experiences. But, as William James points out in *Varieties of Religious Experience,* most conversions are long, slow processes, with many starts and stops in need of discernment to trace patterns of authenticity. A second complication is that human beings are formed through a variety of life experiences. Not all can be characterized as religious. Not all can be dismissed as irreligious. Lay people, in particular, are formed in an ongoing way by events, persons and settings that are not within church and are not explicitly religious in orientation. Vatican II acknowledges that family, work, and socialization are formative by calling these lay settings the "web of existence" for Catholic lay men and women.

The following is the "tip of the iceberg" when it comes to formation. But the five kinds of formation described represent in part realities that *influence formation in faith.*

One Kind of Formation—Our Createdness

Early one April morning while I was gazing through a window in Vermont wondering if spring would ever come, I was invited by five year old Nicole to make a few acorns. "I'm making a house (from a Kleenex box) for Teddy Bear, and you can help if you want, Gran."

As she and I drew, colored and cut out acorns, I gestured to the window and said, "From tiny acorns like these grow great big oak trees. It's very mysterious."

"I don't think it's mysterious," Nicole mumbled. Still intent on her crayon on the paper, Nicole pointed to her nine month old sister. "Look at Renee, Gran."

I looked over to the corner where Renee was drawing clothing from her Grandpa's duffel bag. With a little "whee," she tossed each item to the wind. Nicole then put her crayon down and looked at me. "Once Renee was this little." Niki put her two hands close together. "Now she's that big." Niki pointed toward Renee. "Someday she may even be as big as you, Gran." Niki moved her two hands as far apart as they could go, which I felt was an innocent exaggeration. "It's not mysterious, Gran. It's just the way things are!"

The little scene came back to me again and again in the following week. Growing, changing, being different from how you now are—that's the way things are. It's not mysterious. Nicole had put her finger on one of the striking differences in how a child and an adult experience and, therefore, perceive life. For most adults, change (whether in a waistline or a habit or a friend) is to be noticed, evaluated, grieved or celebrated. For a child it's just the way things are. Children anticipate the body changing, the mind changing, the heart changing. The embedded adult ambivalence about change means that spiritual growth sometimes is not anticipated.

In addition, the Christian tradition with its emphasis on baptism may diminish in value the formation that happens as we are "knit in our mother's womb," as Psalm 139 reveals. Recent research on newborn infants indicates that they distinguish their mothers' voices and respond to them. Hearing tapes of the mother's voice caused increased suckling on a bottle in contrast to hearing voices of the father and of other women.

To Nicole that would be "the way things are." To me the way things are reveals the mystery of our formation by God.

Formation Through a Profound Experience of God's Love

Until recently, church leaders seemed to have underestimated the significance of formation regarding the call of lay persons to engagement in mission. To put it another way, an expectation for mission action may be laid on lay people without realizing that *preparation* is necessary to persevere in that call. Or as Cardinal Pironio of the Pontifical Council on the Laity puts it, ". . . all the fruitfulness of our presence in the world as witnesses to the resurrection, our capacity to change from within the structures of injustice, depend on our capacity, as a church, to manifest clearly and communicate effectively the mystery of God's love for the human person. This means: forming 'witnesses of love,' men and women who have *a profound experience of God's love.*"[7]

Without a formation process that enables us to discover "a profound experience of God's love" (and to remember and savor those experiences in prayer), we may be weak witnesses. The world may run roughshod over our mission efforts. The central call to the church *internally* is not sustaining sacraments or dioceses or movements or church buildings or schools. The central call is *to enable the formation of lay believers to be "friends of God and prophets" on mission in the world.*

Community—A Third Kind of Formation

Community is not a substitute for formation. Community can enhance formation by providing a setting for experiences of God's love. Community also reinforces the meaning of connectedness in our lives, connectedness with God, with other believers, with world, and with self. Being part of a local community or movement may also enhance the process of individuation that happens when God gives God's Self to us.

Without a sense of *individuation,* the only mission that laity engage in may be communal. Because, from this perspective, our spiritual identity and church identity are seldom considered apart from a "group," we may lack a mission consciousness during all those hours each week when we are not part of that group. In addition, dependency on community presents a danger when lay adults are forced to move or when the community, for one reason or another, dissolves.

Community, on the other hand, can be instrumental in the formation of spirituality and a mission consciousness. As Rosemary Haughton puts it, "It may help a little to remember that one of the ways of recognizing increasing spiritual maturity is by noting an increase in areas of full consciousness. The spiritual breakthroughs of life always make consciously available areas of personality previously unconscious."[8]

Participating in community, if it is authentic community, helps to enable that process. In her book *The Passionate God,* Haughton notes the benefits received from members in a community: ". . . the common experience of this adventure, the support they give each other, the discoveries they confide to each other . . . deepen and widen the scope of their human awareness, first of each other and then of themselves as part of a greater whole, many of whose members suffer dumbly and remediably."[9]

A Fourth Kind of Formation—Spiritual Awareness

One week recently I met with five believers who are adult in their work life, and, of the five, three believers who are adult in their spiritual life. How was that spelled out in our sessions together? Bob, Sharon, and Fran were (a) easily reflective, (b) able to listen to interior cues, (c) responsive, not reactive, in their engagements with God, and (d) experienced in concentrating their attention on their "spiritual state." Bob, Sharon, and Fran have overcome that embedded adult bias against change. In regard to their own spirituality, the three *expect* to change. In particular, they have learned how to take their cues for moving forward with God from *the inside*—from what they sense *within.*

Bob, Sharon and Fran have been through a *spiritual formation process.* Each has had the opportunity to develop a *consciousness* about his or her "interiority." They have engaged in a process that was intended to help them understand how they function spiritually. (For many of us in the church, if that happens, it's accidental.) They learned how to keep track of patterns in their relationship with God, how to "stand outside of themselves" and consciously notice the intersections between their life and their prayer. They are able to discern psychological and spiritual "movements" within and to perceive how *change* characterizes these movements. They are comfortable with change; they anticipate it, desire it, know that change often represents progress in the spiritual life.

The other two believers, Kay and Don, want to be part of the mission of the church, but they have not participated in a formation process. Having little consciousness of their interior spiritual "ups and downs," they often feel frustrated and burned out when they attempt to minister or engage in mission in family, workplace, and civic community. Don puts it this way: "I feel as if I'm in the middle of a pitched battle, and the supply troops are three states over in covered wagons. I'm about ready to give up on the whole thing!"

In *Formation of the Laity: Twelve Theses,* Cardinal Pironio begins by referring to scripture: "Let us begin with a text we read a few days ago during the liturgy of the mass, 'Although alone, she (Wisdom) can do all; herself unchanging, she makes all things new. In each generation she passes into holy souls, she makes them friends of God and prophets . . .' (Wis 7:27–28). Friends of God and prophets! That is the goal of our formation."[10]

Rosemary Haughton perceives Wisdom in a Pauline sense: "Paul knew Wisdom in another way, which thrusts . . . the experience it expresses and the fact itself into a different category, the category of fleshiness; not just 'penetrated' by Wisdom but as herself, as a body, 'planted' in a people. In that people she grows in and through them as the point of exchange in such concrete and ascertainable ways . . . until the final breakthrough makes possible another kind of bodily being. 'The Church is Christ's body,' says Paul."

Becoming friends of God and prophets, being part of Christ's body, is difficult for some lay believers because a pastoral deficit exists in their local parish regarding spirituality. That they do not want that pastoral deficit was revealed in the consultation of the Synod on the Laity. As Robert Kinast puts it, "The desire for and necessity of lifelong formation is high on the laity's priority list . . .

(particularly) growth in the spiritual life." Unfortunately, spiritual development for lay parishioners may be looked on as an "extra," something one goes beyond the local community to find as if this pastoral deficit had no connection with the ministry and mission the parishioners are called to activate in this real world in which we all exist.

Formation for the Already Formed

Human, animal or vegetable, if she, he or it is in the adult phase of life, another phase, another time, other events preceded this adult phase and helped bring into reality the adulthood now experienced. Adult means having a history on which to reflect. That is how we gain self-knowledge and self-understanding. By *tracing* that history, that life experience, adult believers begin to identify ways in which they have been formed to be the adult Christians they are today. This approach dovetails with the capacity for change given to us by our creator God, the formation enabled by community participation, and the practices of prayer and reflection we have developed in explicit programs of spiritual development.

Lay adults are in many ways already formed. What I fear the most from emerging formation programs is that some programs may treat lay adults as if they are "clean slates"—ready, willing and able to be fashioned in any form a professional staff minister sees fit. Adulthood implies that personality has in many ways already become established, that some habits and attitudes are fixed, that the routes taken in achieving adulthood can be traced.

Helping readers trace, in an explicit way, their faith journeys as experienced *in church-related activities* is not the purpose of this book. Effective ways to engage in that kind of formation process can be found. Instead we will consider *webs of experience in our past and how these have been formative.* This approach evolved from questions I have asked myself during the past few years while working in the area of spirituality. For example, does our Christian formation happen only through church activity and worship? Do parental figures, friends, the places where we have lived, the work we do, have a spiritually formative impact? If these elements *are* formative, I feel it is essential to examine them and how they have made us the Catholic Christians we are today.

In testing this approach, we will reflect on the formative aspects of relationships with parental figures, friends and spouse. Work and callings as well as relationship to "place" will be considered. Place, the cultural context that influenced us as children and has an impact on us as adults, will be central to our reflection because mission takes place in particular places and is motivated by our sense of bonding to places we inhabit.

The reflection described above *is foundational for lay mission.* By this I mean that discerning the source of our values and how we have enfleshed those values within the web of our own lives would seem to belong in formation programs for lay adults.

Putting Away the Things of a Child

Some commentators feel that the small communities emerging in the church since Vatican II are no accident. Within them believers have discovered the adult reality of others, of themselves, and of God. Experiencing the reality of God and experiencing the reality of ourselves as adults often go hand in hand.

Community experiences have given some believers the courage to face experiences that happened in the stages of life prior to adulthood. The developmental routes to adulthood are paved with the particular events and the varied processes we experienced as infants, children, adolescents, and young adults. We sometimes resist reflecting on these routes and take detours around them. But the particularities and processes we experienced have *formed us* to be the adults we are. To eventually "put them away" in order to engage wholeheartedly as Christian adults in mission, we must not foreclose on them prematurely. We have to look at them and face their realities.

One of the most significant "processes" I experienced as a child, one that formed me in particular ways, was living with an alcoholic. Living with an alcoholic is a particular process. As an adult I had to confront this process in order to understand myself *as an adult* even though it was a process I experienced as a child. For some time I delayed facing the impact of this process on me; I thought faith would compensate for whatever happened to me in childhood.

The truth of the matter was that living my life as an adult Christian in fidelity to God was hindered because I denied that process. It was a *spiritual* gift to recognize, finally, that what I went through as a child affected not only who I was as a child, but also the particular Christian adult person named Virginia.

As an adult child of an alcoholic I have something in common with all adults who were and are children of alcoholics. For me, being the daughter of an alcoholic father influenced me in ways I might not have been influenced were I the daughter of an alcoholic mother. Being the child of an alcoholic father who stopped drinking when I was nineteen influenced me in ways I might not have been influenced were I the child of an alcoholic who was a drinker until he died.

Through a childhood process that many people have experienced, some things particular about me were formed. Is this a spiritually significant fact? I believe it is.

It took me twenty minutes to think through and write down these statements of particularity about myself. It took me *twenty years as an adult* to come before God and share them.

While living at home and for more than one decade after I left home, I made statements to myself *about my father* with no realization that my identity was being shaped by his identity. During the novenas in high school I prayed fervently for him, but never for myself. Later, I came before God as a member of the group by which the church seemed to identify me—one of those "trying to be a good Catholic mother" types. Then I became involved in social justice issues and came before God as an activist believer trying to enhance justice in the world.

These *roles* were spiritually convenient. They allowed me to pick and choose the who within me I revealed to myself and to God. I thought I was doing what I was supposed to be doing, even after I received the letter from the columnist in *St. Anthony's Messenger* referred to earlier. The advice in that letter I felt indicated how I could present myself to other people—not to God.

I told God who I was. I didn't listen to what God wanted to say about the topic. In a way, *through foreclosure,* I resisted God's formation.

That doesn't mean God didn't know who I was. But it did mean that I hid part of who I was from God; in turn that meant that my heart was deaf to hearing anything God might have to say to me *about that part of myself, about being an adult child of an alcoholic.* I could not be naked before God as Jesus was. I could not be fully formed by God.

Until lay believers are able to hear all that God might have to say about any facet of themselves as adults, they may remain stuck on a spiritual treadmill. *Roles (good Catholic mother) can help us deny our true identities.* My faith in God, the very thing that enabled me to survive as a child, played tricks on me as an adult.

If naming your particularities is not part of who you are in the church, then admitting these particularities to God may be difficult. Implicit in St. Paul's dictum to "put away the things of a child" is *decisiveness,* indicating action. Putting away is not a process of denying, nor hiding, nor disposing of by throwing out. What has been formed deeply within us is *beyond our own power* to "throw out."

Putting away means facing what is there and dealing with it. There is no authentic formation process without facing and dealing with how we have been formed by the past. That is how we are enabled to put it away.

When we put away things in everyday life, there is always the possibility of retrieval. The analogy is apt for our spiritual life. What we don't put away we are apt to trip over. But when we put away through a process of facing and sorting through what we put away, we can move on freely yet retrieve in trust what we have put away. No matter what stories we may tell ourselves, if we have not faced what we think we have put away, we have not yet really put away.

In my own life, living with an alcoholic was a crucial formative dynamic. When I finally dealt with it as an adult, I took that decisive action that enabled me to put away yet be able to retrieve. I was then able to *break away* as Jesus did.

The most basic kind of preparation women and men need is formation for adulthood and formation in faith. The two can go hand in hand, as Jesus reveals.

Jesus on the Way to Adulthood

Breaking away from dependency in order to become spiritually mature is portrayed for us in the New Testament in three gospel accounts, each revealing Jesus breaking away from being parented in order to be *wholeheartedly at one with God.*

The first takes place when Jesus, at age twelve, is found in the temple.

> After three days they found him sitting in the temple, sitting among the teachers, listening to them and asking them questions; and all who heard him were amazed at his understanding and his answers. And when they saw him, they were astonished; and his mother said to him, "Son, why have you treated us so? Behold, your father and I have been looking for you anxiously." And he said to them, "How is it that you sought me? Did you not know that I must be in my Father's house?" And they did not understand the saying which he spoke to them (Lk 2:46–51, RSV).

When I pray with this passage from Luke's gospel I see the child Jesus breaking away particularly from Joseph—telling his father Joseph that his call is to be about the business of his Father Yahweh. Because there is afoot in our world someone who bears a familial sense (Abba—dearest Father), someone who transcends the natural gift of family, the call is to shift allegiance. And in my imagination I see Jesus peer into the angry, frightened, sad eyes of Joseph as he bluntly breaks the news of his breaking away from the *vertical* dynamic that human parenting is.

Later in the gospels we find the passage about the true relatives of Jesus.

> While he was still speaking to the people, behold, his mother and his brothers stood outside, asking to speak to him. But he replied to the man who told him, "Who is my mother, and who are my brothers?" And stretching out his hand toward his disciples, he said, "Here are my mother and my brothers! For whoever does the will of my Father in heaven is my brother, and sister, and mother" (Mt 12:46–50, RSV).

"These are my mother and my brothers and my sisters."

Parenting often has a horizontal, nurturing dynamic as well as a vertical dynamic. Mary calls him to be with her and his brothers. In response, Jesus seemingly disowns them by owning, in a familial way, his relationship to those who hear the word of God. "These are my mother and my brothers and my sisters." And in my imagination I hear Jesus bluntly *choosing* the horizontal dynamic of friendship which transcends the natural order that mothering and sibling relationships represent.

Interestingly, these two stories seem to parallel the two great commandments. A vertical transfer happens in what the child Jesus was formed to feel for his father Joseph, his mother Mary, and the Jewish master of the universe whom Jesus puts into a familial context (Abba—dearest Father, the one whom believers are to love with the whole of mind, heart, and spirit). In a similar way, what the child finds evocative in being family in a horizontal sense, Jesus transfers to friendship experienced beyond family. With those linked to him by faith, those whom he names as intimate to himself as mother, brother, sister, Jesus teaches us how to love neighbor as one loves self.

As his mission intensifies, Jesus breaks away again.

And they came to Jerusalem. And he entered the temple and began to drive out those who sold and those who bought in the temple, and he overturned the tables of the moneychangers and the seats of those who sold pigeons; and he would not allow anyone to carry anything through the temple. And he taught, and said to them, "Is it not written, 'My house shall be called a house of prayer for all the nations'? But you have made it a den of robbers" (Mk 11:15–18, RSV).

The third gospel story that exemplifies breaking away is Jesus' turning over the tables in the temple. I imagine it as a warning to those who insist on parenting God, who lust to have God belong to the temple rather than having the temple belong to God. Breaking away from perceiving church only as a parental figure to help form church into a community of disciples whose relational purpose is God and neighbor, not church itself, is taught vividly in this scriptural lesson.

Breaking away; severing the apron strings; the inevitable rebellion against parents—in whatever lingo we put it today, what Jesus did each of us has to do. It is the essential formative process in becoming adult. In order to do it we often need to understand, not back away from, the parental figures who have formed us. If we attempt to substitute an immature filial relationship with *church* for a robust, *adult* relationship with God, we, in a way, sell our souls.

No one is excused from the breaking away process that Jesus went through in claiming his adulthood. Some try to delay the stages. Many of us know men or women, in their thirties, forties, or fifties, who confound church as a structured community of adult disciples by making infantile need-fulfillment the business they are about. "Mother me, father me," they cry.

Or the message may be, "Let me mother you, let me father you." Between the lines of this concern may lie: Let me praise or blame you; don't ask me to join you as another companion of Jesus, as a fellow disciple of God.

In the passages I have cited we see Jesus modeling the way to a spiritual adulthood of deepened intimacy with God. Lay believers understand the wisdom of Jesus when they struggle with their vertical parenting agendas internalized as innumerable "shoulds" that stymie their thrust toward mission. They discover the love of Jesus in their struggle with the horizontal parenting dynamic in favor of a generativity that frees them from being only with "my own" kind to feel secure. They taste the courage of Jesus turning over the tables when they struggle to lessen the hold of church as a parental figure by ratifying with their own lives that church is a community that belongs to God for the sake of neighbor.

Scenes of breaking away, even in the gospel, evoke chaos, confusion, challenge. Growth is never neat. If we expect it to be, we may mutilate the process by "spiritualizing" it, never really growing up, never developing the depth of adult personhood that is the only foundation for spiritual maturity. To walk the path through this chaos we often need mentors such as Mary was for Jesus, mentors who have faith in our destiny.

Breaking away in order to come into adulthood is a blessing initiated by Jesus in his earthly life. If lay believers disown this blessing, activated by themselves with the help of the Spirit, and attempt to do mission, they may give a good spiel, but they run the danger of ending up standing behind a table selling pigeons. Like Jesus, they are called to let go of dependencies by engaging in the challenging process of breaking away from the need to be parented by others or to parent others, or to have the church be about the business of being their parent instead of being a house of prayer for adults and a catalyst for holiness and mission, owned by God. Part of the process of putting away in order to break away and be wholly available for God, is to reflect on how parental figures in our lives have formed us.

PART TWO

1

FORMATION THROUGH RELATIONSHIPS: PARENTAL FIGURES

The Private World That Prepares Us for the Public World

Intimacy is a crucial factor in formation. Intimacy is a process, a process within a relationship. Intimacy is one way to be related to another, whether that other is a parent, an aunt, a grandparent, a friend, a spouse, a daughter or son—or God. Engagement in this process of intimacy leads us to an awareness of the other—to his or her particularities of personality, spirit, habits, and so on. Intimacy gives us a special kind of knowledge about one another. Where intimacy has been formed we dare to be vulnerable.

The home, the bedroom, the fireplace are images that suggest intimacy. To reveal intimacy on film the close-up shot is used. The world of intimacy always seems like a small world, confined, contained, cocoon-like. Though a small world, intimacy can prepare us for encounter with the large world. And the world of intimacy is what heals us when the slings and arrows of the large world leave us wounded. Our effectiveness in the public world of work and civic concerns, the world we associate with Christian mission, depends in no small part on how we have been formed in the small world of intimacy. The lessons we learn about self-respect, respect for others, and standing up for our convictions are often lessons shaped within childhood on which we can reflect.

The intimacy that prepares us and the intimacy that heals us may be intimacy within family, with friends, alone with God, or with God through family or friends. It may be the intimacy of the gathered community in prayer with God.

How we meet the larger world we migrate to in adulthood may

depend on the capacity we have for intimacy. If within the relationships we've had in childhood I feel affirmed and loved for who I am, then I may encounter the wider world with confidence, free to exercise my gifts and competencies and stand by my convictions and values.

This is an essential part of formation because the journey to adulthood is not only a conversion of identity, from child to adult; it is also a process of conversion in intimacy. *As an adult,* my behavior will be inappropriate if I exercise intimacy as if I were a child. As an adult in relationships with others, I must exercise intimacy as an adult.[1]

Intimacy is not an escape from reality; rather intimacy integrates self and reality. In other words, when I am intimate I am in relationship with another or others, and I realize that fact. This relationship is a bonding. You matter to me, I matter to you—in the reality of who we are *as persons.* I reveal my reality to the ones with whom I am intimate. They reveal their reality to me. In addition, we both invite the reality of the world, and other relationships, into how we are related. When these last elements of reality are missing, *romanticism substitutes for intimacy.* In our culture, and even in our church, the two—romanticism and intimacy—are sometimes confused. For example, a co-worker may feel that he is on intimate terms with a colleague because he has shared his vulnerability with her. But if she has not responded in kind, the relationship is not intimate. At times the romantic has its unique value, but because romanticism in our culture is often equated with intimacy, Christians cannot forget that *reality,* not make-believe, lies at the heart of intimacy.

The *interior* dynamics of who we are as persons become apparent within intimacy. From this fact, we can infer a tie between intimacy and spirituality. Friendship is not really friendship, or marriage really marriage, unless two persons share interior dynamics. In a similar way, a sharing of the heart with God (as well as sensing a reciprocation from God) is what "having a relationship with God" means.

In addition to intimacy with another or with others, it is possible to be intimate with oneself. *Self-intimacy,* a vital component of spiritual maturity, is not always valued. We live in a "doing" society, and this "doing" dynamic has seeped into the church, causing us to think we can get by without seeking solitude and befriending what's going on inside ourselves. I am not talking about being self-absorbed, an adolescent phenomenon that reveals insecurity about self. I am talking about *"knowing" self.* But self-intimacy also means *caring about self* as well as knowing self. The former has been affirmed in Christian tradition while the latter, the caring about self, has sometimes been denigrated.

The quality of one's self-intimacy is often shaped by attitudes and values within the home. For example, as I was growing up, humility was valued. If I brought home a good report card, it would receive a compliment, then be put away with a caution about thinking I was "better than the rest."

"I don't want you growing up conceited. Don't think too good about yourself," my mother would say. Consequently, I came to believe that considering myself in a favorable light was an occasion for sin. This was reinforced by the fact that the only time I ever spoke about myself in church was in the confessional where I enumerated what was bad about myself. As a child and as an adolescent, having a good image of myself would have been a miracle. Later, in early adulthood, when I let an authentic awareness of self emerge, I often felt uncomfortable. Unable to own myself, it became second nature to me to let others own me. It took a very long time to learn that self-esteem and self-possession are necessary foundations for self-discipline.

Intimacy and Childhood

The intimate life of the young child includes those creatures who seem inanimate to those of us who are adults. Halfway through the Nutcracker ballet one Christmas, four year old Nicole moaned in a loud voice.

"What's the matter?" her aunt and I hissed simultaneously.

"Poor polar bear," cried Nicole, forgetting to lower her voice. "Polar bear's in your pocketbook, Gran, and can't see the dancing!" For a moment all three of us felt guilt for depriving polar bear of this special occasion. The gift of intimacy with which small children are blessed can sometimes lead those most hardened by life into the enchanting world of imagination that children's familiarity with intimacy creates.

Surprisingly, it can be difficult to describe formation within a family where the gift is a sustained quality of intimacy that forms children to become whole persons as adults. The way family members relate can have a taken-for-granted ambiance, one that prevents seeing what was so good about the intimacy in that house that formed the kids to grow up to be remarkable adults (not in achievements but in character). "It seemed like such an ordinary family," we say, or, "It seemed as though things were always on the brink of disaster but look at the way those kids turned out! Makes you wonder!"

Young children, from birth, need a world of affirming intimacy. Blessed are those who create this formative path into adulthood for them.

Within the process of intimacy variations occur. For example, one is not intimate with offspring the same way one may be intimate with one's spouse. "One big happy family" with mom and dad always being mom and dad rather than husband and wife may not be one big happy family. A person may not be intimate with friends the same way that person is intimate within family or with a parent. The intimacy that characterizes a family with a missing parent may be different from the intimacy that characterizes the family that includes, besides two parents, a grandparent and an exchange student from Holland. The intimacy that characterizes an Arab family may be closer to the intimacy that characterizes an Israeli family than the intimacy within a Scandinavian family. Yet throughout the world, the kind of intimacy one experienced in childhood often indicates how one will handle intimacy as an adult.

Intimacy shapes personal and adult identity. There are at least three "frameworks" for family intimacy. In a framework evocative of affirmative intimacy, not only is affection openly expressed, but realities are also acknowledged. "Who I am" may get under the skin of other family members at times, but "who I am" is not pre-judged or condemned. We "rely" on one another, and we "come through" when we are relied upon. Quality time together is apparent as is time for honest exchange. *The responsibilities accepted and the authority exercised in this type of family emerge from the seedbed for family life—affirmative intimacy.*

The second family framework evokes a *negatively intimate*

atmosphere. When abuse characterizes the relationships within family, suffering can be experienced with particular intensity *because* the family is a limited world; what is felt is felt with exceptional intensity because the persons *are* related. Children caught in such a world may become psychologically deformed—the opposite of formed—and spend a lifetime undoing this process of deformation.

A third framework is lack of intimacy. Although in the United States at this time there is a necessary focus and concern about wife and child abuse (negative intimacy), *lack of intimacy* may be even more prevalent. Family members may not be demonstrative with one another. Not only does this mean that hugging is not a family practice, it also may mean that the good "give and take" of fighting never crosses the threshold. Grace may be recited at every family meal, but graciousness is not felt. Solace is seldom sensed, as expressing sorrow is seldom allowed. Spontaneous fun is experienced less than scheduled, structured family activities. Being with one another is not often experienced as joy.

Parental figures shape the kind of intimacy that becomes the framework for family, and the world of family intimacy may not be a world conducive to health, psychic or spiritual. Ingmar Bergman portrayed such intimacy dramatically in *Fanny and Alexander* by revealing the contrast between the family world the children experienced one Christmas with their natural parents and extended family, and the family world they entered when their mother remarried after becoming widowed, an intimate world characterized by diabolical cruelty. In the film the children experienced what can happen when the framework for family intimacy shifts from positive to negative.

Within family it is no easy task to trace the fault-lines that lie beneath the surface. Yet no family is without them. When we come to realize that *love expressed as intimacy is the first and most essential formative experience of childhood,* we begin to search for those fault-lines.

Ancestral Figures and Intimacy

"My oldest memories are a hundred years old, or perhaps a bit more," said Gaston Bachelard.[2] He speaks for many of us. There is no denying that many of us were formed by stories of ancestors heard in childhood, stories that may go back a century. Hearing these stories of ancestral parental figures, we experience the security of sensing our roots.

Aspects of ourselves are formed by ancestors whose stories are "bred in the bone." For most of us these ancestors remain a mystery. But a group, interviewed recently, revealed how famous yet distant ancestors formed them. Reading the interviews, I realized that there's more to our formation than meets the eye.

"I'd never want to get into an argument with her because I know I'd lose. She was very opinionated and spoke her mind. But in some ways I'm like her: I talk a lot and so did she," says the great-great-grandniece of Louisa May Alcott.

Nathan Hale Shapiro, great (times five) nephew of the early patriot, has reflected on his formation. "I think I take after his risk-taking side. I work on scaffolding (as a painter). I do kung fu and skate boarding." This descendant recognizes gifts from both of his lines of descent. "I think I have the best of both worlds—I'm proud of the colorful people in my mother's lineage and of my father's side, which is Russian Jewish. They're two extremes, but I think they're the best of both worlds. I think the combination says something good about this country."

"Bloodlines—Don't Leave Home Without Them," the title of the article in *New England Magazine* from which the above stories came, suggests that the bloodlines of ancestors, many of them mythical parental figures met in childhood, contribute an intimate dimension to childhood. In them we hear the story of our own formation in deep and colorful ways. Hearing the stories makes my particular "history" *my* particular history, forming, in a way, my personal identity.

Parental Figures

According to Sam Keen, "the disappearance of a sense of place, of the significance of particular spaces and locations, is one of the deplorable characteristics of our time."[3] For immigrant peoples like the waves of Catholics who came to America in the 1800s, place and people easily became fused, not only by city but by parish and by neighborhood. For example, in one part of Boston people often introduced themselves by naming first their parish. Parish established their "people," their neighborhood, which established who Timmy or Tommy, Molly or Bridget was as a person.

Some Catholics were eventually forced to move beyond their ethnic group. Artist Frank Stella, in *Growing Up Italian,* describes the dilemma that emerged in his family from the lack of schools in the Italian quarter where he grew up. In the same book, Bishop Francis Mugavero of Brooklyn describes some who desired to move *beyond* their ethnic enclave, like his brothers who did not marry Italian-Americans. "Marrying outside your culture was, I think, part of that *looking up,* that wanting to rise out of your own class into the class that had made it."[4]

Between Catholic ethnic groups all was not always harmonious. In childhood I never lost sight of the fact that my heritage came from two different Catholic ethnic peoples. In his worst moments, my father would refer to my mother by the epithet for her native stock. He also accused her of believing that she had married beneath herself because marriage had forced her to move from a college town, with little overt ethnicity, to the mill town where he lived.

Although my mother never went beyond an eighth grade education, she may have felt she *had* lowered herself by moving from the college town to the ethnic mill town. She never tired of telling me that in France her ancestors were large land owners, and I felt awe when she told about our heritage in goods and treasure sinking into the Atlantic Ocean on the voyage to Canada taken when our ancestors emigrated. That our ancestors were lost too was barely mentioned. My mother always moved on to the story of our second cousin Giselle, an opera star in Paris, whom we would someday visit. Such is the stuff of children's dreams!

But Daddy was as proud, for different reasons, of his grandfather's escape from Ireland as a felon for having poached on the king's land to feed his starving family, and of his mother coming alone at age eight by steerage from Ireland.

How do these stories form a child? Who can ever know the dimensions of meaning and hope they create within?

When I was a child, every few years my father would take me on a day-long trip to the Berkshires in western Massachusetts where we would visit the house where he grew up in Williamstown. Sometimes the lady in the sweet red house by the river would invite us in to see the tiny rooms inside. When our own children were adolescents, we lived in the Berkshires and made a pilgrimage to this ancestral house at least once each summer. We now have photos in our album of our granddaughter visiting the little red house with us, connecting her with a great-grandfather she knows only through stories. In a recent renovation of the house, the new owners discovered beams that go back to the 1770s.

This "family history house" continues to reveal *its* history, enriching the stories that are handed down. Knowing "I have a history" expands my horizon of time and place as a child. In families, one way to begin to connect children to global realities and mission is by helping them become more aware of the history of their own families with its broad horizon of time and place. As we mature we come to the realization that some of these ancestral figures were the parental figures who formed our own parents. That consciousness can bear the fruit of gratitude or forgiveness.

Intimacy, Responsibility, and Authority

Lineage empowers. The glory and majesty of Giselle the Parisian opera star, the courage and perseverance of Katherine Sullivan who came by steerage from Ireland at age eight, formed my daughters as well as myself. Someday we will be ancestral figures, but today *as parental figures,* whether we be mothers and fathers, teachers, aunts, uncles, priests, sisters, or lay ministers, we empower or impoverish those who come after us by *the way we combine intimacy, responsibility, and authority.*

In reflecting back on our childhood, most of us begin to realize that there were many parental figures in our lives—mom and dad for sure, whether missing or present, but also aunts and uncles, older siblings, teachers, neighbors, nuns and priests, the cop on the corner, the doctor, the dentist—the "big people" in my place, big people who, in one way or another, helped or hindered my formation.

In one way or another, in order to grow up and claim our adulthood, we eventually must deal, interiorly at least, with these parental figures who formed us. For some believers, conversion to the identity of an adult believer may be impeded by memories of church parental figures. Finding a place for the healing of these memories in the church is a needed dynamic *within* the church if we are serious about lay formation. Because there has been little opportunity to do this in many church settings in an honest way, the stories are told (sometimes in an exaggerated way) in more public forums. The number of Catholics who have flocked to plays like *Sr. Mary Ignatius Tells It All* reveals the need for healing within the church.

The Aunts

One June a few years ago, when Nicole's age was still counted in months, I put her in a backpack carrier and walked with her around the circle that was my neighborhood growing up. I remembered the family in house after house after house on the streets that framed my street. I told the stories of those families to baby Nicole.

Two weeks after the morning walk in my old neighborhood, I started a thirty day retreat. Memories of the walk and the neighborhood emerged in my first prayer of that retreat. And then I saw the "aunts."

Because life at home when I was a child had its ups and downs due to difficulties between my mother and father over his drinking, I was often farmed out. My aunts took care of me and took the edge off the loneliness I felt as an only child. In the first prayer of the retreat I savored each of them: Aunt Peg who let me sometimes mind the corner store she and Uncle Peter owned; Aunt Edith who taught me to cook by letting me cook alongside her; Aunt Laura who took me to the race track and let me pick out the horse for the last bet of the day, but who more often took me to a nearby city where we saw a double feature in the afternoon and another double feature in the evening; Aunt Nora who taught me how to sew and how to see the world through creative eyes; Mrs. LaPrade (whose husband always called her Mrs. LaPrade even in front of their own family) who took me on vacations along with her own nine kids.

As I contemplated my aunts (only two were blood relatives) I heard myself now and again say "angel" in place of aunt. The prayer ended with an outpouring of deep love within me for these aunts who had been angels for me in my childhood. They were also role models for me in adulthood, signifying perseverance and vitality. One became a housemother for a college fraternity while in her sixties. In her eighties she almost took a home for the aged to court when administrators there told her she was too old to apply for the position of cook. Another, until six months before her death at age eighty-three, drove fifty miles round trip each day to work as a hostess in a restaurant!

Doing Things Together

The extended family of the Catholic ethnic cultures often had a variety and richness to it lacking in other more "American" family systems.

With each of my aunts there was a bond of intimacy born of our doing things *with one another.* This natural intimacy had intimations of both authority and responsibility whether we cooked together or sewed together or minded the store together or went to the race track together. As we did together, we talked together. One aunt had had a painful childhood. She would sometimes recount it to me, and then always say, "But when children have a hard time early in life, God gives them a special gift when they grow up. You'll get one, too, just as I did." In the toughest of times, that bit of folk wisdom gave me the strength to persevere. It formed me to hope.

The authority of my aunts' own experience, not their exercise of law or position, blended with responsibility and intimacy to nourish and form me in my childhood. As adults we come to realize that we have been formed by the values that emerged from the customs and attitudes revealed to us as children. We learn that often we discovered intimacy through ordinary activities that encouraged gentle affection, sharing, and the give and take of responsibility and authority.

My mother's style of being a parental figure was not the same as my aunts'. The highest Christian virtue to my mother was doing *for* others rather than doing *with* others. She would take me anywhere I wanted to go in the car, drop me off and wait for me, but she lacked appreciation for our ever doing "with" one another. The house buzzed with her hundred and one projects, but she preferred to do them alone. I was too slow. I was too fidgety. I was too young. I was too awkward. One day I did help with the laundry, but my arm got caught between the rollers of the washing machine, and I had to be rushed to the doctor. Didn't that just prove I was too much of a nuisance to ever help out? I could "go along outside and play." I could "read a book, dear." I could "listen to the radio for a while." But I could not be together doing something with her, the one I called mother. Perhaps growing up in a home with a dozen siblings, she had never done things *with her mother.* Generations form generations.

"Let me hem that skirt—your stitches are uneven." "Let me fix your hair—you make a tangle of it." My mother's forte was doing *for* others. Others, however, could not do for her.

"All I want for my birthday is the grace of God." Year after year it felt like a waste of time to buy or make a present for her. How could it compare with the grace of God?

I'm sure my mother saw absolutely nothing amiss in our never doing anything together. I'm sure she felt it was more saintly to form me in a perception of doing "for" others, setting the example by doing for me, even though she gave me no chance to practice the lesson. These dynamics bred a different style of intimacy, one that was equated with being affectionate but not sharing responsibility.

Authority and responsibility were separated out from intimacy in my relationship with my mother, unlike my relationship with my aunts. Responsibility exercised by an "I do for you" but "you can't do for me" leads to dependency. (What on earth could I do well for myself?) Because we did not *share,* responding to authority became a matter of *obedience,* not a matter of *cooperation,* as it did with my aunts.

"Yes, Momma." "Yes, Momma." "Yes, Momma."

One of the hard struggles regarding faith in my adult life has been dealing with the sense that intimacy, responsibility and authority within the *church* operated from a dynamic identical to the one I experienced with my mother—obedience rather than cooperation. When such a dynamic is habitual it lacks spiritual validity because it militates against adult conversion. The believer lacks the interior freedom to break away from natural or church parental figures to fully and freely embrace God as the absolute in one's life.

Doing Things with Daddy

Although my father's drinking caused incredible suffering and harm to our family life, when he was not drinking he was the companion I did not find in my mother. The only things my father did at home were read and tend the garden, a large, marvelous garden, filled only with flowers because "flowers must be cherished as much as food." He let me putter around in the garden and even argue with him about the flowers. "Don't put in zinnias again this year, Daddy. They're ugly!" He would say something about that being an interesting view of zinnias, then give a little lesson on how sturdy zinnias were, ugly or not, which made them good border plants. But the point was that I could express my opinion on *our* project. I might be wrong in my *conclusions,* but I was never judged wrong in my feelings or my perceptions.

Reading is an activity one tends to do alone. But my father still read the funny papers *with* me long after I could read them by myself. When I was around eleven, he started to buy the *New York Times* each Sunday so we could read it together. For two years all I read were the write-ups on the parties and weddings. On some Sunday nights I'd tell him about the classy New York social affairs. He always listened keenly, often responding with a gentle little sociological perspective, then he'd summarize for me "The News of the Week in Review." If I was puzzled, he answered my questions. If I got bored, he'd find a new topic. Never once did I suspect it was teacher and pupil. I was convinced that we were doing the *New York Times* together, *with* one another. Eventually I read more than the society pages, but, of course, I did it because his authority was always exercised within the realm of intimacy which invited me, in a gracious way, to follow his example.

At age eighty-three, confined to the hospital by a small stroke, my father fell victim to a massive cerebral hemorrhage at ten o'clock on a Sunday night while doing the *Times* crossword puzzle. Of personal property possessions, all he left that moth and rust could consume were books and four large boxes of *Times* crossword puzzle books. In an age that believes that the only things of value that can be left behind are what moth and rust consume, that may seem paltry. But while he was living *he passed on his love for words* in a way that reveals what formation at its best truly is: his oldest granddaughter, Leslie, has been since childhood an omnivorous reader. Pamela at age thirteen started to write a novel; she continues to write and has taught English as a second language. Kerry speaks four languages fluently. Tierney makes words come alive on stage.

Destiny is decided, in part, by the parental figures who have formed our lives. My father's drinking made him an ambivalent parental figure for me. But that stopped when I was nineteen. The parental figure he was for me as an adult, and as a grandfather for my daughters, was a rare blessing. He never gave beyond his own gifts: a love for story-telling, a love for words, a love for nature, a love for the "real" people as he put it—and a love for us.

These gifts were remarkably *formative* because they emerged within shared experiences that evoked responsibility and authority within intimacy. Whenever that happens, the younger generation is empowered to assume maturity in adulthood.

The Integration of Intimacy, Responsibility and Authority

Children encounter the land of adulthood like immigrants encounter a new country. How they settle in and meet the challenges of the land of adulthood depends on the quality of the voyage the parental figures in their lives navigate with them. The formative power of family is unsurpassed.

In families of parents too busy to be parents, or of overworked, lonely single mothers and missing fathers, a loss related to an expectation is experienced. A wound can fester that dinner out and a movie will not heal. The kind of intimacy a child needs in his or her formative years is not just sharing occasional physical affection, it's the *ongoing* work of home in everyday activity, activity that invites sharing of responsibility within a give-and-take ambiance of authority and within an intimacy that reveals feelings.

The initiating events for this formation are often simple

experiences shared together—some chosen for the festive spirit they evoke.

One Christmas when our older girls were in primary school, they and I spent a day making Christmas decorations and cookies. Way past bedtime we were still at it. My mother had given us a fancy wooden rolling pin with designs etched out. Although the designs were supposed to imprint on the dough, the dough kept getting stuck inside the grooves. We were finally so exhausted we brought the pan of dough to the coffee table where we could sit around to work on it.

At last the back door opened and in came the father of the family from the factory Christmas party. For the first and last time his kids saw him tipsy. This evoked massive giggles followed by a recounting of our plight with the rolling pin.

"You do it, Daddy." (Assigning responsibility)

"Don't be silly. Daddy can't cook!" (Authority)

"But he'll feel left out if he doesn't have a turn. Won'tcha, Dad?" (Sensitivity)

A crooked smirk. "Just watch me do it!" A quick flip of the rolling pin. Voila, each cookie was beautifully imprinted.

"He did it! He did it! He's drunk, but he did it!" Hugs, kisses. Celebration of the great victory.

"Cut the cookies, I'll put 'em in the oven." (Authority)

"Why don't I get the potholders." (Responsibility)

"The first one's for Mom because she let us stay up so late. But the second one's for you, Dad." (Sensitivity)

"Even though he's drunk which he's not 'spose t'be." (Authority)

"He's not drunk. Are you drunk, Daddy?"

"Nope. Just slap-happy!"

"Which he's 'spose t'be cuz it's *Christmas!*" Giggles.

Parents earn the right to authority by paying the coin of intimacy—taking the time to show they care in the small, shared events of life. The child may suffer for life if this coin of the realm is not paid. Authority sustains structures that allow intimacy, but intimacy is the process that insures cohesion within the family, with God, and within the church.

If, instead of integrating intimacy, responsibility, and authority within shared events, authority moves on one track and intimacy on a separate track, responsibility either falls between or gets linked to one or the other of the two tracks.

When intimacy is isolated, it can come across as superficial or smothering affection. Developing a sense of responsibility in a child from this base often leads to manipulation or bargaining. If the development of responsibility is linked only to authority, obedience becomes the imperative, leading to passivity or rebellion. As adults, offspring may then lack the interior freedom to break away from dependency.

The Christmas cookies story may seem trivial, but important dynamics for Christian formation were taking place. The story exemplifies a way of being related that includes shared responsibility, flexibility in authority, and various forms of intimacy (kidding, showing feelings, sensitivity, affection). As a result, when the "work to be done" among us as family was talking about Sandy, our dog, being killed by a car, Daddy being fired, Mommy losing a baby, we were ready and able to do that work together.

Multiple traumas happening at once (it never rains but it pours) can shatter a sense of family unity. When this happened, George's temper and my tendency to fade into the woodwork, or pick on the girls, impeded our relating to one another as a family unit. We were far from perfect parental figures, and we all had to face and deal with that as our daughters moved toward their own adulthood. But some of the dynamics initiated in the small, ongoing and ordinary experiences of our lives together, experiences that let the children eventually break away and become individuated adults, gradually bore fruit as the following story reveals.

Relinquishing Authority for Vulnerability

In 1984 my husband was with his mother in Utah for a week before she died. There was a wake and funeral in Salt Lake and then another wake and a church service in Massachusetts on a very icy December morning. The weather caused our youngest daughter to miss both the church and the graveside service. But she was able to come to the homestead. Before returning to Boston, we brought her to the airport to return to Manhattan.

We sat in the airport's restaurant, exhausted and quiet. Then

George said, "Tierney, I want to tell you how it was as your grandma was dying. I mean how I felt and all."

"I want you to tell me, Dad."

He took my hand. She put her arm around him. He spoke softly but steadily, sharing with her what he had shared with me the day before. Tears coursed down his cheeks. It was as if they were alone in a deep wood, not in a crowded restaurant where people kept glancing at them.

She cried. She held him. They had turned themselves totally over to one another. He let himself be held for a long time. It was the Pietà for me.

That is the power of authentic intimacy, power that enables both vulnerability and the relinquishing of authority. In turn, it engenders shared responsibility. Within family, that is what God asks of us. No more, but certainly no less.

A few months later Tierney called George from New York and said, "Instead of going straight to the Berkshires Friday, I'm going to fly to Boston and drive there with you, Dad."

"But that's way out of your way. Go directly there."

"No, I'm coming to Boston first. I want for us to stop at Grandma's grave. The cemetery's on the way. I didn't get there the day she was buried. And I really want to go—with you."

"I understand, honey. But you don't have to do that!"

"But I'm going to do it! She was my grandma. I loved her and I love you. I want us to do that together."

That's authority, responsibility, and intimacy becoming one. That's the adulthood our children are called to assume. The process that leads to that kind of adulthood is formation through the gradual relinquishment of parental authority and responsibility. This is what God expects of parental figures, in the church as well as in the home. No more, but certainly no less.

2

FORMATION THROUGH RELATIONSHIP: FRIENDSHIP

Friendship, a Process of Love

Good friends are mirrors. A friend helps me to see myself with a clarity the mirror on the wall or over the sink seldom affords. We learn a great deal about ourselves in the protective yet sometimes vulnerable setting of friendship. The discovery may come from perceiving differences between yourself and a friend, or by perceiving similarities.

Our love for God and our perception that we are loved by God are often strongly influenced by our relationships in life. Right from the start lifelong dynamics regarding relationships are initiated. As children, we are formed by parental figures. Friendship also forms us. Authority, responsibility, and intimacy—the dynamic interplay spoken of in the last chapter on parental figures—can affect our religious attitudes and our image of God, as the following story illustrates.

One afternoon in February, when I was in the fourth grade, I went to the Methodist church after school with my best friend. After cutting out pictures from magazines and pasting them in scrapbooks for the children at the Shriner's Hospital, the nice lady in charge said we'd form a club called the Epworth League. I was elected secretary.

Three days later, late in the afternoon, the curate from our parish showed up at our front door. Fr. G____ removed a clipping from his pocket and passed it to my mother, saying, "I cut it out before the pastor got to the paper this morning. You can imagine how shocked he would be."

"Virginia, the newspaper says you were elected secretary of the Epworth League at the Methodist Church!"

"It does!" I couldn't hide my excitement. "I did get elected! They didn't make me feel awful for being Catholic."

Because Father was patient, I was not made to feel guilty. Because Father was patient, it finally got through to me that what was *wrong* was the *Methodists,* not what you *did* with them. Helped by my mother, Father was able to get me to agree to resign immediately. He even made me feel like a conspirator in the matter of "never mentioning the incident or the newspaper article" to the pastor. Before leaving, Father assured me that he would say special prayers for me during Lent in case the Methodists had confused me about my faith.

The *Methodists* weren't confusing me about my faith . . .

The next day the Methodist minister called my mother. Seeing the name Sullivan, he had doubts about whether the new secretary was really a Methodist. "I almost called the pastor at the Irish church, but I thought what we might have here is a mixed marriage."

"Imagine that, Tom! He almost called Fr. D____!"

"Then your little deception with the curate would have been down the drain," my father laughed.

I stopped listening then and started worrying again about *the* question: "Why did God love all us Catholics and none of the Methodists? Including my best friend!"

A poignant desire stirred within my heart that God love my best friend. She was a wonderful friend and wonderful girl, and I had never before known how much I wanted God to love her and take care of her the way God loved me and took care of me. The *desire* that I felt indicates that a significant step in my Christian formation was happening: the discovery that I cared as much for a friend as I cared for myself. Unfortunately, for the first time in my life I also felt the need to choose *between* caring for someone else and caring for God—two who suddenly seemed opposites to one another. To choose *either* would put me in opposition to the other. In an uncanny way I felt—because I loved both—that I was betraying both God and my best friend.

Dimensions of Friendship

This kind of best friend story gives us a feel for the consolations and contradictions, bounty and betrayal, that friendship evokes. To introduce a working definition of my use of "friend," let's look at a few characteristics of friendship.

Friendship seldom happens in isolation. The relationship with a friend is part of a context that includes other friends, family, colleagues at work, etc. The relationship with even one friend is seldom static; expectations, desires, resentments, disappointments are the stuff of the intimacy that flows between the two. There are *authority* dynamics within relationships with friends. We jealously guard the exercise of our naming who our friends are. We do not relinquish easily the authority to choose our friends.

There is also an "ally" dimension within friendship. The phrases we use for this are familiar: "go to bat for you," "put in a good word," "stand up for you" as well as "stand by you." Conversely, on being thrust into a situation devoid of friends one feels vulnerable as well as lonely. You know there's no one to "go to bat for you," "to put in a good word," "to stand up for you" as well as "stand by you." Stress and fear, as well as loneliness, can then become your companions. "I'm on my own!" The *responsibility* dimension that friendship provides is missing.

Paradoxically, a public display of affection is not always appreciated. Declarations of intimacy made to others without our permission may feel like an invasion of privacy. Intimacy and secrecy form an alliance. Privacy protects the alliance.

Intimacy, Responsibility, and Authority in Friendship

Deep friendship is a process of love, one we need to become Christian adults.

Because we learn the dynamics of intimacy, responsibility, and authority from our own *experiences of life,* reflecting on our concrete relationships contributes to formation for Christian adulthood and mission. The relationship called friendship, an openended, growing process with strong emotional dynamics, spells itself out in how each friend uses authority, assumes responsibility, and protects intimacy.

How well we relate in friendship provides one key to how well we will relate in ministry and mission. If holding onto friends poses a problem for us, we may try to turn the people to whom we minister into friends out of our own needs. If we are shaky about exercising authority within friendship relationships, as some Christian adults are, we may send a mixed message when we offer Christian service, inviting others into a friendship our hearts do not sincerely want.

Family contributes to our formation for friendship. Siblings and birth order play a role in shaping attitudes toward others. Because my mother was raised in a family with a dozen siblings, socializing daily with friends is as necessary to her (even at age eighty-nine) as breathing; because I had no siblings, having some time for solitude each day is of like importance to me. Because our twins, Kerry and Pam, experienced "community in the womb," their perception of the meaning of friendship varied from what Leslie and Tierney perceived. There is no one "right" way to all of this; God helps us to use the various strengths that have come to us through our varied placements.

The natural give and take among siblings eventually protects us from being victimized by every parental figure on the block, including friends who try to be parental figures. This give and take of sibling relationships is one way we test out how to be a friend.

Sorting through our life experience helps us discover how we have been formed to be Christian adults. Even the simple stories we tell about friendship in childhood may reveal the formative subsoil for the Christian values we embrace later in life. For example, knowing the "ally" dimension of friendship helps us to experience solidarity with others; knowing the advocacy dimension inherent in friendship encourages us to advocate for others as part of our Christian mission; knowing the privacy element in friendship enables us to protect confidentialities; knowing the authority dimension of friendship strengthens us to be true to ourselves. Parental figures have an opportunity to assist formation through friendship by encouraging children to initiate and experience, in horizontal relationships, dynamics of intimacy, responsibility and authority. These bear fruit in adulthood.

Friendship enables us to become, in a non-threatening way, *conscious of the experience of others.* We learn to walk in another's shoes. Through sensitive awareness of another person we discover how to relate to the *whole* person the other is, the key to enduring relationships.

When our friendships are at their deepest, freshest best, an honest openness flows between the two of us or among a group of friends. *Companionship*—the being *with* and doing *with* components of relationship—is vital to vibrant bonding. From this intimacy flows a sense of responsibility. On the other hand, if we try to impose a sense of responsibility on a friend, the relationship may become little more than an endurance test.

Unlike family, the only authority we have in friendship comes from "the bottom up"—from our actual experiences of intimacy and their consequent call for responsibility. And that authority is exercised as between allies, with its intimations of advocacy for one another. In other words, if I feel you are being reckless by flirting with drugs, and I feel that this risk you are taking is spoiling our time together as well as your own life, then I will exercise the authority component in our relationship and confront you. If intimacy has not flowered into responsibility and authority, I may simply drift away, or I may talk about you behind your back but not confront you, or I may kid you about it rather than making serious inquiry.

Best friends can confront one another because they are confidantes to one another. Being able to keep secrets is integral to the responsibility and authority dimensions of every deep relationship. In contrast to children, adults in a long-standing relationship do not feel forced to reiterate over and over, "Promise you won't tell." Awareness of one another and of relevant outsiders makes us savvy about what can be shared beyond our relationship and what cannot. Without trust, the foundation for revealing secrets, I can never truly let my hair down. Without the capacity to let my hair down, what passes between us may resemble friendship outwardly but we're really buddies, not friends. Responsibility is missing.

Real life experience within close friendship is what engenders *fidelity*—the primary spiritual quality of friendship, the quality that sustains friendship and encourages depth between two people or within a small group or community. Friendship, a significant formative process, is a *school in relationship,* a school whose lessons about fidelity and betrayal affect how we love self, neighbor and God.

The Equality and Mutuality of Friendship

Within friendships we learn about sharing in ways not always available within family life. *With* (not *above* or *beneath*) characterizes true friendship. "With" engenders empathy, which, in turn, motivates caring.

The sense of equality that pervades in good friendships insures that we can "be ourselves" together. Neither party assumes a *role* which means that neither party opts for any sense of ownership over the other. Responsibility for the quality and the permanence of the relationship is shared by both; authority is mutual. We own our friendship collaboratively; neither of us owns the other as person.

Unlike family, there is no differentiation in naming. I am called friend; you are called friend. For our intimacy to have quality, the naming must be identical for each of us. The terms co-worker and colleague imply a kind of equality in the workplace. But within the workplace roles also flourish, often unequal in status and power. That inequality is named: supervisor, boss, president, foreman, CEO. Within family and church, role names also flourish.

When equality is not present, pejorative terms creep in. For example, a bully is a person intent on owning the ones called pals. A wimp is one who lets himself or herself be owned. These terms seem to emerge more frequently in male relationships because the male world often fixates on power. Power generates competitive dynamics that can mar friendship.

Shared ownership, or equality within the relationship, does not mean *sameness*. You may smoke; I may not. You may be more patient than I am; I may be more practical than you. The equality that bears the fruit of shared ownership refers to *respect* and *care*. It means that I respect you for who you are, and you respect me for who I am. We reveal ourselves to one another with an honesty and openness that differentiates the friend relationship from the parental figure relationship.

Intimacy Lasts a Lifetime

Two years ago I had a unique experience in friendship. Eleven women friends and I arranged to have a reunion. We had lived together for two years in the same house as undergraduates at the

University of Massachusetts in Amherst. While some of us had kept up a Christmas card correspondence, most of us had not seen one another for almost thirty years. Would we feel like strangers? Would we feel so awkward that the weekend would seem interminable?

The feeling of closeness that emerged during our first evening of being together was uncanny. Until three A.M. we telescoped our lives and told these stories to one another with as much or more openness than some of us share with those who know us now. Compassion welled up with force in response to the narratives of suffering that some of us shared. At times the authority dimension that is part of friendship erupted. The fly on the wall heard us shout, "You don't have to take that!" "Confront them! Don't let them walk all over you!"

No one couched her outrage behind a polite shield to be socially acceptable. Some of us had been badly hurt; the rest of us felt wounded. A bonding that had been formed among us within a few years, yet not been attended to for over thirty years, was more vibrant than it had been when we lived together. Our being seasoned by the joys and sufferings of the intervening years helped us to contemplate one another and deepened what we experienced together.

Parting on Sunday was not easy. During the following week, contemplating our reunion, I felt both gratitude and awe. If we had a disappointment, it stemmed from the dimness of our memories of events from our college days. To me that made all the more poignant the intense caring for one another that we experienced, a caring that revealed a love that had stayed sheltered in our hearts for years without our even realizing the love was there. But memories may have also played a part in the poignancy we felt—memories of the young, spontaneous, smooth-skinned, slim women with whom we had shared secrets thirty years ago contrasted with the full-figured, worn and weary women with salt and pepper hair who came to the reunion. Each held up a mirror that told us that none of us had escaped the process called life. The reunion was a felicitous setting for embracing what most humans admit only in the abstract—I am irretrievably joined to the cycles of the human condition. Embracing that reality is essential to Christian adulthood. But it is always a poignant embrace. At the reunion, part of the compassion that welled up inside each of us may have also been a response to contemplating oneself.

Contemplative Dynamics in Relationships

Adolescence is the bridge between forming relationships helped by structures that outsiders provide and forming relationships from which authority and responsibility emerge through shared intimacy. Contemplation plays a crucial part in how that bridge is formed.

Contemplation is natural to us as human beings. In other words, it is a God-created dynamic as much as breathing is. If you have ever climbed a mountain and sat absorbing the vista when you reached the top, you have contemplated. If you have ever sat on a beach gazing at a sunset on the ocean's horizon, you have exercised your contemplative gift. A contemplative vista draws us *out of ourselves.* That's why we need mountains, rivers, lakes, oceans, and sunsets. We need to feel the pull of an attraction that draws us away from self-absorption, that lets us lose ourselves in something that makes us feel "restored."

Some of us only contemplate nature. Others of us learn to contemplate life, friends, ourselves, God. What is God-created— nature, persons, myself—as well as God is what attracts us and what we let draw us out of ourselves.

Adolescents are naturally contemplative creatures. This dimension is not always endorsed by the parental figure who notices that Michael has been staring out the window for the past twenty minutes.

"What a day-dreamer! He should be finishing his homework," the study hall monitor murmurs.

"Michael hasn't moved from that window for a half-hour. He should be finishing his homework!" Michael's dad mutters.

"Michael, shouldn't you finish your homework instead of staring at nothing out the window?" Michael's mother worries.

"Michael's grown so quiet and moody," Michael's aunt Teresa whispers. "He used to be so fidgety. Now he's dreamy."

Michael is staring at the side of the garage but he isn't seeing its gray shingles. He sees Beth's face. And instead of hearing his mother's warning, he hears Beth's voice.

Michael is in love.

For a long while Michael just stays with contemplating Beth's face and voice. Then he begins to day-dream about being with Beth at Friday night's basketball game.

Puppy love is God's gift to us. Puppy love not only moves us onto a different level regarding friendship, it also expands our ability to contemplate. Someday Michael may be able to contemplate his wife, children, friends, the wider world, and God. Through contemplation he may envision a calling or mission action. Now, however, Michael's heart is engaged in a long, loving look at Beth.

Beth is a real young woman—there is no doubt about that. But the Beth whom Michael is contemplating may be a composite of the real and the ideal. Michael may be *projecting* onto his image of Beth all he desires an adolescent woman to be as well as his own interior dimensions of femininity, a process called transference.

But Michael's teachers, father, mother, and aunt Teresa need to learn to trust that what Michael is going through as he wastes time is preparation for adult life and commitment. As Morton Kelsey and Barbara Kelsey put it, "Perhaps God gave us the capacity to project so two people with their own bad self-images and their fears of relationship could be drawn into living with each other. For many people, real committed relationship would simply be too threatening without the sauce of falling in love. Almost all studies, however, show that until two people can move beyond these romantic feelings, through genuine communication, to a state of knowing and appreciating each other, their relationship is not likely to last."[1]

Fidelity in relationship depends on our ability to contemplate the *real* friend or friend-spouse. According to John of the Cross, *Pure contemplation lies in receiving.* Fidelity becomes the destiny within a relationship when we can *perceive and receive* this friend as a completely other person from myself. Only then can we embrace and confront the one whom we contemplate in all of his or her own *reality*.

Being Reflective Together

Developing our contemplative gifts can affect *the way we communicate with friends.* Communication that has a contemplative dimension I call "being reflective together." This mode of communication is exemplified by the way two friends, Maria and Gloria, relate.

Every evening around ten, Gloria puts the kettle on the stove. By the time Maria enters the apartment a half-hour later the tea and small plate of sweets from the bakery are on the table. Gloria and Maria are quiet while they eat, but by the second cup of tea, they are sharing morsels of their day in an easy, gentle way. Sometimes they linger over an experience, musing about the day the way one might shine a cherished copper bowl. If either is agitated the other gives her a chance to vent her feelings. Then they gaze at the feeling as if it were one of the sweets on the plate, considering all its dimensions with their hearts. Sometimes Gloria unbraids her thick ebony hair and Maria brushes it while they talk. Eventually, Maria lights the candle by the Virgin's statue and Gloria puts out the pin-up lamp that hangs on the wall near the kitchen table. They stand by the candle in silence before preparing for bed.

Maria and Gloria have perfected *being reflective together.* Being reflective together is not discussion. It is not putting our heads together to analyze situations that have emerged during a given day. It is not being judgmental. The purpose of being reflective together is not to weigh on a scale the good or bad of every incident that came to pass.

It is not the morning after. There are no Monday morning quarterbacks, replaying every move in order to suggest how the move or the game *should* have been played. Being reflective is not indulging in a litany of regrets or mea culpas.

Being reflective together is soft-edged, slow-paced and sensitive. Because of that, there are few relational dynamics that surpass it. It is done in the simplest ways—friends meeting for a quiet cup of coffee; either initiates or either offers a response until there's a sense of completion.

Formative Values

Being reflective together is often the first thing we let go of when life gets busy. It should be the last because it is the spiritual glue that holds relationships together. There is no shorthand that can substitute for it. When it happens with regularity a range of feelings can be expressed. Divergent feelings become acceptable. It provides practice for those times when expressing feelings might be problematic. Being reflective together as a family process helps instill a thoughtful attitude within offspring, one that can bear surprising fruit. One of our daughters in high school started to spend time with a new group of friends. Late one afternoon she came home in a quiet mood. "I don't think I'm going to hang out with those kids anymore. They're not at all reflective."

"What do you mean?" I asked.

"Well, I'm no one to brag, but they *never* pause for a second before shooting their mouths off and they never think before—or after—they do something. They just seem to *bounce* from one thing to another."

A *value* (being reflective) she learned at home (as part of her *formation*) became a *standard* she used to evaluate friendships. Without a lot of fanfare, she exercised *authority* over her own life. The above is a key to formation. Being reflective together, something that was experienced within family, became *a formative value,* a good, something to hang onto. This value then became a *criterion* for measuring other ways of behaving. With a standard in hand, so to speak, one that was internalized over a period of time, *authority over self* was enhanced. From this came *decision* and *action.*

From intimacy within the home emerges accepting responsibility about relationships beyond the home (for evaluating new friends in relation to self) and exercising authority (deciding to continue or not to continue the relationship with the new friends).

Relational values are the bedrock for ethical choices. The best gift that parental figures can give young adults is *to contemplate them*—to receive them in their reality, to love them in that reality even as one harbors hopes that they will grow and change. It is harder to love and to teach the lessons of love than to lay down the law—as Jesus found out. But the lessons of love are what Christianity and adulthood, what friendship and family, are all about. And they are taught through "formation," that is, through the example and experiences of love that the adolescent and young adult receive from mentors. These form the relational values that enable wise moral choices.

Christian Formation Through Friendship

Some friendships may be short-lived; others may be lifelong commitments linked to intimacy and mission, God and spouse. Within the company of friends we learn to make the discernments that inform us about how to make our way as Christian adults through the thicket called world. Formation through friendship prepares us for relationships in the peer world of adults—marriage, work, civic and church community. We need *years* of this maturing in discernment to develop wisdom about the myriad relationships that are the gift of life.

Christian formation does not happen apart from formation by family, friends, and culture. Christian formation, in other words, does not happen only in church. It happens through the quality exemplified by the Christians around us and by others who may not name themselves Christian but who reflect a value system allied with what is best in our Christian value system. A consideration of just some of the American political leaders who received Catholic formation in childhood—William Casey of the C.I.A., Joseph Biden, Geraldine Ferraro, Edward Kennedy, Bruce Babbitt, Oliver North—reveals how very different are the paths of Catholic formation and how differently they manifest themselves today.

As our tradition has always put it, grace builds on nature. Attempts at Christian formation that don't connect with the natural reality of our lives as adults, or with the natural reality of the lives of our children, are a gloss that will rub off in time. Formation that negates the import of our past lived experiences (the places, family, and friendships that shaped us) is often skin-deep formation. A one-size-fits-all formation process seldom becomes rooted in who the person truly is.

On the other hand, formation by "life" is not equivalent to Christian formation. Culture plays a strong role in formation; without active participation in a religious tradition, trends within a given culture may contribute powerfully to the shaping of the child or the adult if that individual does not have a religious faith and community through which to filter the culture.

Without the development of reflective skills for wise discernments tied to life experiences, the spiritual development that Christian adulthood demands falters. Then the lessons about Christian life taught by the school of friendship may not become apparent on a *conscious* level. Growing up as a Christian and having friends may be perceived as two *separate* tracks in my life. Although they have been the most influential factors in my formation, the value and power of family and of friendship in shaping who I am *as a Christian* remain undetected. In other words, I am not aware of my own formation.

Community, Friendship and Faith

A dozen years ago we moved from the country to the city. A year after our move, our youngest daughter, looking perplexed, said to me one day: "I don't understand the church down here. All my friends talk about 'belonging' to their parish. And they say strange things like, 'I went to the Saturday night mass, my dad went to the early mass on Sunday, and my sister and mother went to the noon mass.' " Growing agitated, she went on, "Church is more than going off alone to mass; church is families of friends worshiping God *together!*"

Our daughter had found church more meaningful when it was "families of friends who worship God together." By families we weren't talking about the idealized nuclear family of mommy who stays home, daddy who has a professional job, and perfectly behaved kiddies. The latter may be a kinship group, not a family. In the Vineyard Community prior to our move to the city, church was a community of families of friendship and faith, whether kin or not, whether single, divorced, widowed, or married. Each person —adult and child—was part of a cluster that felt like family and evoked the trust found in solid friendship. Christian community with this dynamic enables both "being ourselves together" and being open and honest about what our faith requires.

For many families of friends who worship together, the responsibilities to which they are called and the authority they are given to exercise eventually unfold into mission beyond the mission of supporting one another. Lay spirituality is enhanced through the sharing of the ups and downs, the trials and joys of their lives. This *intimacy*—this being who we are within a group of God-related friends—is a mainstay for the intimacy between those members who are married.

When local church is truly a community, we learn how God is a parental figure and how God is a friend.

Unity among families of friends who worship together is not new to our tradition. As Joseph H. Lynch points out, "Spiritual kinship was an important social institution in western Europe from the sixth to the sixteenth centuries."[2]

Baptismal sponsorship evoked a form of voluntary kinship "which took its place alongside kinship by blood and kinship by marriage as a fundamental social bond."[3] At each baptism a "spiritual family" emerged within which members "were expected to treat one another respectfully and honorably, to have love for one another," as a seventh century source put it.[4] Four distinct relationships became apparent through baptism. The first was the relationship between the sponsor and the infant being baptized. (Often children went to live for a time, when they were older, with a godparent.) The second was the relationship between the baptizing priest and the infant. Third, the sponsor and the natural parents became co-parents *to one another.* Adults in this kind of spiritual kinship came to the immediate aid of one another. And finally a "spiritual sibling" relationship existed between the baptized child and any children of the sponsor. Intimacy, responsibility, and authority, shared among Christian lay adults, is not an invention of the twentieth century.

Family, Friends, and Transformations

Friendship is the solid ground that enables us to walk forward when the never-ending shifts in family life leave us feeling bereft, as the following story illustrates.

Four years ago the season of spring was overflowing with celebrations in our family. Friends from the Vineyard Community shared the joy with us. In May our daughter Pamela, along with other lay students, women religious, and Jesuit priest candidates, received a master's degree from Weston. Two weeks later she was sitting on a lawn a mile away on Massachusetts Avenue in Cambridge watching her fiancé, Richard Magahiz, receive his Ph.D. from the Massachusetts Institute of Technology. As this was happening, George and I were sitting on folding chairs in Washington Square Park, watching our youngest daughter, Tierney, receive her bachelor's degree from New York University.

Although my mother was a bit confused (she told her day-care friends about Pam's degree from the Weston School of *Technology* and Rich's degree from the Massachusetts Institute of *Theology*) she stood tall and proud, walking with me on one side and with her great-granddaughter, Nicole, on the other, as we led the procession down the aisle a week later when Pam and Rich married one another on June 15.

Their meeting at Eastern Point Retreat House in Gloucester linked friendship, family and church in a unique way. During the time I was a campus minister at MIT, Rich and I began to meet for spiritual direction. Later Pam and her dad came one Saturday in May to Eastern Point to visit me while Rich was on retreat. Rich "broke silence" to become acquainted with Pam. The next fall, on the day they became engaged, Rich and I met for our last hour of spiritual direction. "You don't want your mother-in-law as your spiritual director!" George said that night, his first bit of in-law advice.

Two days after the wedding I went to the Berkshires to recover from exhaustion and to savor the abundance of joy experienced during our season of celebrations. One night at the end of that week, the phone rang. I answered it, did not recognize the voice, and asked who was calling.

"Pam Magahiz," the voice replied.

"Who?" I asked again.

"It's me, Mom. Pam. We're back from our honeymoon!"

The next afternoon I kept hearing her voice on the phone— the confident way she said, "Pam Magahiz." Why didn't she just say "Pam" or "Pam Finn"? Or just "It's me, Ma"?

Why so formal? So married. So gone from our lives.

By late afternoon the sudden sadness I felt drew me to prayer where tears finally came as I told God that it had all been wonderful

but there had been in one month too many changes tumbled together. *Too many leave-takings and no homecomings.* "Please let
me know you don't intend to leave," I begged God.

Then the phone rang. I reached out for the receiver, said a few
words, and heard a voice of concern. "You sound awful! What's
the matter?"

"This woman called last night named Pam Magahiz. Do you
know someone named Pam Magahiz?" My voice broke.

"Stay where you are! I'll be right over. I'll bring us a treat!"

We sat out back. I slowly sipped the frappe she brought, letting
myself behave like someone sick with the flu. We talked for hours.
We talked about being women, and being mothers, and being
wives, and the way some folks in a family grow up which means
others grow older. Finally I said, "I do know Pam Magahiz. And I
love her and I love Rich very much."

My friend left then.

Seldom has God answered a prayer as swiftly as on the day my
friend called while I was praying, and came right over, and let me
know that I'm still who I've been for ever so long—her friend.

3

SPOUSE: FRIEND OR ENEMY?

> At a recent wedding reception, my husband walked across the room to join me and a gentleman I had just met. My new acquaintance asked, "And who is this, a friend of yours?"
>
> By way of introduction, I said, "This is my husband, Bruce . . ." Picking up where I left off, Bruce said, "I'm her friend, too."[1]

As this letter to the editor in a recent magazine reveals, spouse is the person who straddles both sides of the fence. Spouse is family. That is undeniable. Spouse is also called to be one's friend. From the "school of lay spirituality" we become aware that it is through experiences in marriage, family, and friendship that we learn most profoundly the meaning of fidelity and of betrayal. Our own faith in God may be tempered by how we have, through the teachings of real life, learned these lessons. It is a rather common supposition that mission occurs beyond the web of existence comprised of family, friendship and work. Because the fabric of marriage, family and even friendship is in such disarray in the North American culture, however, we may need to become more cognizant of how *these settings* provide a witness to mission.

Every year I learn more about this mission from my own experience of marriage and from my daughters who are married. Sometimes the lesson that the latter teaches startles me. For example, about a month after Pam Magahiz returned from her honeymoon, George, my mother and I made a trip to visit her for an afternoon. Our get-together was initiated by our going out for lunch as Pam did not suggest having lunch in their new apartment. As we ate in a nearby restaurant, Pam rather proudly told us about the stuffed grape leaves her husband had made for a party, the casserole he had invented the night before, the soup he had prepared, and so on. Finally my mother asked what new recipes *she* had tried.

"None. I don't like to cook, Grandma."

"What do you mean, you don't *like* to cook?"

"Just what I said. I don't like to cook."

"But you're a wife now! Like doesn't come into it."

"Grandma, it's no longer the dark ages! I prefer to clean. Rich prefers to cook." Pam reached for a piece of garlic bread.

"Your grandfather never had to wonder who'd cook his supper after a hard day's work!" was Grandma's rejoinder.

"If Rich is tired I *will* cook supper, Grandma. But he loves puttering around the kitchen. I don't!"

"You should have taught her how to cook," Grandma pointed a breadstick in my direction. "I've never heard a wife say the things she's saying, Virginia."

And on and on it went. (I refrained from asking my mother when she thought she had taught me to cook.) This incident helped me to realize that Pam and Rich are trying to reverse the roles earlier generations took for granted. Will it work? Only time will tell. But I certainly don't wish on them our approach to early married life.

Spouse as Worst Enemy

George and Virginia had seven years of friendship before becoming husband and wife. Soon after our marriage, in the early 1950s, role superseded friend. It was the primary catalyst for our first big fight, a memorable occasion because it happened on Christmas Eve. Around nine that evening we arrived at our tiny apartment after last-minute shopping. Our small, fresh, table Christmas tree, along with pieces of wood, nails, hammer and himself, went out onto the second floor back porch. I wrapped gifts and then prepared a festive buffet for midnight. In the middle of the preparation I realized that George had been missing for about an hour and I stepped into the back hall to check. The string of cuss words I heard from the porch put me in reverse and I backed into the kitchen. By eleven the buffet was set in the living room, the candles lit, the table by the window ready for the tree.

At eleven-thirty the tree stood on the table. Half the needles were missing, a major branch was fractured, and the tree itself listed like the sinking Titanic. "You decorate it," George said as he put it on the table. "I'm exhausted. I'm going to bed."

"But it's our very first Christmas together!" I exclaimed.

"Whaddya mean! We've had seven Christmases together."

"But not as husband and wife!" Tears came into my eyes. "I fixed this beautiful buffet. Especially for us."

"That tree got the best of me. I'm going to bed!"

I sobbed for an hour. I took sheets and blankets from the linen closet and made up the living room couch as my Christmas bed. Unfortunately, the street light illuminated our yet to be decorated, forlorn tree. How could a small tree like that defeat a big man like my husband? Then I remembered previous times when a much smaller screw or nail had defeated him. But he was a husband now! Husbands are supposed to know how to make a Christmas tree stand! And do it in twenty minutes, not two hours! And do it without taking half the needles off! What kind of a husband was I married to?

Wasn't I doing *my* best to be the best wife a husband could have? Suddenly, all the Christmases before our first Christmas as husband and wife flooded my memory. Each hung on a branch of the battered tree like a jewel. Why had they been so much better than our first Christmas as husband and wife?

The next day at Christmas mass we sat in separate pews.

Thirty years later, in my mother's comment regarding Pam's cooking—"What's like got to do with it?"—she was saying, "Wives cook. Period. Marriage means putting likes aside in favor of roles and their responsibilities."

Thirty years earlier, in my consciousness, the *persons* George and Virginia actually were had little to do with the husband George was *supposed* to be or the wife Virginia was *supposed* to be. For at least five of the seven years of friendship prior to our marriage, I knew that George and tools were enemies, not friends. But I never integrated that fact into the expectations about husband that flooded my consciousness once we were married. The standards that dictated role expectations emerged from the culture that accompanied us into adulthood and into marriage.

Marriage as Metaphor for Friendship

Today it seems ironic to me that marriage meant shifting my eyes from my beloved, my dearest friend, to the role he was supposed to fulfill as husband and to the role I was supposed to fulfill as wife. Spiritually marriage promised a deeper experience of friendship, a giving over of self to the other in a *completion* of the trust signified by other friendships in life. This ultimate level of intimacy was not missing in our marriage, but it was eroded by our giving ourselves over more and more to roles and over to judgments about the fulfillment of those roles.

For husband and wife to remain "dearest friends in the world" to each other, *responsibility and authority must emerge from their own experienced love and intimacy.* As a couple, George and I allowed standards for responsibility and authority to emerge from beyond our bond of intimacy. Our local church, certain members of extended family, and the culture itself operated as *parental figures* toward us after our marriage. In many ways they inserted themselves between who we were, not only as husband and wife, but also as George and Virginia. These parental figures determined how we shaped responsibilities and handled authority far more than our beleaguered intimacy did.

It took years of hardship and suffering for us to discover how to let responsibilities and authority emerge from our own intimacy. Today, the parenting that the church and the culture does may be far less *explicitly* directed toward young couples but it is felt nonetheless. Consequently, a young husband or wife may have expectations regarding success or sexuality or socialization with others that are not rooted *in who they are as persons and as Christian adults.*

Early in our own marriage—as early as the first year—the intimacy dynamic and the responsibility/authority dynamics started to travel along separate tracks. Intimacy happened during those rare and special moments when George and Virginia as dearest friends revealed themselves to one another (sometimes in *honest* anger, sometimes in great affection). In everyday life, through shoulder to the wheel engagement in the responsibilities to which each of us were committed, we let intimacy fall through the cracks.

Neither of us had any understanding of the place of mutual

authority in marriage. One reason for that is that we belonged to a church that had *no models of mutual authority.* Each of us perfected our responsibilities and watched the other to make sure he or she was doing the same. Consequently, husband George and wife Virginia became Husband george and Wife virginia.

Marriage is meant to be the *continuity* of the friend relationship that preceded it, not the disablement of the prior relationship. A continuity of friendship into marriage is not easy to sustain because we all bring expectations to marriage, but it offers the best promise that marriage will have as its bedrock sustained emotional and sexual intimacy.

Faith that God is working to enhance the profound friendship marriage is meant to be supports the very delicate process that takes place when intimacy unfolds into new contexts for responsibility and authority. The post-conciliar affirmation of the value of the human person in his or her own right has evoked a quiet revolution regarding Christian marriage in some settings within the church. Where this is apparent, church as well as faith provides a structure that enables a marriage to flourish as the fruit of the deepest relationship between a man and a woman that life and God can provide.

Best Friend as Blood Relative

Some husbands and wives perfect roles to enable a smooth couple functioning that operates *as if* it were marriage even though the partners are far from being best friends. This *kinship group* may win the prize in the parish for best family of year, but is it in reality Christian marriage and family? What I am suggesting is that your spouse, if you have a spouse, is called to be your best friend. If there are six other people in your life with whom you can be "who you are" with more freedom than with your spouse, then your spouse is not your best friend.

The language you speak with your spouse may not be the same language you speak with a close friend of the same gender. For example, my husband does not often enjoy the detail I might invest in sharing about nuances within family relations that a close woman friend appreciates. I don't follow in my mind or heart the nuances of a Celtics game or trade that a male friend of his appreciates. But there is an *affective* language between us that differs from what we share with others, a language that has emerged not only from our own relationship but from what that relationship has created—family and home.

The essential meaning of friend and the essential meaning of intimacy is divestiture of role. Authority and responsibility are still operative but the naming is done, not by "outside forces" but through an integration accomplished by the two who are intimate. Sexual love-making, protected by the bond between the two, ratifies this integration. On the level of authority, one partner says to the other, "I give you full authority over my body. And I take responsibility for yours." The response given by the other mirrors that intent. There is a trusted exchange of ownership. "Own me; let me own you," our bodies, hearts and spirits cry. This unity of intimacy, responsibility and mutual authority says, "I trust you with all that I am. You can trust me with all that you are." In that kind of trust a most profound experience of love is enabled.

Tragic results occur when there is a holding back by one partner or the other, i.e. "I'll give you my body but don't expect my emotions." Or, "I'll give you my emotional love but I'm afraid to relinquish my body."

The unique relational aspects that marriage provides are the links between friend and family that spouse engenders. There is no other model of relationship in which best friend becomes relative —blood relative, in a sense, once children are born. The family relationship that this spouse-friend provides often becomes nuanced in varied ways, i.e. husband, father of our daughters, son of my in-laws, in-law of my parents. As wife-friend I have to relate to husband-friend within all these nuancings. Systems of support for the *spouse-friend* dynamic, not only within the churches in the United States but also within the culture itself, are critical if our society is to have any stability. No other personal relationship within a society exhibits the internal intricacies marriage does. After decades in which we as a society have done little to sustain and protect not only the structure of marriage but also the intimacy that sustains that structure, Americans are responding to the issue with a soberness that is badly needed.

The sublime challenge of marriage is for the two friend

partners to have faith that the sense of responsibility they need and the authority they are called to exercise can emerge *from the intimacy* born of the relationship between them. Even in a post-conciliar church it is not easy to trust that God is actually present within that intimacy of relationship, helping to bring to birth the kinds of responsibility and authority appropriate to who wife is as person, who husband is as person, and who they are together as one.

Everything changes if husband and wife are no longer best friends to one another. Intimacy, responsibility and authority cease to be integral to the relationship and travel along separate tracks. Rather than flowing from intimacy, responsibility may begin to *substitute* for intimacy. Discipline may replace desire. Going through the motions of affection may mask the fact that discipline is substituting for a desire to care about the other. But discipline is draining. Feeling drained, one is easily led into the temptation of using authority as a weapon. Mutual authority is no longer the buttress for stability it was when intimate love generated the energy within the marriage.

The Struggle for Authentic Generativity in Marriage

Later in this book we will deal with mission within the broader world. We short-change millions of Catholic lay adults, however, when we disregard or underestimate the mission they are already activating by responding to their destiny in relationships of friendship, parenting and marriage. Within these relationships they give witness to the values of fidelity, generativity and lay spirituality, sometimes in ways that counter the values of the mainstream culture. In this chapter we will consider how challenging the mission of fidelity and generativity can be.

Friends of ours, a husband and wife, both teach in the same public high school. When they recently celebrated their twentieth anniversary, their students, many of them from broken homes, expressed amazement that a man could be married to the same woman and a woman to the same man for twenty years. "Sometimes," the husband said ruefully, "I feel like a rare collector's item."

Being Catholic may have had something to do with that sentiment expressed by the husband. But if "staying the course" has been more habitual for Catholics than for some others, the inference should not be drawn that all the Catholic couples who have stayed together have stayed together in wedded bliss.

When my husband and I look over our years of marriage, one period that evokes gladness of heart is the occasion of our twenty-fifth anniversary.

We didn't celebrate it.

Everyone urged us to celebrate it, inquired about how we were going to celebrate it, made suggestions about how to celebrate it, e.g. a special Mass, a big party, a sit-down dinner in a restaurant. One Saturday, after a month of deliberating, we woke early and went out for breakfast. The memory is indelible. Sitting over a second cup of coffee at Andy's Restaurant, one of us said, "Let's not."

"Let's not?"

Then, with tears in our eyes, we reflected together about the need to face the hardship those twenty-five years had been, the failures and sorrows those years had contained, how seldom we faced that fact, how desperately we needed to face that fact. We decided that morning to spend the year of our twenty-fifth anniversary reflecting honestly together on those twenty-five years. So, there was no party. On the night of our anniversary we had a sandwich at a deli and went to a movie.

We are still incredibly proud of our decision to go against the crowd and the custom of the culture to be exactly and honestly who we were at that moment of our marriage—to one another. If we were to spend the year facing the past in a rigorous and truthful way, it was important not to initiate this by glossing over our pain with a party.

We were true to our promise to one another made that Saturday morning at Andy's. Once a week during that twenty-sixth year of our marriage we sat down together, often on Saturday morning, to be reflective together. Each of us would bring up a memory and share with the other all the feeling that memory evoked. Often the feelings were bitter, angry, hurt, fearful, sorrowful. Miraculously we had come to the point where we could share the feelings quietly.

Reverencing the truth. And reverencing our God who is found *in the truth of our real lives.*

We talked about the years we had stayed together, taking seriously our *own* experiences and feelings about these experiences, not letting the shadow of the church impede the process. We talked about the years we had stayed together, not because we had made promises on our wedding day to one another, but because we had made a promise at our wedding to God. We talked about the years when Jesus saying "Love your enemies" characterized our relationship more than "Love your neighbor as yourself." We talked about how little, for so long, each of us had loved self because we belonged to a church that never encouraged that part of Christ's commandment, a church that for so long never helped a believer learn how to love self, yet expected that unloved self to love neighbor.

We never prayed together during those times of sharing. We had never been able to do that well, much to the disappointment of one of us and the relief of the other of us. Toward the end of the year, I made an eight-day retreat. On that retreat I listened to records that the retreat house had in its music room. While listening to one of the records, I experienced God's love in a particularly vibrant way. After that I prayed with the record daily. Each time the blessing of love was encountered again. After the retreat, I told my husband about the record, and he said, "That's the music from the movie we saw the night of our twenty-fifth anniversary."

There are many times that I wonder where on earth God is in our lives and in the lives of others on earth. But my conviction runs deep that God was with us in our decision about celebrating our twenty-fifth anniversary. The Spirit was with us, generatively enabling us to share. And the Spirit would be as generative, recognized now by us, in the years to come.

Twenty-five years "after the fact," we embraced *our destiny.* One reason why we were able to do that is because we had a Catholic marriage. The church kept alive our hope in God; the church also provided the means for us to appeal to God over and over through those years.

One reason why twenty-five years of marriage passed before we were able to embrace our vocation of marriage as our destiny was that we had a Catholic marriage. During the first *decade* of our marriage, we did not own our marriage. God did not own our marriage. The church owned our marriage.

One Saturday morning we felt a sense of desolation as we remembered how separated we became, within the confines of our marriage, through the obedience we gave to the law of the church. After having three babies within seventeen months, we appealed to the church and the church counseled abstinence. Sexual intimacy then became the enemy. It wasn't long, we discovered, before emotional intimacy also became the enemy because emotional intimacy, in those early years, so easily led to sexual intimacy. Any look of affection, any word of affection, became dangerous ground, to be avoided at all costs.

Our byword became: avoid the one you live with and you love. It worked—some of the time. In place of intimacy, we concentrated on responsibilities. Lord knows we had enough of them. It wasn't a difficult displacement. We focused on authority—battling about who had it over whom about what, day after day after day. Responsibility and authority, disconnected from intimacy, helped us to avoid thinking about intimacy, to avoid feeling any intimacy.

One Saturday morning we held each other close as we remembered how hard it was to be faithful to the church and its law when our hearts longed for us to be faithful to one another. We felt a poignancy as we remembered an instance now and then when we turned our backs on the law of abstinence to obey the law of love—such as on the anniversary when we treated ourselves to dinner out, a dinner by candlelight, a dinner when it was so difficult to defend oneself against the enemy across the table.

Our anniversary baby didn't live. We grieved for that miscarriage. Three other miscarriages, the outcome of attempts to practice the rhythm method, were grieved for on those Saturday mornings during the non-celebration of our twenty-fifth anniversary.

Letting the church own our bodies was the tragedy of the first ten years of our marriage. In order to be *physically* generative at all times, we eventually surrendered to the church (rather than to one another) not only our bodies but also our hearts and spirits—out of obedience. We gave our marital authority over to the church, gave up the consolations of intimacy, and gave ourselves up to the many responsibilities of family except the responsibility to love one another. Out of obedience to what the church demanded, we eventually abandoned our destiny of love fulfilled in marriage. During that time there was hardly an hour when either of us recognized within ourselves what we really felt about what we were experiencing. That is the hold the dynamic of obedience can have over people—engendering interior paralysis.

Because the twins were born so soon after our oldest daughter, she was *forced* to grow up rapidly rather than living the natural, God-intended, process of slowly growing up. One of our twin daughters had cerebral palsy, a mild case, yet one that was hard to diagnose and heal, one that crippled her left leg. She didn't walk until she was over three. She wore a brace until she was thirteen. Meanwhile her twin sister was beginning a bout with chronic illnesses, accompanied by high fevers. From age four to seven, when it was finally diagnosed as a congenital kidney problem, she didn't gain a pound. What was tragic, truly tragic, during that time was that their parents lived as enemies to one another because the church owned their bodies, hearts, and spirits—enemies trying *individually* to love the fruit of their bond, enemies lost in sorrow, unable to offer one another the consolation the sacrament of matrimony demands.

It is hard to absolve the church of such a sin. And we did not try in those early years. We, instead, feared the authority of the church and dreaded the power of the church and forgot God. This was not of God, we could see twenty years later, because whatever is of God bears fruit, especially the fruit of love. And our love for one another was law's captive.

We spent more than one Saturday morning, the year of our twenty-fifth anniversary, savoring the time when we turned the corner. For me, pregnancy meant staying in bed for most of the "duration," and avoiding any sexual encounters. Waiting for our youngest child to be born was a gentle time for us. The older three were in school and I felt a great sense of anticipation for this new life within me. But there was a sense of finality, too. Having toxemia, I gained seventy-five pounds, and the doctor urged us to make this my final pregnancy.

During that advent time of awesome waiting, we began to trust ourselves to small affections, to let personal intimacy flow between us. During that long hiatus, we also began to form intentions, to make plans. Being friends again felt sublime. We would be bold and let it continue after the birth of the baby. We held hands over the mound that was my middle and would become new life for all of us. At that blessed place we vowed that, for a change, we would be best friends with all the intimacy that implies for a husband and wife. We would be friends and recognize how the church had become our enemy.

The year of our twenty-fifth anniversary we did not celebrate our wedding, we dealt with our marriage. It became a generative experience for each of us as persons as well as for who we are as a couple. Sharing the truth, in the context of love, is always what I call generative, what engenders a sense of new life.

Those months of confinement waiting for our youngest child became a time of solitary prayer for me. Prior to the pregnancy I had been head of the parent educator organization in the parish and a first grade religious education teacher. A month after being put to bed, I called the curate with whom I worked on these projects and requested that he bring me communion. He refused, annoyed that I had asked him and annoyed that I was to be confined to bed for so many months, adding to his burden in overseeing religious education.

The heartache I felt at being deprived of communion for so long drove me to solitary prayer. My confinement became my hermitage. My entire being sought God and then leaned on God— God without the church between us. Looking back I sense that in that hermitage time, *I heard the call to love my husband and children unconditionally.* Doing that mandated letting go of the conditional love I felt the church was imposing on marriage and family, i.e. that they qualify as Christian, uniting us to God, only *on the condition* that husbands and wives obey the law of the church.

Our Paschal Mystery

During our twenty-fifth anniversary year, we removed the fig leaf covering the story of our sexual bonding and let go of shame for what we perceived as the "messy" story of the early years of our marriage. Having the courage to do that enabled us to embrace *our sexual story as the spiritual story* of the first decade of our marriage. Such a declaration is not easy to do in a celibate-governed church. Unlike what is found in the Bible, we tend in the church to circle around sexual stories in the telling of spiritual stories.

From 1954 to 1964 our paschal mystery, our laying down of our lives, was bound up in many ways by how we regarded our bodies. This affected us, this affected our children. To me it now seems ironic that within a church founded on God-with-us, God *enfleshed* among us, it is still difficult for so many Catholic adults to embrace a story rooted in embodiment and mating as a primary dimension of their spirituality.

Parallels Between Spirituality, Sexuality and Church

The stories we told to one another that year helped us to own these stories as *formative* elements of who we are today as Catholic Christians. It is a sorrow to us that so many similar stories in the lives of other lay Catholics will be buried untold. In the public forum of the church we so often still hear an idealized rhetoric about marriage, instead of the reality of married life told by the voices of those who live this generative calling. They are the ones who can reveal the reality of that destiny. They should be doing that revealing in an honest way in the public as well as the private forum of the church.

Because the true leadership that only lay Catholics can give to marriage and family is withheld, the church, in place of generativity, still symbolizes *negativity* on many issues related to marriage, family, and sexuality. Our secular culture is in chaos regarding sexuality and marriage. The proclamation of the church can no longer be limited to deploring broken marriages, abortion, homosexual activity, and sex education within public schools. Converting this negativity into generativity mandates releasing from the bondage of silence the lay women and lay men who can evangelize if they are encouraged to articulate the struggle to be faithful and generative from the reality of their own lives.

Generativity, the life-enhancing quality that reveals care about future generations of life, has become a crucial issue in North American society in a way that wasn't apparent in the 1950s, when care beyond self was reinforced in many ways by our culture.

Today we live in a decade that seems to ratify self-indulgence. If it weren't before our eyes day after day, we might say unbelievable self-indulgence. Self-indulgence, the antithesis of generativity, is adolescence adopted as an adult stance. Regarding sexuality, Catholics will be weak witnesses of an adult Christian stance as long as they feel they must remain mute within the institutional church.

What kind of *revelation about generativity* am I talking about? One example might be that God can be entrusted with our sexual story as part of our personal story of longing for love. God can be trusted even if we sense mistrust rather than understanding from church representatives. Another example might be that the best nourishment for vibrant personal and sexual intimacy is rootedness in fidelity.

Within the Jewish tradition in ancient times the husband had a *religious* obligation to satisfy his wife sexually. Christian tradition eventually came to stress that the wife was to submit to her husband whether he was drunk or sober, enraged or sweet-tempered. The woman's role was to give pleasure to the man. This mockery of married love, this sexist irresponsibility, this misuse of authority still haunts the church.

How can adult lay Catholics hope to be comfortable about articulating a positive message about fidelity and sexuality if this heritage insists on lingering on?

In Catholic tradition the same principle became operative regarding marital fidelity and religious fidelity: *fidelity can be separated out from intimacy, from love that is generative.* In the preconciliar church, fidelity to God through obedience to church law, not through intimate relationship with God, became the ultimate value. Church law also controlled sexual relations between wives and husbands. Relations intended by God to sustain fidelity became perceived solely in reproductive terms.

How we as a people have suffered from these aberrant interpretations, from the collapse of fidelity into obedience to laws, from the separation of spiritual intimacy from responsibility and authority! Perhaps these came about because separating fidelity out from intimacy began to *characterize the way the church itself functioned.* In the pre-conciliar church a pattern similar to the phenomenon I described regarding the early years of my marriage developed in the church. Early in marriage, George and I stopped letting responsibility and authority be the generative *fruit of our intimacy.* Excursions into separate exercises of authority and responsibility began to *substitute* for intimacy. Eventually we looked at one another as rivals. An abyss descended between two people who had loved one another.

In the pre-conciliar church a similar abyss sometimes descended between bishops and priests, superiors and vowed religious, pastors and lay people. Part of the upheaval within the post-conciliar church is related to realigning the dynamics of intimacy, responsibility, and authority through co-discipleship, collaboration and shared responsibility.

In many church settings, priests, vowed religious, and lay adults are reclaiming the good news that *intimacy, responsibility and authority are as indissolubly linked in the church as they are in the home and in relationship with God.* Base Christian communities, alternate communities, church associations, innumerable parishes and even some dioceses are refusing to sever responsibility and authority from intimacy, *from communal love generated among the people* in this given place, in this place and people given by God.

Unlike the experience of the early church, for centuries the tradition lived by the myth that relationships based on love—love among lay people and love between lay people and pastoral leaders—was unnecessary. Such intimacy could be dangerous to both celibacy and authority; responsibility and authority are primary, not love. Responsibility and authority can substitute for intimacy between pastors and people. Eventually this substitution led to obedience and authority becoming the symbol for the fidelity of the church *to God.*

For centuries before Vatican II lay people accepted the separation within the church between intimacy and authority. For centuries this was also the norm for interactions within both the home and the culture. Because a separation between intimacy, responsibility and authority is no longer the norm in many homes, lay adults find its continued existence within the church intolerable. They insist that "See how they love one another!" as a sign of church is a mandate meant for today and not only for the first century A.D.

Destiny comes to us through a call. In order to be fulfilled, destiny has to be embraced by the heart and not just understood by the head. The subject of this book is formation because I believe that formation is the process of internalizing values significant to one's sense of destiny and of discovering the motivating forces that propel one into mission. What we are going through at our present time in the church is facing the hard truth that a renewed sense of mission as our destiny cannot be imposed the way law or rules were imposed in the pre-conciliar church. Spiritual intimacy, community and mission are integral to one another. Embracing mission with the heart is often a long, formative process akin to what is meant by internalizing. Married life is the primary ongoing process of formation for innumerable lay Catholics. The vitality of this relationship is their primary call to mission, but it is not their only call.

4

CALL AND CALLINGS

Some of us have job descriptions in a drawer at home or in the office; some of us may be sorting through new job descriptions right now. All of us are commended to the job description we find in the New Testament—the job of mission. Vatican II put fresh heart into lay believers by revealing that we are called to be heralds of God in family, work, social activities, and civic endeavors within the web of our ongoing existence.

Recently at a Sunday liturgy on a university campus we remembered in prayer brothers and sisters who have gone on to various new places and who are living out the call to discipleship and mission in their new settings. Some have married and are beginning families since I last saw them; some, one hopes all, have new friends in their new "webs"; some are teachers, others engineers, some social workers, some starting a career in management. And right there in Houston and St. Louis, Denver and New York, in these new callings to personal relationship, new callings in the world of work, they are attempting to live out discipleship—through the mission of Jesus Christ. In many diverse ways, they will reevangelize and humanize whatever place has become their new setting in life.

Before Vatican II most of us thought that the work called mission was work done only by missionaries. That expectation turned a corner in Vatican II. From Vatican II to the Synod on the Laity in 1987, it has become more and more apparent that all lay adult women and men are being encouraged by hierarchical leadership to take mission to the marketplace, to *live out the call to discipleship and the call to mission through their callings in life.*

Being motivated to do this doesn't automatically happen just by going to mass on Sunday. To be effective in mission, to sustain a mission thrust within the workday world, mandates pastoral re-

125

sources to match the call encouraged in Vatican II and the Synod on the Laity. The tradition in the church is that to be engaged in mission means to be engaged in discernment, an interior process of sifting options, negotiating with oneself within oneself in the presence of God and with God's help, to discover the next step in living out one's faith. This sorting through one's gifts and talents, as well as blind spots, helps believers determine what bolsters or enfeebles discipleship and mission. It is crucial to have skilled pastoral persons to assist in the discernment process necessary to deal with tensions between call and callings. To proclaim the mission call of the laity without offering resources to enable effective response is unethical and unjust.

Call Through Callings

In the movie *Chariots of Fire* the runner from Scotland was tested by the tension between call and callings. Running in the Olympics beckoned to Eric Liddell. The call to be a minister had long gestured with great strength.

In a poignant scene on the side of a hill, Eric tells his sister Jenny that he intends to go to China to be a missionary, and then says, "I've got a lot of running to do first."

"I'm frightened what it all might do to you."

"Jenny, Jenny, you've got to understand," Eric says with urgency. "I believe God made me for a purpose. For China. He also made me fast, and when I run I feel his pleasure. To give it up would be to hold him in contempt . . ."

The call to go to China as a missionary was felt by Eric as his destiny. The calling to run in the Olympics emerged from gifts embedded in Eric's createdness. Running fast was a gift from God; running fast was part of Eric's identity as a person. Running fast became linked to Eric's spiritual identity. To ignore this gift and calling would be to fail at acknowledging God. In order to be the true person he was in relationship to God, Eric had to run.

So Eric Liddell competed in the Olympics. Within that setting he found himself revealing the call of discipleship. His refusal to run on the sabbath upset the establishment, giving Eric the opportunity to witness in an *explicit* way to his faith, to proclaim values besides competition and winning.

Chariots of Fire is a parable of faith and holiness. The movie revealed that there is something holy about exercising one's gifts from God even if companions in faith imply that it is unholy. Letting a calling have its way with you and letting it be an amplifier for your call is likewise holy even if secular figures mock you for it.

Every Christian through baptism receives the call to discipleship, to ministry, and to mission. This call is an invitation to be in close relationship with the one who personally calls us, an invitation to fidelity. Evidence of response to the call to discipleship is expected of every Christian in intentional ways within both the private and the public settings of life.

All Christians are called to *salt of the earth ministry* based on their discipleship. Day in and day out, year in and year out, in whatever setting they find themselves, with whomever they encounter, they try to comport themselves according to Jesus' teachings as remembered in the gospels. Each person they meet is valued; each exercise of intimacy, responsibility and authority has accountability within their relationship to God. But they do that from their own reality as human persons, persons who have feelings, who have acknowledged weaknesses, who have needs, and who suffer when those needs are not met.

Christians are called to mission, lived out generatively through *callings*. These callings are diverse. They include relational callings like parenting, marriage, friendship, and participation in voluntary ministries within the local church. Some of these callings are societal like active citizenship, working for justice and peace, and mentoring the coming generation. Some of these callings pertain to a life-work like carpentry, medicine, engineering, or bookkeeping. Some of these callings are avocational like environmental pursuits and the arts. Modern men and women, adult Christians, often have *more than one calling.*

Callings Based on Giftedness

Discovering one's callings seldom happens overnight. It often takes some discernment. In *Chariots of Fire,* we actually saw the following three stages regarding discernment: (1) Identifying gifts, recognizing these gifts, claiming the gifts. (For twenty years I worked with children and adolescents who were disabled, emotionally or mentally. It was rare to find a young person without gifts; some had the gift of "running fast.") (2) Our gifts are such a part of us that we sometimes take them for granted and forget the source. That my exercising my gifts brings delight to God, as Eric Liddell pointed out, is a spiritual insight rarely found within believers. If as Christians we claim to want to please God, then never admit we do, we've got a terminal case of false modesty. Discerning how to live out our giftedness now and in the future sometimes means we negotiate one calling with another as Eric Liddell did. (3) Part of our destiny as Christians is to incorporate, within the response to a calling, *a mission dynamic.* We do that by being prepared to initiate mission in our own particular setting, taking a stand of advocacy for others or for honesty and justice when the occasion demands. We are blessed if like Eric Liddel we perceive that living out our giftedness through callings and mission gives pleasure to God.

In *Chariots of Fire,* Eric Liddell felt that the occasion of the Sunday Olympic running meet demanded that he take a stand. Although he didn't run in the heat, he did watch it. His companion asked him if he had any regrets.

"Yeah," he replied. "No doubts though."

That is a mission stance.

Callings, Church and Culture

The culture in which we live can influence the value placed on particular callings. Culture can encourage the development of certain callings, and it can impede the development of others. Church cultures play a role in this as well. Women today have perhaps more sensitivity to this issue than men because women have, in striking ways, felt the impact of culture and church on their callings.

That I love being a grandmother and sense it as a real calling is readily apparent to those who hear my innumerable grandchildren stories. For me being a mother was a real calling; perhaps that is why being a grandmother is such a delight. There was a time, however, when our children were grown and I was more reflective, that I felt a sense of betrayal because mothering for me was limited for so long to sheer "care-taking of basic needs."

The first year our twins were born the only time I left the house was to go to mass on Sunday. Because of their fragility, it was advised that no one besides my husband and I care for them. I never picked up one of them or their older sister without giving a hug, but the time and energy to get to know, to play, to cuddle for a while, to "waste time together," to teach—to "mother" in its emotional and spiritual sense—was in short supply. In addition, the contrast between the glorified image the church held up concerning motherhood and the motherhood I knew I was exercising contributed to my guilt. How was I not a failure?

My maternal grandmother, with thirteen children, a husband and a hired farmhand to feed, saw her calling to be a mother likewise erode into sheer "care-taking." My mother remembers many late afternoons when my grandmother, in respite from chores, would lie on her bed and sob. When her children were older, she sometimes took them to a matinee, but my mother remembers no time when my grandmother did not knit socks, when she went visiting or in the dark as she watched a movie.

When our oldest daughter was three and the twins two, George lost his job. Fortunately I was able to get a teaching position, and my mother volunteered to take care of our children. During that whole year, I don't remember one Friday night when I did not sit in front of the television set and cry all evening from complete exhaustion.

As a grandmother there are two joys I savor. One is loving and being with my grandchildren. The other is watching my daughter live out *fully* the calling she so deeply desires—being a mother. That doesn't mean she is not, at times, exhausted. It means that she was not forced to rush into more than she could emotionally and physically carry.

Within the women in our family, it took four generations for the calling to be a mother to be lived out with the respect that the woman embracing it deserved. My grandmother endured without openly questioning her "marital duties," including being a mother of thirteen. My mother felt ambivalent about the callings and roles that she embraced, but she did not fully understand because the modeling for mothering she received symbolized care-taking and exhaustion. My desire to mother was intense, but the modeling for family life I received had more heartbreak than joy within it. My grandmother's great-granddaughter found the freedom to be who her mother, her grandmother, and her great-grandmother wanted to be.

Was the church to blame because the women of three generations were unable to attain self-respect and self-regard related to their calling? The church should not carry all the blame; culture and ethnicity played a part in telling women who they must be rather than inviting them to reveal who they desire and feel called by God to be. But the pre-conciliar church surely meddled where it took no responsibility, had little expertise and less interest. Its rhetoric and demands concerning the calling of motherhood hindered my responding to that calling, a calling I *genuinely desired.*

What of the post-conciliar church? Has it learned to work *with* lay women and lay men to nourish and enhance their callings? The verdict does not seem to be in yet.

Callings and Jobs

Sometimes we take jobs just to put bread on the table. We have no sense of calling for these jobs and we may even dislike the work. Knowing what we're about "clears the air," and it may enable us to see that assuming responsibility for ourselves and for others by our willingness to engage in the work is profoundly valid spiritually. Our willingness reveals the embrace of responsibility that comes with living an adult Christian life. In addition, any workplace can be the setting for salt of the earth ministry.

We run into trouble (and we often do) when we equate a calling *with a job.* Having a calling does not always mean we will be *able* to live it out in a job. It is also possible to lose a sense of calling.

Lanford Wilson illustrates this in his play *Angels Fall* when the character who is a teacher remonstrates because he has lost all zest for caring about students, all interest in the subject matter he teaches. In contrast, Zap, a tennis player, speaks vibrantly of *finding* his calling:

It was really weird. I was like in the fifth grade and I was watching these two hamburgers on some practice court, and they took a break and one of them hands me his racquet. So I threw up a toss like I'd seen them do and zap! Three inches over the net, two inches inside the line . . . Right down the line. And the thing is, that's where I wanted it . . . that was it. I hit the first ball and I said, "This is me. This is what I do. What I do is tennis." And once you know, then there's no way out. *You've been showed something.* Even if it's just tennis, you can't turn around and say you wasn't showed that. So I went to church and said a novena for those meatballs, 'cause they didn't know all the butterflies that was in my stomach, that they'd been my angels. But, man, on the way home, anybody had asked me what I did, right there I'd have said, "I play tennis." Didn't know love from lob, didn't matter. That's what I am.[1]

Zap lets a calling most people would consider an avocation have its way with him—own him, in a sense. In memory he reveres the day he discovered his calling because his calling *showed* him who he was.

Sometimes we come into a calling through mentors. For some time my husband's avocation was acting. From childhood our youngest daughter was asked to run through his lines with him; she sat waiting for him at rehearsals; she sometimes secured a small part in a play in which he acted. When she was in high school, they both had roles in a professional production of *Charley's Aunt.* They shared early supper hours, incredible parking problems, an insufferable director, and a unique sense of companionship.

Today acting is her vocation. The mentoring in this process was subtle and natural, much of what family generativity means in its best sense.

Life Without a Calling

In his play *Angels Fall* Lanford Wilson seems to be posing the question, "What do we do in a society in which a tennis player has a greater sense of calling than a teacher?" What we do with ourselves in such a culture is take a good look at ourselves to assess whether we still own ourselves or whether the culture or our job owns us! If either does, then we most likely lack the inner freedom needed for discipleship and mission.

To remedy the situation we may have to begin at the beginning and learn again how to distinguish between jobs and callings. We may have to admit that what I do day in and day out has little to do with what I perceive as a calling.

There are times when it isn't possible for us to have a job that is a calling, but if there is no area of our life in which we are pursuing a calling, life can become flat, stale. After a time the lack of a calling can affect our physical, psychic, and spiritual well-being. In contrast, when one pursues a calling (whether as an avocation or a vocation) one feels a spiritual connection to what is beyond the here and now—the actual moment and the actual task. That's often why we persevere in difficult tasks in spite of the challenges that confront a calling. In the midst of the turmoil and tensions we may not sense what we commonly define as "spiritual" but sometimes the value of our endeavor to the value of life is affirmed in an elusive but real way. We are "shown" something. These dynamics link us beyond the moment and the activity to the Creator who creates the *gifts* that draw us to particular callings, ones that sometimes engender religious experience, a sense of the Spirit filling us with vitality.

Sometimes to understand a sense of calling we are helped by reflecting on what nourishes us during leisure time.

1. Engaged in an activity that is avocational we are removed from the world of *shoulds*. The goal is a sense of *being* regardless of the activity engaged in.

2. An avocation often encourages intuition and feeling rather than reasoning and analytical thought. It draws us out of the immediacy of our lives. Avocations expand the boundaries of our world.

3. Engaged in an avocation we get a different sense of ourselves; we touch the human rather than the functional side of ourselves. We know what it is to be the same as myself. Role is forsaken, person is revealed.

4. Pursuing an avocation, we may find that questions emerge that have no immediate answers. This helps us to understand the human journey as quest, as a mystery to be lived, not a problem to be solved.

If some of the above characteristics also describe our engagement in the world of work, then our life-work may be a calling as well as a paid job. On the other hand, if none of the above is apparent in our life-work, then our job may simply be an *occupation*. The goal is doing, not being; shoulds are internalized and sometimes heard even in hours away from the workplace; every question has an answer; there is little sense of being the same as myself because at work *role* dominates. I am functional and rational and utilitarian and reactive, rather than contemplative and receptive and responsive; spiritual values are reduced, rewards become values. To use an old phrase, I am part of the "rat race."

The character played by Danny de Vito in the film *Tin Men* illustrates the above. Who he was at work became who he was, period. Losing his wife meant little more than losing a sale. When he was alone, he repeated to himself the defensive arguments used with others on the job to prove he was right. The Danny de Vito character in *Tin Men* evokes the type of adult who never changes, who seems incapable of change, who is possessed by the secularity of the life he or she leads.

Denied a Calling in the World of Work

There are few of us who don't have times in our lives when we work only to put bread on the table. The idea of a calling during those times may be felt as a painful mockery in contrast to what we must do day after day even though what we do is an honest day's labor that contributes to the general welfare of society.

Some of us spend most of our lives working for a minimum wage doing work others don't want to do. As a Salvadoran refugee puts it, "We have to work. So we do the work that the American people don't want to do. It's just a fact we have to accept. We adapt ourselves to that fact to survive."[2] Teresa Amott, an economist, describes that kind of minimum-wage survival: "You borrow. You depend on charity. You depend on relatives. You furnish your home with stuff you find on the street. You have crowded living conditions. You scrape. You manage . . ."[3]

Christian minimum-pay laborers may exemplify salt-of-the-earth ministry in their jobs. They may have the opportunity to evangelize and desire to do that. They may have a wonderful sense of the meaning of calling in relation to family, because they sacrifice so much for family. But they know it will be their children, not themselves, who have a job someday that lets them live out a calling. As Catholic Christians we have the responsibility to hasten, by our individual and communal actions, that day for their children as well as easing the burden of our brothers and sisters who will never have the privilege of that day for themselves.

In my own life, if there is little sense of "being the same as myself" because my work role dominates, if I am always functional and rational and utilitarian and reactive rather than contemplative and receptive and responsive, if spiritual values are reduced and rewards have become values, then I may bring home a sizable paycheck but I may also be at the brink of a sizable personal disaster. Time away from work may be spent trying to compensate for this "lost cause" through alcohol, through travel, through competitive sport. I may find it hard to find empathy in my heart for those who are less fortunate and for the survival of humankind on planet earth because my heart has become arid and desolate.

Career Change and Calling

Within our culture in recent years, some adults have found the means and the courage to shake the dust off their feet and leave a job that denies them dignity and inner peace. They have found that the movement from work that is an occupation to work that is a calling is often a spiritual journey. In the great movement in the 1960s and 1970s toward career change these risk-takers packed it in and ventured toward fresh, new work, knowing in their hearts that a calling, even when laborious, energizes more than it drains. And it energizes by giving *meaning* to a day's labor. Work without a sense of calling, even if it is not strenuous, drains us because it becomes labor devoid of personal meaning.

In the mid-1960s my husband made such a career change. After a decade of work in manufacturing, George was in charge of production control for a plant that made surgical implements. The plant was close to our home. We both knew something was radically wrong when he came home for lunch day after day, ate in silence, and then said "I hate it!" as he left the house to go back to work.

What did he hate? That wasn't an easy question to answer. "I just hate it—that's all I know." For a long while that was all he could say. He could name easily what he would rather do—be a town or city manager. He had served on the city council in a medium-sized city when we lived in another location. Calling came through *then* loud and clear. Gradually George was able to name what he hated about his present job. "I am so tired of the tyranny of *things.* Year after year I feel as if my whole worth rests on our producing things. I also hate the fact that every escalation in the (Vietnam) war is savored like a victory at the plant because it means there will be more wounded, more sales of surgical implements, more profit. That makes me sick!"

He compromised. Rather than pursuing civic jobs, George began to consider jobs that would utilize his business skills in any setting that was people-oriented rather than object-oriented. This realistic compromise brought light to the end of the tunnel of his job vs. calling crisis, a crisis of such intensity it almost shattered our marriage. Effective pastoral help would have facilitated the process with much less blame and pain.

George took a position in school administration, living for a year in one state alone while I remained with our daughters in another. The change meant a cut of $7,000 in salary. Two of our children had recently had major operations. Further drain on our financial stability seemed downright reckless. Nonetheless, self-respect mandated abandoning caution in favor of the promise of fulfillment.

That September George moved. Being a business manager at a boarding school was nothing he had ever dreamed about, but it became a dream come true because it reinforced his hunch that work with a sense of calling had an entirely different flavor and vitality than work without a sense of calling.

In his new setting he discovered how work can have a ministerial dimension though at the time we did not recognize it as ministerial. Students from broken homes turned to him and came to rely on his wisdom, caring and advice. There were as many tensions and tedious times as in his former setting. Most of his time was spent on administrative tasks, but combining this with a ministerial dimension gave special meaning to his work. What we gave up financially has been repaid a hundredfold in the rewards of mentoring and collegial relationships. It has also been repaid by the value that *meaningful* work bestows and by the development of the ability to be reflective and discerning about work itself.

The initial impulse to break away from what had become a predictable and patterned existence emerged from the engagement in *civic* responsibility—serving others on a city council. Years later an avocational pursuit enabled a similar change. One school setting where George worked proved to be a dead end. Not only did he have no contact with students but his authority and responsibility were severely curtailed, making his work repetitive and routine. His self-esteem diminished daily.

At that time life was bearable because his participation in his avocation as an amateur actor increased. He had a role in a small independent film about a woman leaving prison, and another, coincidentally, in a stage play about a woman leaving prison. *Getting Out* by Marsha Norman had a long run, including performances for prison inmates. It was chosen the best Boston production of the year by the *Boston Globe* drama critic. George was asked to join a repertory company. Opportunity comes occasionally to do what is a heart's desire—but what will never be done because financial responsibility to family comes first. To be stuck in a job you hate, yet refuse a job you'd love, is heart-wrenching.

It wasn't until a few years later that George himself realized what those exhausting months of being on stage each night and being behind a desk all day really did for him. He put it this way. "When my self-image was at its lowest, the acting itself and the response to my acting gradually repaired a sense of self-respect. At work I was feeling so defeated I began to feel trapped. Paralysis set in. But as I regained self-respect, I regained a sense of freedom. 'You damn fool,' I said to myself, 'you may not ever become Paul Newman, but you sure as hell can get a different job!' " And he did.

Civic and social service as well as avocations sometimes awaken dormant dimensions of ourselves that may lead to a change of consciousness and a call to risk. Discerning, on a periodic basis, why I work where I work is essential for the Christian adult. Is my work a duty or a calling? Can I distinguish between avocations and work, or do I make work even of avocations? These are important questions to answer. More people than we may want to admit are in spiritual crisis because of their work. Yet work is a life experience seldom brought into the churchplace. George claims that he waited twenty-five years for that opportunity. Then, when it came, the pastoral leader pushed a mission theme on participants without first establishing how each personally perceived his or her engagement in work.

Only when calling and career mesh can the call to mission be heard. Without a sense of calling and a sense of mission, we expend most of our energies simply trying to survive the day on the job. And we may easily fall into patterns of television addiction or alcohol addiction. In a similar way, without avocations and participation in social justice and civic leadership, we too easily become self-absorbed, involved with one world, the little world we feel we own.

George and I share a common mission regarding the workplace. In different settings, we are jointly committed to the viability of the small educational institution in higher education. Our mission bond reinforces our marriage bond; our marriage bond reinforces our mission bond.

The freedom we have had to move to new positions in the workplace is not available to everyone. Two practical dynamics that have enabled this freedom: (1) competencies that have transfer potential; (2) pension plans that are not tied, in an exclusive way, to particular institutions. We belong to a retirement system for people who work in non-profit institutions. The freedom that lay adults have to leave jobs that may not cohere with a calling and a Christian value system is influenced by such practical issues, especially if the Christian adults are responsible for families.

Formative Approaches to Callings

Without play and daydreams, without leisure and avocations, few callings become activated in the young Christian. Without a flexible, hopeful image of self and times for self-intimacy, the young adult can easily take cues about who I should be and what I should do from the external culture rather than from the interior spirit. Without mentors who encourage "stretch" and a vibrant relationship with the world, the young person may grow up to be insular, self-satisfied, and complacent. Without an introduction to the God of creation, the God who loves me, the spiritual link between oneself, one's callings and the world may never be forged.

Callings are related to mission because callings help us to *envision* our place in the world. Without this envisioning, we may drift aimlessly or cling feverishly to one familiar spot or secure job. Without a sense of ourselves as embedded in this world purposefully by God, there may be no *depth* to our sense of mission. Bouncing from cause to cause, we burn out or equate being religious with being messianic.

Within our culture the most popular way for people to discern what to do with their lives is the *occupational* approach. The focus of this approach is career. "Plastics—go into plastics," the first words the Dustin Hoffman character in *The Graduate* heard at his graduation party, were remembered because they reflected a reality within our culture.

"You can make more money than I ever dreamed of being able to make if you go into business," a parental figure will advise a youth who may look up to him or her and thus, without reflection, heed the advice. "If I could live life over I'd be a doctor. You have that opportunity. Don't throw it away."

In each of these instances the focus is "out there," in the work-place. The target is the job. The goal is success. The young person is sized up to fit the bill of "making it." It may mean suppressing desires, lopping off gifts and talents that don't "fit the bill," denying crucial facets of oneself. Who you are matters less than what you do.

Schooling can reinforce that. At MIT, for example, in some departments it is difficult to avoid defense supported funding and defense oriented careers. One graduate student put it this way, "I'm not naive. My degree may say MIT, but it's coming from the Navy. The Navy put up the money. All MIT did was provide the lab."

A more generative approach is the *formative* approach. In the formative approach the focus is always on the person: Who is she? Who is he? How does she perceive the world? The future? How does he relate to others? To self? What gifts and talents, avocations and interests, have already been revealed in her? What personality traits predominate? What spiritual values does he want to enflesh in his life-work? What is the heart's desire? Is mission stirring within?

In the formative approach the hope is to further self-understanding so that the young person will make appropriate choices out of a sense of *who I am in relation to the world.* Parental figures, including campus ministers, may assist in the discernment of giftedness and shortcomings. Above all they need to be generative by respecting the need within the young adults to develop their own sense of personal identity. Mission *follows* formation. Mentors enhance this process when they *walk with* rather than ahead of young adults, lending support but not manipulating the formation that God, through developmental processes, is trying to enhance.

The issue of mission lived out in the world by the lay adults can be confused and clouded if freedom was lacking when they embarked on adulthood. If Mary Jean took her cues from what the culture called lucrative careers, if Phil went into business because his uncles urged him to take that route, if Eddie joined a volunteer corps because the college chaplain persuaded him, then the *integrity crucial to living out a mission stance within callings has already been compromised.*

For the young adult, seeing self against the horizon of the world can be intimidating. Yet this is often the reality of the lay believer. We must not forget that many young lay believers spend most of their time thrown against a horizon of non-belief or of belief not made apparent. A church professional, spending day after day surrounded by colleagues with a deep faith, has a buffer zone between self and secular reality, one that can lead to underestimating the challenge facing the lay believer.

Competitive, consumer-oriented cultural standards that *homogenize* is what we see spelled out day after day in commerce and in the capitals of our states and land. We may forget that the Yuppie phenomenon is a *formation* phenomenon, the impact of older, over-achieving adults within the secular culture on the educated young adult. To counter this trend, individuation, not individualism, needs to be pursued vigorously in our church communities. A Christianity that makes short shrift of who a person is—the delights and desires, the sorrow and trials of this person of faith in this place of no-faith—is a Christianity that encourages what it thinks it resists—*homogenization.* Young Christian adults, alone and up against the horizon, may not have a notion about how to interact with this horizon in ways we call mission. They may be at a loss regarding how to humanize and evangelize the secular setting where they have been "thrown" because these young lay adults never experienced humanization and individuation within their church.

What are the roots of this lack of generativity in the church? It is time to consider this question.

PART THREE

1

GENERATIVITY AND CHURCH

Vatican II spoke forcefully about the mission of the church in the world. While many Catholic believers felt affirmed by the council's implementation process, for others the upheaval and unevenness of the implementation led to an eventual alienation from the church. Although the focus of this book is the active Catholic, I feel that we must not lose sight of the estimated twelve million American Catholics who are estranged from the church. That figure represents over *one-fourth* of all baptized American Catholics over eighteen.

A few years ago a believer caught in this estrangement confronted me: "Why do you stay in? For the life of me I can't figure out why you're still so tied up with the church!"

Dick was an old friend, but we had not seen him for eight years when we received his call from Long Island saying he had business in Boston. Could he stay with us for three nights? The pallor we noticed on our old friend's face when he arrived disturbed us. Dick admitted that he hadn't been feeling well, but it wasn't serious, and he didn't want to talk about it.

Each night after supper, he badgered us about the church. His attack was relentless, his complaints about the church a laundry list. He and his wife had tried this parish and that parish. None of their five grown children, all educated in parochial schools, had held onto their faith. When Dick and his wife saw their kids abandon the faith they had tried to instill, they were upset. But now they felt the kids might have been on the right track all along. He was amazed that we hadn't seen the light.

Two weeks after Dick left we received another call from Long Island. It was Dick's wife telling us that, after a brief period of hospitalization, Dick had died. Looking back, I think that this book started to write itself within me the week Dick died. While he was with us, we heard complaints, criticism, and challenge concerning the church. We reacted defensively. We did not hear the deep cry in his heart. Dick didn't come to Boston on business. He hardly left the house. From what his wife said to us after the funeral, Dick came because he was dying and he was desperate to connect with God whom he felt he had abandoned when he abandoned the church. The three of us, regrettably, could not get beyond that church.

The week we went to Dick's funeral we also went to Jerry's funeral. Both were in their early fifties. Jerry's death was more sudden than Dick's; he too left a widow and five children. Jerry like Dick was exasperated with the church. His community had recently lost its priest and its chapel. Perhaps Jerry had at times felt an anguish as deep as Dick's, but it didn't seem to entrap him. Jerry was too involved, along with others, in trying to hold his community of faith together, writing to diocesan officials, advocating face to face with the bishop. Jerry loved a people, and these people were going to live. Jerry and others stepped into a governance role regarding this people; they assumed responsibility. Jerry had a mission.

Dick and Jerry responded quite differently to pastoral deficits in the church. It is futile to ask why Dick couldn't develop the adult autonomy Jerry had. For all the talk about reevangelization, when one considers the massive cultural change in the church since the early 1960s, efforts have really been minimal in assisting alienated Catholics. Calling them prodigal sons and daughters, as one program does, is not "assistance."

That is one reason why I am not sanguine about a Catholic Church that is little more than a conglomerate of moralistic strictures and populist sects emerging from movements or small communities, as vital as the latter are in the life of the church. The emergence of a populist/authoritarian hybrid church would inhibit the broad vision that the Catholic "place" engenders as well as any hope for the availability of consistently available pastoral services. Without many theologically educated and spiritually formed leaders in every area of the country, including lay leaders, we can continue to expect a reduction in the meager pastoral services available locally for most Catholics and a greater reduction in the witness and mission of the church within mainstream secular cultures.

The Reduction of Pastoral Leadership

The emergence, in some dioceses, of mixed teams of pastoral leadership (vowed religious, professionally prepared laity, and clergy) ministering collaboratively within parishes is a sign of an adult church. On the other hand, the diminishment of clergy on local church levels poses an ominous threat for the future if non-ordained personnel are not hired as replacements. We are just beginning to see the dramatic changes that lie ahead from this threat. The announced closure of *over forty parishes* within the city of Detroit may be a portent for the future. You'd have to be Pollyanna to believe that mission effort in the workplace, in civic settings, and in social justice endeavors won't be affected as the coming upheaval in pastoral ministerial leadership accelerates. Resistance toward alternative leadership exacerbates not only injustice but also the morale of existing leadership and the quality and quantity of pastoral service available. If the institutional church, with its right hand, calls for greater lay mission effort, while its left hand removes pastoral support through budget cuts and resistance to non-ordained personnel, lay believers have a right to question and challenge.

Denial of the reality about to descend upon the church in the United States seems tenacious in spite of the obvious rise in the median age of vowed religious and priests and ratio of people to priests. One diocese in upper Michigan will, in eight years, have twenty-four priests for eighty-five parishes. At a recent church gathering on the future of the church a diocesan priest exclaimed, "Are the people going to be abandoned?"

That may be a legitimate and timely question. It appears safe to say that we have crossed the threshold of crisis. The uprootings to come make the uprootings of Vatican II seem like child's play. Retired or ineffectual priests are being drafted into service as the priestly personnel shortage intensifies. Lay volunteers, pressed into service, may be given increased responsibilities but seldom are given increased authority. Three years ago in one very large mid-western diocese, the pastors of twenty parishes losing a priest who would not be replaced were asked whether they would like a non-ordained pastoral associate. Eighteen pastors replied that they would not!

To me this represents a *shunning of the pastoral needs of lay women and lay men.* Abandonment often builds on the tradition of shunning.

The Power of Shunning

Shunning the laity is not a new invention. The breadth and longevity of shunning within the church reveals a remarkable and pervasive strength. Many of us remember the subtle shunning en-couraged when the wedding ceremony for a mixed marriage was relegated to the rectory, when divorced Catholics were forbidden to receive communion, when public school boys were not allowed to be altar boys, when the sons and daughters of divorced parents were denied entrance into some religious congregations.

Shunning is socially acceptable, sanctioned sometimes by the example of clergy, sometimes by church regulation. Lay adults are often adept at shunning.

When lay eucharistic ministers were introduced in a nearby parish, my mother and her neighborhood friends, in confabs after daily mass, decided they would take communion from all the lay eucharistic ministers except for Harry Johnson.

"What's the matter with Harry?" I inquired.

"He's a convert. We'll go to Father when it's Harry's turn."

"Ma, Harry became a convert twenty years ago!"

"That doesn't change the fact that he's still a *convert.* A eucha-ristic minister should be a cradle Catholic. It keeps things on the safe side."

Shunning is a weapon of both primitive and patrician societ-ies. Shunning turns potential saints into pharisees. By keeping things "on the safe side," shunning blunts the mission impulse of its vitality.

Shunning goes on today at all levels of the church. Vatican leaders appear to shun the input of local bishops in selecting new bishops. (The tradition of electing bishops was shunned and disposed of centuries ago.) Shunning the vitality of national episcopal conferences was apparent during earlier years of this century and was apparent in some of the criticism heard at the 1988 NCCB meeting when the statement in response to the Vatican document on episcopal conferences was discussed. An intervention offered at Vatican Council II by Cardinal Spellman of New York shunned in a way the entire body of bishops: ". . . the authority of the supreme pontiff is supreme and full in itself. It is not necessary that he share it with others, even if these are bishops, whose collaboration in governing the universal church . . . is neither necessary nor essential."

Lay leaders are often shunned regarding church governance. Hispanic and black Catholics still feel shunned in some white parishes. Catholic voters in 1984 were told to shun certain Catholic candidates for political office, candidates who were criminalized within their own tradition. Female children who want to be altar girls are shunned, and former priests who want to serve in ministries are shunned in some dioceses.

What woman in the church, at one time or another, has not felt shunned? Sometimes the shunning descends to the level of direct insult. A dozen years ago I went to a liturgical conference with many clergy in attendance. One priest, who had seen me at another conference, asked me in a voice full of contempt if I were a "camp-follower for priests."

Shunning is practiced by right and left alike. Because there is often no legality involved in shunning, a structure or process enabling just response is lacking. Shunning is seldom perceived as a sin. Self-righteousness removes that sting.

Perhaps the shunning that shocks me the most is the shunning of realities leaders don't want to face. Even dialogue about particular subjects can create a risk for those who work in the church. The 1989 statement on priests' morale by the NCCB Bishops' Committee on Priestly Life and Ministry revealed that some priests are frustrated because certain solutions to the crisis of declining vocations i.e. expanding ordination, can't even be discussed publicly.

Although two hundred priests in North America have been arrested for pedophilia, causing grave spiritual dilemmas within lay adults, especially parents, very little is heard on the topic from hierarchical leadership apart from specific cases. We are urged to continue to pray for priestly vocations but never urged to pray for the children so severely damaged by this tragedy that afflicts all of us.

No family, no business or other secular institution, would survive if it swept under the rug of silence what it found uncomfortable to discuss, a reason perhaps why so many lay people refer to their realm as "the real world."

Lastly, one of the most pervasive and serious examples of shunning within the institutional church is the shunning of the *real life experience of innumerable lay believers.* The paradox of being called lay people yet feeling the necessity to leave one's "layness" behind when one participates in church activity is still endemic within the church. When the reality of one's life reaches crisis proportions it may receive pastoral attention, but until then the dilemmas and stress of daily work, the tensions and joys of parenting, the challenges of participating in the ongoing political and civic life of one's city or country, and the pleasures and problems attendant on one's sexuality too often fall under the mantle of silence. Recent documents that urge lay adults to engage in mission in their multiple settings of life still fall short by failing to urge the means to bring these encounters back into the church for articulation in local, diocesan, and national communities.

Shunning, during the heyday of the Land League in Ireland, provided a way, a church-approved way, for the Irish people, particularly those whose towns and farms were owned by English landlords, to fight their oppressors. Unlike the Fenian uprisings, shunning was not violent, but it was a weapon. Thomas Flanagan in *Tenants of Time* reveals the power inherent in shunning. ". . . there is a fine line between shunning a man and raising your arm against him. . . . In that rich hive of a society, community clotted like honey in the comb, it must be a peculiar torment to be 'shunned.' As though life had turned its back upon you, denied you not existence but identity."[1]

An existence but not an identity is what lay women and lay men still experience in some church settings. In the Land League War, shunning was using the weapon of the oppressors *against* the oppressors by the oppressed. For centuries shunning had been the way aristocrats dealt with those considered beneath them; "downstairs" permitted its party so long as its party-goers didn't crash the party "upstairs."

Reverse Shunning

Reminiscent of the Land League War, some lay Catholics are engaging in what I call "reverse shunning."

Traditionally, women have been the mainstay of the Christian churches, providing crucial voluntary service to the local community. Many Catholic women are becoming disillusioned about their service role. Some are just plain tired—tired of "taking it" as much as tired of providing the service itself. Tired of hassles with pastors, tired of trying to reconcile factions, tired of being taken for granted rather than affirmed and appreciated. As the bishops say in the first draft of the pastoral letter on women:

> Clearly, women feel alienated when clergy patronize them, treat their concerns as trivial, take their contributions for granted or simply ignore them. . . . (Women) are ready to assume roles and responsibilities beyond those usually identified as theirs. When they undertake such roles, they do not want to be treated as children or feared as threats.[2]

Denial of ordination of women may increase the amount of shunning practiced by laity. In 1974, 29% of Catholics approved women's ordination. In 1985 the figure in an identical poll was 47%. Interestingly *more men than women favored women's ordination in both polls.* According to Dean Hoge, "the support goes far beyond the women's movement."[3]

A second form of reverse shunning by lay Catholics is to limit what is given to the church from the wallet. Bishop William McManus summarizes recent data on pocketbook shunning:

1. Catholics in 1984 contributed *less* to the church than did Catholics in 1964.
2. *Church-going Catholics* in 1984 gave less than did church-going Catholics in 1964.
3. From 1964 to 1984, Catholics moved up—not down—the economic ladder. They have much more gross and disposable income.[4]

Most directly attributable to actual shunning is the sharpest decline in financial donations—offerings from lay Catholics who participate in liturgy *on a regular weekly basis—from 2.7% of their income in 1963 to 1.8% in 1984.*[5] Should this decline continue by 1994 "the level of Catholic contributions would be 0.8% of income."[6] Protestants, on the other hand, have consistently given 2.2% of their income to their church.[7] If the Catholic situation is to be remedied, church leaders can no longer afford to play deaf to lay complaints. As Andrew Greeley puts it, "It would be a mistake for those who lead the American church to mislead and deceive themselves on the subject of lay anger."[8]

A Destructive Dynamic

Shunning is one of the most destructive dynamics operative in the church today because, unlike responses that erupt from freely expressed anger, *shunning is both subtle and sanctioned, pervasive yet dimly perceived.* We shun because we don't dare "fight clean." Shunning, a form of fighting, is an interior weapon used by those who have entrenched negative attitudes yet have no means for venting their anger. Often they are not even conscious that they are fighting. Shunning, in other words, is akin to passive aggressive behavior.

Communities with passive aggressive shunning operatives are death-dealing. We seldom see vibrant mission and forward mobility in dioceses where priests and people inflict passive aggressive behavior on one another. What we may hear in such dioceses is a great deal of scapegoating—blaming the laity or blaming the clergy or blaming the bishop for all problems and lack of progress. So long as all governance in the church is tied to ordination and obedience, so long as local preferences for episcopal leadership are ignored, passive aggression and shunning will flourish.

Rolling back the stone of passive aggression happens when believers, on all levels of the church, discover an interior freedom based on trust that enables the believers to deal with one another frankly out of respect for one another as individuated adults with varied gifts and talents. Authority and responsibility emerge out of being *with one another for the sake of God's kingdom.* In this kind of community, honest and open "give and take" emerges because each participant wants the gifts and talents of others to be donated to a vision that is collaborative and not self-serving.

Risen Life

What I find most amazing at this time in the church is that so many do "go on"—go on engaged in vibrant mission, go on in faithful service within the church, go on in deep fidelity to one another and to God alive in our midst.

Perhaps we go on because these are *the best of times as well as the worst of times.* When I get discouraged, I go to prayer and let the discouragement move into tears or erupt into anger. Later I sometimes find myself "rewinding to the resurrection." I savor the many instances of risen life I have experienced in the church in the last few years. If the darkness impedes mission life, the light of resurrection engenders it.

One day recently I spent an hour in late afternoon playing scenes of risen life against the yellow clapboards of the house next door. These memories healed my heart and gave me the hope and courage to go on.

The Memory of a Conference

Since Vatican II, through participation in ministry and in associations, more and more lay believers have developed a sense and appreciation for life within the church, beyond their local setting, by attending regional or national conferences.

Early one summer, hundreds of miles away from where I live, I watched a six foot nine inch tall bishop and a bearded abbot from a monastery dance down the aisle of a church that looked like the French church of my childhood. In procession, behind the bishop and the monk, a black choir sang and *really* danced. We were at a gathering to share insights on American spirituality, in particular lay spirituality. The reflection and sharing was among lay leaders from organizations rooted in spirituality.

Slow-down seemed to be the motif; at informal gatherings in the evening, being contemplative about one another was the way we learned about one another's spirituality; knowing one another as persons was more important than knowing one another's arguments about piety. Because of this ambiance, Saturday's session on social justice and spirituality was lucid, direct and sometimes confrontative rather than a rhetorical harangue.

On Sunday, leaving the conference, I pondered what we had learned. We learned that would-be competitors can be companions. We learned that, in the church, we may be passing to a time that needs no fundamentalism or revivalism, no new popular piety or new devotional dynamic, a time rather of *spiritual deepening.* At a church conference where the ambiance was slow and contemplative—finding God in "a long, loving look at the real"—we discovered that contemplation is not an *activity* one does once a day. Contemplation is the day lived out with God, the path many believers are verging toward in their hunger for greater intimacy with God.

Whether bishops sit on thrones or dance down aisles, so long as some believers still glide like angels into God's heart, so long as they let their lives be led into mission by God, so long as they deepen their friendship with God through prayer and reflection on the life they are living, the church will go on.

The Memory of a Diocese

Against the yellow clapboards of the house next door, I see the couple I talked with early one morning in Saginaw, Michigan. Tim was a lawyer who had taken early retirement from Dow Chemical. He now practices law full-time as a voluntary service for Legal Aid, working primarily for women who have been abused by their husbands. Phyllis, after training in a special program in a neighboring diocese, serves as a spiritual director in her parish. Both feel that their service is a gift to themselves as well as to others.

"After a career in corporate law, it is really a great experience to be on my feet in a courtroom! And great to know I'm directly helping others by what I'm doing," Tim says.

Both had been enabled to discern where God was leading them, now that their family is nearly grown, through participation in the two year program at the Diocesan Ministries Institute, a program that includes spiritual direction for each participant. Later that morning, the three of us participated in one of the classes in the Summer Ministries Institute.

The first person I met when I arrived at the former convent next to the cathedral was a sixty year old mother of eleven children who had just returned from a conference on prisons in Appalachia. Bessie explained how her participation in the Ministries Institute programs has led to visiting inmates on a regular basis, a ministry she hopes to intensify.

One member of the class I was teaching owned a furniture store. He has been instrumental in convincing other owners of furniture stores to open a shop with used furniture for those existing on very limited budgets. A lay woman who had been through this creative program, designed and led by Sr. Roberta Koloza and Sr. Jo Gaugier, has organized and opened a human services agency in a part of the diocese lacking that kind of outreach.

In my travels throughout the country in the last decade, I have seldom encountered a group of lay men and lay women as mature in their faith as the people it had been my privilege to be with that week. Absorbed in the task of discerning, through the program, whether God is calling them to ministry in the church or increased mission engagement in a secular setting, they are a people with a purpose. There is no sense of floundering or flailing out at the church on the part of these lay adults who not only know their lay identity but also rejoice in it.

The Memory of a Parish

In Milwaukee, Wisconsin, the parish family at Gesu prays together and grows together spiritually. Many are discovering how to let their lives be led by God through spiritual direction and retreats. When an eight day individually directed retreat is held in the parish, a special chapel is created where other members of the parish community come to pray for their brothers and sisters on retreat. Margaret Peterson, a lay ministerial staff leader at Gesu, was invited recently to be godmother for a baby whose mother Margaret had guided through a 19th Annotation Ignatian retreat while the mother traveled the deep journey to the birth of her yearned for, prayed for, new baby.

At Gesu, the Jesuit, women religious and lay staff ministers know that the spiritual deepening of their church community will not be effective unless the faith of the team members is also deepening. An hour is set aside at each staff gathering for prayer and for sharing with one another the consolations and desolations each has experienced since the last gathering. Collaboration is the dynamic of this parish setting.

At Gesu the spiritual often bears fruit in social outreach. The parish is a member of a fifteen year old central city consortium of ten churches that sponsor a food pantry and operate a shelter. At Gesu the St. Vincent de Paul group is creative as well as active. There is a full-time social justice staff member whose responsibility it is to integrate a mission consciousness into all components of parish life—liturgy, spirituality, adult education, parish council. Each catechumen serves in a soup kitchen or shelter as part of the R.C.I.A. program.

It's hard to hear about such remarkable means for vitality within a parish like Gesu without savoring the openness in such a setting to the Holy Spirit. Where this has occurred in parishes or movements or small "ecclesial" communities, God becomes, for the people, close and caring within the immediacy of their lives. The invitation to lay down one's life for the sake of the kingdom can often be more readily embraced in a spiritually supportive community.

(In this instance the gospel is not being interpreted in some radical new way in the United States during the latter decades of the twentieth century. In Christian history we find abundant evidence of lay outreach to those who suffer. Within parishes in the thirteenth century, for example, peace fraternities emerged and maintained buildings for charitable as well as religious purposes. In one fishing village, lay leaders collected tithes from parishioners, distributing one-third of what was collected to the poor. According to Michael Mollat in *The Poor in the Middle Ages,* lay confraternities often supported almshouses and leper hospitals. One founded in 1187, and dedicated to St. Eligius, is still active. The building of bridges, many supporting a hospice, was also the mission of lay organizations. Mission enabled by the laity has a long tradition in the church.)

The Memory of a Lay Community at Prayer

My last memory played out against the yellow clapboards was of a holiday, Labor Day, and a gathering of the people of the Vineyard Community in the Berkshires. Now without a church building and a priest chaplain, the Vineyard Community gathers monthly in homes of members for prayer together. On Labor Day we came together at the home of June Thomas where we eventually formed a large circle. Each of the more than twenty lay adults had brought a "tool" used in a work setting and each shared something about the tool and something about faith and work. At first we felt a bit awkward. Then Mike Cancilla lifted up the ophthalmascope he uses in his work as an eye doctor. Mike told us about the invention of this "tool" and how it helps him to see inside the eyes of his patients. "Maybe three or four times a year I help someone from going blind because of this small instrument." Mike paused and then said quietly but feelingly, "That means a lot to me—to be able to do that."

We savored Mike's sharing in silence for some time. Then Judy showed us a puppet she uses with nursery school children and explained how the puppet helps them to express what's going on inside them. Later her husband, who is also a teacher, told us that when he started teaching, one child in his class came from a broken home. Last year most of the children in his class came from broken homes. Responding to their needs is his ministry.

Mary June showed us her hand trowel used in her avocation of gardening; Norma held up a thimble and talked about making wedding dresses for new brides; Barbara and Jane had both brought appointment books, symbols of their work as therapists; John held his hands out, his tools for creating ceramic pieces; George showed his calculator, used in his work as a business manager of a school. Each also shared in a reflective way how faith contributes to their work or how their work contributes to sustaining the world—ears for listening from a nurse, a microscope for detecting blood diseases from a medical technologist, a dishcloth from a homemaker, an Exacto knife from an artist, a pen from a salesman, a description of a goncometer from a physical therapist. When it was June's turn, she gestured in a way that encompassed the room and said, "This home is my tool." A widow with a young special needs daughter to care for, June offers weekend hospitality to teenagers in a diocesan faith-building program.

The stories told both moved us and filled us. Some of us may not have known how we ourselves perceived how we lived out call through callings or the worth of our work *until we were asked to share.* As we moved into our closing prayer, we included our children, many now young adults with a sense of global consciousness. Dan was back from Africa but John was now in Africa as a volunteer for the Peace Corps. A young African had come to live with one family to attend high school in the United States. Other offspring were in Canada, Ireland, and Mexico. More are scattered across the country, beginning diverse careers. The creative arts dynamics in the Vineyard has helped to form the callings of others —two are in theater, one is a weaver, one is a writer, another works in graphics, two design clothes. One has committed himself to the calling of monastic life, another is a diocesan priest. Of the fifty families that once comprised the Vineyard, some have moved away, some have drifted away, but all were remembered in our afternoon of prayer on Labor Day.

Paschal Mystery

Hardly a day goes by that my heart is not in sorrow for lay people who don't experience the risen life found in the above stories. Some are trapped in places where oppression is what the church has become for them. Except for saints, and sometimes even for saints, unrelieved darkness courts despair. William Macready claims that we may lose a generation of young adults if local churches continue to discourage the most creative parishioners and slight their ideas and offerings.

Some of the tensions and shunnings relate to the issue of *lay empowerment in governance.* Since Vatican II, models of lay participation in governance have emerged. I say models because in so many Catholic settings these dynamics, though called forth through the council, are not the ordinary way of doing church:

—parish councils, diocesan pastoral councils, diocesan synods with many lay representatives

—new local, national and international lay associations and councils

—the expansion of lay ministries within the church

—lay pastoral administrators in parishes without a resident priest

—consultations with the laity

—collaboration with the laity

—co-discipleship

Some people are fearful, others are grateful, that the collapse of governance and ordination into a single and singular mode of church leadership is loosening. In small incrementals, governance has inched forward as a responsibility to be shared with the people of the church. Whether one fears or rejoices in this manifestation of a lay voice, the church will be diminished in power and effectiveness if this lay voice is silenced. Without the public proclamation of lay mission experience within the church, lay participation in governance may continue to meet resistance and be seen as engendering polarization. That we lay people are still perceived as objects in the church was noted by Robert Kinast in his commentary on the synod's working paper:

> Although the overall tone of the first part of this document is affirming, there is still a tendency to speak of the laity in the third person and the church as someone other than the laity. There is an unmistakable, hierarchy-centered perspective which gives the impression that *the laity are being looked at rather than lived with* (*nos. 12, 13*).[9]

On their deathbed lay adults no longer cry to be dressed in the habit of a monk or a nun in order to gain more ready entrance into heaven. Nonetheless, though 98% *of* the church is lay, lay people *in* the church are still too frequently treated *symbolically and corporately* as its stepchild, or as a *separate* "secular extension of the church" as one bishop has put it.

Removing Barriers

Last Christmas, our daughter Kerry related a story about a concert she attended in the prison where she was working.

> The concert was in the chapel. The inmate choir entered from the back. We couldn't see them as they sang *Joy to the World,* but we heard a real harmony in their voices. [Kerry was quiet for a moment.] There are stained glass windows of Jesus in the chapel. Stained glass windows with bars. Bars between the stained glass and the inmates. It's sad to see.

The image lingered in my mind during the days after Christmas. One cold afternoon in Vermont I gazed from the warmth of the house at a field with two horses nudging for grass under a dusting of snow. There I let the image settle in my heart. As it did I saw a cathedral with stained glass windows. Stained glass windows with bars on the outside.

Keeping the laity out. In my mind's eye I saw scenes from church history reflected on the glass and the bars. A bar put in place when prelates, in imitation of Roman secular leaders, began to wear ornate vestments. Another when lay believers no longer elected bishops. A third when Chrysostom's warning about the risks and temptations to the salvation of one's soul that came with a sacerdotalist interpretation of episcopal office was forgotten. Another with the rood screen separating the laity from the altar in the fifth century. Each bar heightened the lay believer's passivity and dependency within the church.

During Vatican Council II the bars were removed, one by one, and the stained glass windows were opened. The maximum security of those on the inside who approve of bars has been threatened. Resistance has set in. The updating promised at Vatican II is beginning to move in reverse in spite of what James Fowler points out: "At every systems level and in every discipline, dynamism and process are king, and substance, stasis, and immutability have been dethroned . . . the dynamic character of narrative, as opposed to ontological categories . . . reflects a hunger to recover a sense of meanings as connected with history, a sense of disclosure and depth as being connected with experience."[10]

Another Stepchild

If in some quarters the laity is still the stepchild within the church, we share this placement with spirituality. Vatican II invited the lay believer to speak up in the church. North American laity, speaking up in the 1987 Synod consultation process, advocated an increased focus on spirituality. As Kinast put it in his summary of the consultative process, "Spirituality has a very high priority among these faithful. They are living a personal, intentional faith life, and they want to develop it."[11]

The desire within lay adults for resources to help them understand themselves more fully as spiritual persons and to engage in ongoing processes to enhance their spiritual gifts should not be shunted aside. But because there is a widespread belief that spirituality is what the lay women and lay men *get* from the church, unless pastoral leaders affirm gifts that lay believers *bring* to the enterprise the church may still fail to recognize that spirituality is something the laity can *give* to the church.

As Friedrich von Hugel put it, "the great fact (is) spirit *and* Sense, Spirit *in* Sense, Spirit *through* Sense."[12] Von Hugel, who wrote so fully and freely about *spirituality from a lay perspective,* helps us appreciate that mission engagement on the part of the laity will be the fruit of greater lay engagement in the church's reflection, formation and teaching *regarding spirituality.*

Von Hugel suggested that believers bring to prayer all the "worldly" encounters experienced and bring to the world a heart that is deeply authentic, spiritually vivified, one that is free for full engagement in that world. Lay women and lay men need, freely and enthusiastically, to "seek and patiently endure (without scandal to either one's faith or one's humanity) the slow, costly, harmony-in-tension-and-through-history of incarnational existence."[13] *Timidity or ambivalence* about engagement in the secular world can only weaken a mission stance. Watered-down monastic spirituality is not appropriate for the lay believer because it often inhibits vigorous lay mission in the secular world. Solitude is necessary but not as flight *from* the world. We go apart but bring our experience of the world with us. While apart, we have the freedom and silence to contemplate that experience with God.

It is knowing the best of times along with the worst of times that enables Christians to savor the paschal mystery at a more profound level and to perceive it when it emerges in ongoing, everyday life. In the cyclone that seems to be recklessly rushing through the church, we need at times the kind of assurance we can only receive from God. In the church we seem to be living a time of paschal mystery, fearing death, yet awaiting new life. Knowing that changes have always been part of church history and having companions in faith helps us to let go of passivity and dependency and move forward with the One who, on the road with us, helps us to find new life.

New Life and Freshness of Spirit—The World Church

For all the sham and shunning that infect the church at this time, there are graced instances of new life and freshness of spirit bursting forth in local church communities and in mission efforts. In 1987, with two hundred and fifty other North American lay people, George and I went to Rome during the Synod on the Laity. While there we heard stories about new life and freshness of spirit bursting forth in many parts of the world. Some of the stories were heard at the Vatican offices we visited. Other stories were told by lay Catholics from each continent at daily late afternoon panels where we felt more solidarity than we ever expected. We were particularly moved by the stories of Catholics in China, Africa, and Latin America where the paschal mystery is a daily experience for so many of our brothers and sisters.

As the week went on we found ourselves growing adept at taking times for reflection with the art treasures of Rome. Not imprisoned in the sterility of museums like the art in the United States, the sculpture and paintings in Rome are amazingly available. We stopped at a small French church and found ourselves face to face with a Caravaggio. The immediacy made the encounter *subject to subject,* not subject (the viewer) before *an object* as it is back home. Contemplating the Caravaggio, I felt gratitude that our encounter with our lay brothers and sisters from other nations was also "subject to subject."

The second day of the conference a journalist from Ireland

handed me an editorial that said the lay group from America was in Rome to hijack the synod. "How on earth would one ever *hijack* a synod?" I asked the journalist. That was my first inkling that some in Rome found us suspect. My dream for the synod was that large groups of laity from every continent would come and celebrate together in Rome. My vision was predicated on a church in which the quality of the community bonding ("See how they love one another") would come alive for the world to see. My vision was of a church in which responsibility and authority would emerge from this bonding; shunning would become a failure of the past. In my own country I had experienced in numerous settings lay people and vowed religious and priests and bishops coming together and giving witness to the co-discipleship of responsibility and authority through bonds of love. Why did a mere two hundred and fifty of the millions of lay believers in the church, coming to Rome in solidarity with the Synod on the Laity, cause a stir? When all the world hears stories of greater freedom and solidarity in the Soviet Union and eastern Europe, yet hears stories of polarization and repression in the church, how can we hope to be perceived as God's church? During a synod on the *laity,* it seemed strange to think that the institution might fear its people. As one companion in Rome put it, "What kind of church would be afraid of its people?"

Most of us had never asked that question before. Back home George is struck by how easy it must be to belong to a denomination born only two centuries ago and born in one's own native country—a church in which all members perceive faith and life *from the same cultural perspective.* It is far more challenging to belong to a church that is ancient in roots and worldwide. On my return from Rome I asked God to enable encounters between the people of the church and their leaders that are *subject to subject* the way the art in Rome is, the way we related with our lay brothers and sisters from other parts of the world.

At times our *spiritual mission* in North America is to remember that graced instances of new life and freshness of spirit are happening in the church *all over the world.* At times we need to let ourselves become infected with the joy these blessings generate. We do this in order *to go on with the mission to which we are called,* a mission with our brothers and sisters throughout the world church, a mission for the sake of that world which is also our brother and sister.

2

GENERATIVITY AND MISSION

If the *quality* of the bonding among people of faith impedes or engenders harmony within the church, then the quality of the bond between the church and the world, this earthly home for the church, is pivotal in impeding or engendering mission. The lay people *of* the church typify *for* the church this bond with cultures and peoples beyond the church. Any reflection on mission mandates a probing of the relationship that we as humans as well as people of faith have with this world. Our relationship with the place called world, like our relationship with parental figures, friends, spouse, callings and other communities of Christian believers, forms us, influencing our engagement with our destiny: *transforming faith into mission.*

How we understand, how we embrace or reject our mission destiny, how we perceive the world in which we are embedded, are the determinants of how generative and fruitful our mission efforts will be.

In many local church settings and associations in the United States love among the people in a believing community, enabled by the Holy Spirit, spills over into generative love for God's created world carried out as *mission.* I am not talking here, of course, about emotional enthusiasm, but about "spirited" life, about a spiritually organic process that generates life beyond the narrow confines of home, neighborhood, parish. The generating life that I speak of cooperates with God's intention and God's power to transform earthly *place* into the commonwealth (or kingdom) of God.

This is what mission is all about. Community is integral to mission. It is never *my* mission for God, leading to my earning God's approval and, consequently, God's love. It is *God's mission.* When mutual love and intimacy are vibrant between God and myself, and between God and my community, we hear God say,

"Come, live fully your relationship to the world. Share my mission with me!" We hear it as an invitation to the community and as a personal invitation.

As a lay believer, some of the time I may be called to engage in that mission alone within a secular setting where there are no other believers. I may be called to engage in that mission with others within my Christian community. I may be called to engage in that mission with others who are animating mission independent of a church but within the civic community. What matters is that I respond, and that I respond as part of the priesthood of all believers, a priesthood of relationship through baptism, faith, and mission.

The member of the ordained priesthood usually exercises his cultic or sacramental priesthood for Catholic believers. The lay member of the priesthood of all believers exercises his or her priesthood for *all.* When the chalice of lay life is offered, it is offered for all. When the bread of lay life is broken, it is offered for all. Today I may serve a Jew I encounter at work, tomorrow I may challenge a politician who represents my district. Next week with the lay brothers and sisters in my local Christian community I may serve the sick and elderly in a nursing home. Last week I may have joined with a secular advocacy group in protesting the treatment of the homeless. The ordained priest is bound by restrictions in sharing the cup and the bread of the altar. The lay priest committed to mission cannot place *any* restrictions on groups or kinds of people she or he would be willing to serve or confront on mission.

All this may sound too rigorous to accept, and it is if interiorly we are still operating out of paradigms formed in childhood. With spiritual maturation comes courage as well as trust. We begin to realize what Jesus meant when he said that the Spirit will speak for us if we are confronted or entrapped because we discover it happening in our lives. We begin to have faith that Jesus is appealing to God for us. Matthew 10 tells it all. In this account Jesus lays down the guidelines for mission. Carefully read, the passage reveals that God is the supporting one who enables the accomplishment of mission and that God grants the great freedom of "shaking the dust off your feet" and moving on if a mission is not working out.

The lay Catholic embedded in the secular culture never knows when the moment might emerge to extend care to another. The moment might be in the midst of the workplace. It might be in the midst of the leisure place. What is significant is that the Christian is ready, willing and able to *act*. In the following story I do not know whether the woman who "acted" is a Christian, but her action exemplifies for me the instantaneous outreach the Christian is called to enflesh.

The Ownership Option of the Gospel

One evening in New Orleans my husband and I went to Preservation Hall, the setting for jazz indigenous to New Orleans. Preservation Hall is a popular landmark. Sharing a seat in the third row bench with a young woman, I looked around the simple, dark and shabby square room. Before long the players straggled in—banjo, trumpet, sax, clarinet, and piano. Most were along in years. They initiated the set with a peppy tune. A few people clapped, some closed their eyes, others watched the musicians.

After a few moments, I noticed a brown-haired boy about eight or ten, sitting Indian-style in the front row, inches away from the jazz band. He was waving his arms high and making rhythmic noises. His mother spoke to him and he paused for a moment but then began again—his movements even more erratic and agitated than initially. Then he turned his face to his father and I could see from his expression that he was handicapped, probably by cerebral palsy. By then all thirty of us crowded into the room were fixating on the boy. The tension in the air was tangible. The melody ended as did the boy's incongruous movements but not his smile. Many of us, I'm sure, felt torn between compassion for the boy and our own desire to become absorbed in the music.

During the brief break between songs the woman at the piano whispered to the player beside her. He passed the message along to the leader who rose and said the next number would be a song in which we'd all participate by singing and with gesture. Soon we were all letting our voices be heard and waving our arms in imitation of the leader. The room came alive, at first in relief at tension being broken and then in the sheer joy of having become one.

Such an instance of generativity is not seen every day of the week. The woman at the piano, followed by the band leader, had invited us all *into relationship* with the boy by saying, "Let's all belong to him and do what he is doing rather than expecting him to belong to us. Let's not expect him to meet standards which we define as good behavior yet are impossible for him. Let's let ourselves be owned by him."

When the third song began, the boy continued to make erratic motions. We did not gesture, but we also did not find him a distraction. In spirit, we had become one. And in a sense we now owned the room together. It was the boy's room as well as ours so he could be who he is and we could be who we are.

This is the *ownership* option that the gospels invite. Belong to the least if you want to be the greatest. Let yourself be owned by the weakest and you'll find yourself owning all that is valuable. Become one with the ones at the foot of the table and you'll be invited to the head of the table. It's what our God did in sending Jesus. It's what Jesus did with his life. It's incarnational ownership.

We live in the twentieth century. We live in a highly developed nation. Of course we're going to own homes and cars. We're going to become educated if we have the opportunity and we're going to travel to regions other than where we live.

But Jesus through the gospels calls us to do that in a way that gives witness to God and God's mission, to our being owned as well as owning. We are called to reveal that we are, in a sense, claimed by God, through God's love for us. Consequently, we are claimed by those *weaker* than ourselves because the destiny of the one sent by God was claimed by those weaker than Jesus was.

The kind of owning our creator revealed is symbolized by the cross and the resurrection. The cross is the sign of our attempt to own God by owning the one so dear to God. The resurrection is the sign of our God revealing to us that we cannot own God, that those with a claim on God are those who own nothing—the least among us, those bearing the cross like Jesus and those imprisoned and persecuted, who hardly own life itself.

Destiny and Goals

At one time almost every public speaker mentioned posterity as the destiny of the people of a given culture. Posterity was felt to have a claim on the present moment and the people living in that present moment. Today posterity is seldom mentioned in the public forum, eroding the value placed on nurturing the coming generation. Our potential for nuclear holocaust may be one reason for the difficulty in envisioning posterity. As valid as that reason may be, it has contributed to a vicious circle. In other words, without a strong sense of posterity and future, we have come to live in the present moment and have not dealt forcefully with the militarism that might indeed produce nuclear war. As E. L. Doctorow put it, "Once the Bomb was a weapon, then it was a way of doing diplomacy, now it's our economy." We have severed our generational bonds and responsibilities.

One appropriate way Christian adults develop maturity in faith is by noticing the values in their culture and how these values compare with their own values. For example, our culture seldom discerns between destiny and goals. In order to embrace mission Christian adults are called to engage in that discernment. If as an adult I have aligned my life only with the goals I have set for myself, then I am a different person from the person I would be if as an adult I had aligned myself with a sense of my destiny.

Both setting goals and identifying destiny are important functions of adulthood. At this particular time in North American culture many adults seem to favor setting goals for themselves over embracing a sense of communal destiny. The contrasts between the two are striking.

To have a destiny means to surrender self to a "pull" or a life pulse or life force that is (1) beyond self and (2) greater than self. To focus on goals means to take charge of oneself and to assert self in an active way within the world around oneself. Accomplishing one's destiny happens, in part, through goal setting. Without the latter, one may sense his or her destiny but, through passivity, drift vaguely toward the future.

Goal-setting without a sense of destiny is like rooms of furniture scattered on a lawn without a home to house the unconnected chairs, beds, tables, sofa, etc. Particular pieces of the furniture may be elegant but they remain inanimate without the greater whole of a home to bless them with meaning and harmony.

To be a person of faith is to have a destiny. The Israelites in the stories of the Old Testament had a strong sense of destiny, a destiny linked to belonging to a people, a people and a destiny chosen by God. The stories of the Old Testament have as their hinge the Israelites' fidelity or lack of fidelity to the one God, Yahweh. Jesus had an overwhelming sense of destiny, one that was in a way contagious. And we see in his followers a struggle to understand this destiny in order to move forward with it. Throughout Christian tradition, each of the figures of faith who stand out had a strong sense of destiny. Gandhi, a religious figure from another tradition, had a strong sense of personal and national destiny.

The way that having a destiny has been expressed by Christians has differed from age to age. The catechism that instructed some of us emphasized an individualistic destiny: "to know, love, and serve God and to be happy with him forever in heaven." Raised in that perspective, I now see my destiny, though personal, as linked to the people of God, the pilgrim people on mission. In gospel times, through some eras of church history, as well as since Vatican II, *mission* has been the destiny of the church as well as of the individual believer within the community of the church.

The mission destiny of the Christian is *relational*. Destiny emerges from relationship to God and unfolds into relationship with others within our community of faith, our family, our friends, but also with and for the sake of those beyond these communities, those in the settings we call secular, settings called to become God's commonwealth.

Formation and Mission

Mission and generating new life are closely linked in that care about another becomes caring toward others. We sense it in families rooted in authentic intimacy. We sense it in groups rooted in authentic community. We find it in the workplace where people perceive their work as calling. In a culture that is truly generative there is a tangible witness to caring about the one and caring about the many in ways that are life-enhancing, not dependency provoking. There is witness to justice in the singular and the universal, to the person and the public. A generative society is a society with a destiny, *a relational destiny rather than a mythic or manufactured or materialistic destiny.*

Through relationships within families and friendships many adult lay Catholics *have been formed to be generative,* to love in a way that is life enhancing. Many lay adults really don't need to be tutored in how to love. They know how to enable generative love that bears fruit, they know how to enable mutuality that unfolds into responsibility and authority. Although many lay adults have already been formed in generative values, and they model these as capably as pastoral leadership does, this gift to the church is not always recognized in the church. This book is a modest effort to respond to that lacuna.

To acknowledge more readily and visibly lay adults who are already intensely engaged in mission in civic, social justice and work settings is crucial. When it becomes more clear how lay mission is actually being accomplished, it will become easier for others to embrace mission as the necessary fruit of discipleship. A second step is to acknowledge more readily that the formation process of growing up in positive family and friendship relationships, what enables lay believers to be generative, is not always acknowledged as *Christian* formation. Consequently, many lay adults see no rationale for translating their formation (generativity) *into mission within the "wider world."* It is easy then to drift into taking cues for values from what is available—an intensely secularistic culture. Eventually, the values and attitudes in which we were formed may diminish in significance interiorly. Religion may take on purely ritualistic value.

When that happens we may become victims of the "popular individualism" endemic in our society. According to Herbert Gans, popular individualism does not mean separation from others. Instead, it is to live and participate primarily with a small, like-minded segment of society, the network of family, friends, and socialization he refers to as *microsociety.*[1]

Many lay adults have been formed to be generative in a microsociety, but there has been too little leadership or too much conflicting leadership about how to enable this generativity to become mission action within the workplace, in civic settings, on a global scale. Lay adults hear about this cause and that cause and feel confused about which deserves their response. From the pulpit they hear the call to live out their faith in everyday life. A friend tells them about a conference centered on social justice. A neighbor talks about work as the setting for engaging in mission.

In this whirling dervish it should come as no surprise that many lay Catholics prefer to stay with local church ministries rather than to respond to mission in the wider world. According to the Notre Dame Study of Catholic Parish Life, almost one-fourth of the lay Catholics in the parishes surveyed participate in one or more parish activities but in no civic involvements. Almost 35% participate in *neither* parish nor civic commitments.

Formation traditionally comes from "inside" a system. In other words, vowed religious who know vowed religious life "from the inside," who have been tested by its joys and sufferings, are the ones entrusted with formation for those entering religious life. These same individuals are the ones who contribute to theology about vowed religious life through their reflections, writings, and teaching. If the leadership of the institutional church is sincerely concerned about Christian lay formation for mission, it will call on the increasing number of theologically educated lay adults to energize its teaching and lay formation. It will also bring into the heart of the church the mission stories that only lay adults can tell.

Confusion About Mission

Although generative in spirit, mission is often, for the sake of others, intentional in action. Sometimes this action emerges spontaneously. Sometimes mission involves prioritizing or planning approaches or strategies. It can demand the goal-setting spoken of above as linked to destiny.

Let's look at this through a brief example from the workplace. Consultants were being called in to share their expertise for a media project Mary Leonard was working on. Mary felt that a consultant with expertise in ethical values should be invited to share with the staff. This became an uphill battle because other staff members did not see the content of the media project reflecting any moral dimension. Mary "did her homework" and persevered. Grudgingly, the other staff members gave in. The consultant was persuasive, and one part of the media presentation was on ethical questions. Mary accomplished her mission by setting goals and persevering.

Not all of us who are lay believers are so clear about our mission destiny and/or about setting goals for mission as Mary was. Hearing destiny's call, discerning the content of that call, and knowing how to move in response to that call are related yet separate entities, in a way. Each needs fine-tuned attention. Having a strong and clear sense of mission does not always mean having the answers to how to go about fulfilling its call.

Mission generates life and engenders peace, justice, the inclusivity essential to social harmony. Formation develops *values, attitudes and motivation.* Generativity is a meld of motivation, attitude, and action that is fundamental to Christian mission. When generativity is internalized, mission becomes a *way of life* with particular goals. Action is motivated by powerful internal convictions engendered by formation. Because of its consequent effect on action, formation by parental figures, friends, spouse, calling and career deserves attention. When mission is at stake our left hand needs to know what our right hand is doing.

According to the Vatican's working paper for the Synod on the Laity, "The secular feature of the laity makes them indeed the leading characters in the church's mission in the world." If we lay believers are the primary agents of mission, then reflection on our inherent relationship with the world cannot be bypassed. If we are not convinced of the value of mission in a particular setting, we may end up feeling like foot soldiers drafted to fight someone else's battle. Personalized and communal preparation related to the idea of mission comes prior to discerning *how* to invigorate mission through goals that call for action. Without this, ambivalence within the lay believer can lead to interior conflicts that evoke paralysis. Instead of moving out toward a global reality, the lay believer may pull back. That is why one goal of a formation process is to help lay believers *choose* their own mission settings and actions as well as affirm their responsibility and authority within those settings.

The goal of formation for mission is not to enroll the laity in one particular mission project like peace activism or pro-life demonstrations. The goal of formation is to help believers *discern where they are being called* and to enable a response to that.

Corporate Formation for Mission

Issuing a diocesan pastoral letter focused on particular mission action and expecting adherence to the values promulgated without a subsequent formation process for implementation is not a good teaching or good mission strategy. When this is done, I am always reminded of a penmanship lesson during my first year of teaching.

The principal came into the room and observed the class for a few moments, then beckoned me to come into the hall. There she pointed a finger at me and rasped, "What the hell are you doing?"

"Teaching a penmanship lesson," I whispered.

"You were not teaching any kind of lesson. You were sitting at your desk correcting papers."

"The lesson is on the chalkboard." Again I whispered, hoping to lower the volume of her voice.

"Putting something on the board and telling the students to copy it is not *teaching*. Without the give and take of interaction, no teaching and no real learning occurs. *Don't you ever forget that!*" She turned on her heel and left me with an invaluable lesson about teaching and learning.

The Hampton Falls Task Force on Peace of the Diocese of Richmond, Virginia, knows that lesson. To encourage the give and take that real learning and real teaching engenders, a three month "formation" event happened in response to the NCCB pastoral letter *The Challenge of Peace.* In addition to parish activities, four day-long regional events were held in the area that borders the huge Norfolk naval base. The first, on making moral choices, was sponsored for an invited audience of business, political, military and religious leaders. The second, for parish lay people, had spirituality and its relationship to peace as its focus. Its intention was to enable parishioners (military and civilian) to discern and articulate where each was in regard to peacemaking. The third, for staff members from military and civilian parishes, engendered discussion about exercising leadership in educating for peace. The last was a celebration entitled "Affirming Collaboration for Peace."

The *Peace Event,* as the series was called, was designed to enable that "each voice be heard." It was profoundly moving to witness lay Catholics, both civilians and military, share from the heart for the first time what, in their own personal backgrounds,

makes it easy or difficult to talk about peace. A challenging experience for many, the sharing was full of heartfelt meaning. With tears
women spoke of the inability to even consider peace in the world
because there was such a lack of peace in the home. A naval officer
said he had awakened three times the previous night with stomach
pains caused by his fear of coming to a meeting where peacemaking
would be talked about. A craggy-faced veteran spoke with feeling
about the navy before World War II, before technology dictated
policy.

The *Peace Event* is the kind of church effort needed to enhance mission. It enabled people to share experiences from their
own lives *about a global reality* that directly impacts on those lives.
It was an "event," but it was also a formative mission experience.

What an intentional formation dynamic like the one described
above often achieves is discernment of the kind of *relationship that
Christian believers want with the world,* how that coheres with
gospel, and what hinders or helps the living out of that relationship
in a mission oriented way.

In our reflection we have considered relationships with parental figures, with friends, with spouse, with self through callings.
Now we turn to how to sustain a generative, mission relationship,
not only with the persons and callings in our small web in the
world, but also with the entire global entity we call world. The
world is an *immense* place. *Image* is the only way we can perceive
the world. Consequently, our relationship with the world depends
on our image of the world. In North America today the world-
image of many is chaotic. One result is that, spiritually and psychically, our hearts may remain *locked* within the parts of the world in
which we exist.

During the post-war period, restoration of war-torn nations, as
well as development of third world lands, captured the imagination
of many Americans who felt a helping relationship toward the
world. During these years, a psychic and spiritual *connectedness*
flowed between them and other peoples of the world; they felt
related to the world; that was fact—they knew it and they cherished
it. That sense of global intimacy is dead. The Vietnam War helped
to kill that intimacy. Some of us began to feel that we had been
naive. Hidden within the concept of development lurked cold war
machinations.

An intimate, caring relationship with the global world seems to have been replaced by what I call a *reactive* relationship. Within a reactive relationship a range of feelings can erupt: sorrow, numbness, anger, fear, worry. Occasionally an energized attempt to *do something* may break through. A reactive relationship is a distinct contrast to a *consistent and responsive* relationship, the kind of relationship we may have with friends and family.

If things get so bad that we can't bear to look at peoples and places of the world on the television screen—at Cambodian families fleeing, at Ethiopian babies starving, at an earthquake-demolished village in Italy—we may rally around and help for a while. Or we may adopt a neo-patriotic loyalty for the United States. Or we may shift gears into neutral, turn off the television, turn off the world.

Neither turning our backs on the world nor sporadic charitable crisis intervention is what the Catholic Christian stance toward the world is meant to be. Nor is neo-patriotism. Nor is neutrality.

> The world which the council has in mind is the whole human family seen in the context of everything which envelopes it— bearing the marks of its travail, its triumphs and failures . . . (*Constitution on the Church in the Modern World,* Chapter I).

A relationship of mutuality with the world was proclaimed at Vatican II.

> Whoever contributes to the development of the community of humankind in the level of family, culture, economic and social life, and national and international politics, according to the plan of God, is also contributing in no small way to the community of the church . . . (*Constitution on the Church in the Modern World,* Chapter IV).

A vibrant and caring relationship with the world, a *spiritual binding tie with the world,* is fundamental to the mission of the church in the world proclaimed at Vatican II. Unfortunately, the world imaged as America's (or Japan's) marketplace or as an expansive resort setting for affluent Americans (or Japanese) has dominated segments of the media in the past decade. A commercial rather than a kinship relationship engenders a me-centered world image. If we regard ourselves as contemporary Christian

Catholic people living in a global age, if we take seriously the mandate to engage in mission in the world, a deep and abiding *relationship to the world* is the formative task confronting us because it is only through relationship that we become generative toward the earth that sustains our life.

Bypassing the need for formation in favor of immediate and direct action, a short-sighted measure too many believers and pastoral leaders foster, ignores the economic and technological complexities of our age. For example, how our careers impact on global realities calls for quiet and prayerful scrutiny. I will always remember a doctoral student I knew while I was a chaplain at MIT. A dedicated young Catholic, he said he loved contemplating the universe as God's creation because the unknown attracted him in an almost mystical way. But because he had no mentor to reveal the spiritual implications of his callings, he was tormented by what he called "the active stance that Vatican II insists on for lay people." Finally he settled his dilemma by transferring into nuclear engineering. The student summed it up by saying, "I'll probably live out my lay vocation keeping some nuclear reactor humming."

This kind of reductionist interpretation of Vatican II is not all that unusual. The student's story illustrates that formation for responsible global generativity is more challenging than we may realize at first glance.

Image of Our Global World

The sheer size of the earth, as I said above, means that to embrace the world, we, in reality, embrace an image of the world. Dealing with an image is, interestingly, what we do when we deal with ourselves and with God.

Hiding one's head in the sand like an ostrich may help us avoid seeing an image that is intimidating, but it is not a Christian stance. As Christians we are called to love the world as God loves the world. Mission is loving the world as God loves the world, loving it by facing its reality of beauty and woundedness and wrong-doing yet holding it lovingly in our arms. Mission is proclaiming that the world has a destiny: to be a realization of the commonwealth of God.

Catholic lay people are people in the world. They grapple daily with its rawness and its rewards. They belong to a church that is in this world, a church whose leadership nonetheless has for centuries sustained a *culture of its own,* one that is separate from the daily hum of that living, throbbing world. If this real world is to be articulated *within the church,* lay adults, men and women, world-wide must assume leadership roles at every level within the church in order to articulate the reality of the world from the inside—from family life, secular workplace, mainstream civic and political life.

Perceiving Place Settings for Mission

An affirmative stance toward the world on the part of the church is relatively modern within church history. Consequently, some Catholics, formed by pre-conciliar church dynamics, may have difficulty sizing up the meaning for them of the place called world. Seen in a post-conciliar light, the issue of this place called world is an essential focus within the formation of religious maturity.

How are we related to place? Are we *related* to place or only to particular persons in particular places? Do I have a binding tie to the place called earth/world as well as to particular places? If so, what is the significance of this? What response do I make? Is "thinking globally but acting locally" sufficient?

One strength of the post-conciliar church is that different segments of the church have *raised different settings* as the locus of mission effort by the laity:

—work place
—civic and political settings
—international settings
—places where the needy live a barren existence

One weakness in the post-conciliar church is the tendency to make these settings rivals of one another. The need, I believe, is to affirm *all* of these settings. But this must be done within a coherent theology—perhaps a contemporary "layology." The *context* for theology and formation must always be global, but mission will be cramped if we continue to quibble about the *one proper setting or way* for all lay persons to engage in mission.

A second post-conciliar weakness is a lingering sense in some quarters that the earth is no more than a provisional setting, a scaffolding for the heavens as M.-D. Chenu put it. Chenu, at the time of Vatican II, pointed out that the world is not sacred because Catholic believers *make* it sacred by their presence. The world is sacred because God created it. God created it for all peoples, which means that stewardship is not a license permit for domination.

A third weakness in the post-conciliar church is the tendency to underestimate the context of peoples in favor of issues. For example, a tendency persists not only to depersonalize people by referring to them as the poor or the needy (as I did above), but also to mentally "remove" them from their setting in spite of the fact that elements in their setting may be *why* they are poor or needy or homeless. And these elements are caused or influenced by events and trends in the mainstream culture, the place where most of *us* live. Patriotism, for example, indicates a particular sense of relationship to place. Justice indicates a particular sense of relationship to place and the people within a place.

Although we speak frequently about the kingdom of God, with its inherent reference to *place,* we seldom *reflect on place and our relationship to places.* We forget that places invite relationships just as people do. At times we also overlook the lay women and men who are accomplishing mission in local, regional and global place.

3

MODELS FOR LAY MISSION

God intends our integration. Believers who are spiritually mature usually reveal signs of integration. One sign spoken of earlier in this book is the meshing of intimacy, responsibility and authority evidenced in Christian adulthood. Within this paradigm, responsibilities we assume as believing adults and the authority we exercise flow from our relationship with God. The intimacy we experience with God in solitude, in community, in family, and in exercising callings emerges from our giftedness and through the myriad encounters and events of our lives. The dynamic experienced with God is reflected in dynamics found in other facets of our lives. Within marriage, family and friendships the only base for responsibility toward one another and for authority exercised in relation to one another is the intimate mutual love between adults who care for one another, and the caring love extended to children. The same vibrant dynamism can be seen in communities and movements rooted in "See how they love one another." The callings in life through which we live out the call to discipleship, ministry and mission emerge from self-intimacy—a knowing and naming our gifts and talents which, when lived out in avocations, occupations, and professions, give rise to responsibilities and authority within enormously varied settings in our society.

Mission likewise emerges *from an intimate binding tie with our global world* which God loved to the fullness of sending Jesus into the heart of it—for the sake of it. Our authority to engage in mission, and the responsibility we embrace at some cost in carrying out our missions, unfold from the unity of our intimacy with Christ and our intimacy with the world, this world that is our web of life. According to *Lumen Gentium,* ". . . the laity, by their very vocation, seek the kingdom of God by engaging in temporal affairs and by ordering them according to the plan of God. They live in the

175

world, that is, in each and in all of the secular professions and occupations. They live in the ordinary circumstances of family and social life, from which the very web of their existence is woven."

Whatever is the very web of our existence cannot help but form us. The webs of home and work and friendship, the places that have formed us and form us today, have spiritual meaning. Within the relationships and callings prominent in these settings we create, with God, life on earth in ways that countersign mere existence.

How are we doing this? Where is the evidence that this is going on? We seldom find the evidence in headlines or on the evening television news. We don't often find the evidence celebrated at church meetings and conclaves. We may, however, hear the evidence in stories told closer to home.

Mission Stories

When the disciples returned from engaging in mission in Luke's gospel they couldn't seem to wait to tell their mission stories.

Closer to home, mission stories are what are sometimes told when Christian families get together for holidays. When we gather as family we are no exception. Leslie often shares stories about conferences on toxic waste and acid rain that she organizes as part of her job at an environmental law center. Pam, who used to tell us about being a voluntary chaplain one day a week in a local hospital, followed by Clinical Pastoral Education involvement in the same hospital, now describes her part-time work at a center for battered women, and weekend ministry as a chaplain. Recent experiences as the youngest member of a parish council are also shared.

Jeff relates the excitement and exhaustion of heading a rural regional economic council. He attempts to convince clients and boards that the housing needs of potential workers are economic needs significant to work. Kerry has brought insights from her work as a counselor in a maximum security prison.

At a picnic get-together last summer, Pam told us about turning on a local television program and hearing that hostages had been taken in a riot at the prison. Her anxiety level rose as she tried to discover whether her sister was one of the hostages. Although Kerry was at the prison when the riot began, she and other personnel were quickly moved out. In the stress of the event she didn't think to notify her family.

George lets us in on the dangers to health care for the poor that federal budget cuts have brought about. Rich shares the challenge of involving undergraduates in graduate level physics projects. Tierney regales us with stories of what goes on behind the scenes when she gets a day's work on a soap opera, all part of trying to make it as an actress in New York.

We tell our stories. Many of them are mission stories. Some of us have gifts for evangelization; others of us have gifts for humanization. Sometimes we're stymied on how to use those gifts, and sometimes we share a breakthrough we've experienced.

There are times when we gather together and reminisce about the past. Although unintentional, many of the stories that get told are mission stories, for example, stories of marching together as a family in Vietnam War protests. One of us usually remembers going to Catholic Peace Fellowship get-togethers where we experienced prayer, community, and a strong mission ambiance. Or we might talk civil rights and remember sending boxes to Ita Bena, Mississippi, after Jon Daniels from the town in New Hampshire where we lived was murdered for his civil rights involvement. Or we might all savor the wonderful sense of community we encountered living among the black and Hispanic people in the inner city.

Someone will remind Tierney of what she hardly remembers from those days—the night at supper when she was in kindergarten and announced that rocks had been thrown at her at recess and an ultimatum delivered by her white schoolmates. Either play with white kids or play with black kids, but stop playing with both. She insisted on playing with both and won out. And at the end of the year her kindergarten classmates voted her "best citizen of the year." Eighteen years later, in Manhattan, she moved into a tenement building where all the residents were people of color except for Tierney and her roommate Karen.

Sometimes George tells us again about how he won the election for City Council because his four and five year old daughters helped to tie little signs on doorknobs in the ward on election day, signs that said FINN IN FOUR. They don't believe his claim that they won the election for him, but they like to hear the story and the one about Grandma buying him a plate after the election with a scene from the War of 1812 on it because he received 1,812 votes.

Or we might reminisce with Kerry about the summers she worked in the Roxbury section of Boston where her facility with Portuguese helped to integrate the black Cape Verdean youth with the other black youth who resided there. Or Pam might remember the year she was mugged three times while working at a social service agency related to education.

Kerry wins the prize in our family for being the best world-dreaming pilgrim. We sometimes remind her of the New Year's day she spent in a small village in Japan having an appendectomy in a rural clinic where no one spoke English and not even aspirin was available after the operation. The rest of us were in panic at home, not hearing the outcome of the operation for five days.

Our stories wind in and out of family events and compete with time spent planning weddings and worrying aloud about pipes freezing and illnesses. Mission stories can likewise weave in and out of parish life, movement life, and diocesan life. Although we may more clearly associate mission with social justice and civic activity "stories," some *family stories* are exemplary mission stories as well. They need to be perceived as mission stories.

Family Mission Stories

Two years ago, Jane and Ray Hailing, a couple from our Vineyard Community, were preparing to visit their son Dan in Africa. Dan, working in housing for Habitat for Humanity, was going into the bush and would be out of contact for several months. The night before Ray and Jane were to fly to Africa, they received word that another son had been killed in an airplane crash. Within the next few days, funeral preparations were initiated and grief was shared with family and with our community. Then, on the evening of the day Ray and Jane buried one son, they flew to Africa to be with another son. Jane and Ray don't perceive what they were called to do as ministry and mission, but others quietly note the inner strength revealed as they responded as family to tragedy within family.

Engaging in ministry within family requires great patience as well as courage, for mission in domestic settings often reflects the qualities associated with leaven. A spiritual life geared to tracking down peak experiences differs from a spiritual life geared to tracking down the Spirit's revelations of where, in one's daily life, fidelity to God is authentic and where it is sham. Living out our faith day by day (predictable or gray or grimy day by day) reveals whether our faith is skin-deep or the essential factor in who we are as persons.

Domestic mission spirituality means forsaking instantaneous evidence of mission accomplished. Being employed, raising children, sustaining friendships, reforming culture, persevering in the bond of marriage, and caring for aged parents are *mission* efforts in which the fruit-bearing seasons can be few and far between. Community, support groups and spiritual direction can be the brick and mortar for sustaining these mission efforts. No bright beacon lights, no fireworks, no media events accompany the leaven spirituality of domestic mission.

Remembering People from the Past

Each year our daughters love to read Christmas letters from neighbors and friends they knew in the places where they grew up. We also remember those from other places who have shared Christmas with us. The ancient religious sense that through memory the past re-presents itself to us is often manifest in family during holidays.

When Kerry was a freshman in college in California, she brought Manuel home for Christmas. A Spanish-Indian from Venezuela, in New England he experienced his first blizzard. All that day he kept asking whether we were certain that the snow would eventually stop coming down.

One Christmas, Lois, a student from the boarding school where George worked, stayed with us for Christmas. After a year-long struggle she was on the other side of a bad drug habit. Until three A.M. that Christmas eve George and I listened to Lois tell about her trapped existence when speed was her nemesis.

We like to remember the people who are part of our stories.

The folks in New Hampshire who pitched in during Jeff's self-help, solar energy grant project. The actors who share the stage with Tierney when she plays Mary in scenes from Bill Gibson's nativity play *The Butterfingers Angel.* The professional film technicians and actors who donated time to Mark and Eddie's film about a retarded adult lost in New York—and Eddie's grandmother who donated her rosary beads and a generous sum of money for the making of the film.

Sometimes we wonder about the elderly rural home-owners Leslie visited to offer fuel-aid assistance. She can't forget the house where the pipes had broken and that, when she arrived, the elderly couple were standing on ice in their living room.

I remind her of the Christmas eve when the temperature *inside* their wood-stove heated house was 20 above zero because outside it was 25 below zero. And she reminds me of my resistance to their outhouse and how my mind was changed after gazing contemplatively at a mountain one dawn from *that* setting.

Do we have stories! One of us always seems on the way to the poorhouse, but do we have stories!

Many of our stories are mission stories. They never get thought of as "mission" stories. They're just "our" stories, the stories of our life, individually and together. Like most families, however, we do love to tell them. And we are certainly not the only Catholic family with these kinds of stories. Our generation spawned a multitude of Catholic social activists who were also raising families.

Formation in Family for Mission

Within me there are mixed feelings about our mission stories.

One of our twin daughters going off to college told me she thought we had done too much together as a *family,* and not enough as individuals with one another. When empty nest time came, each of our older daughters returned for a year alone with us, perhaps for the special personal attention she may not have received in her growing up years.

In the 1960s and early 1970s when our four daughters were

children and adolescents, George and I had absolutely no *con-sciousness* about how we were living our lives as human beings and as Catholic Christians. If a cause was good, our motto was "Go for it!" Don't think about it or reflect together on it or pray about it. Go for it!

We had little consciousness of the mission value of the callings we lived out in our occupations. We had no consciousness of spirituality needs in those social activist days. Parish meant sacraments, and we were unaware of any range of spirituality beyond the sacraments. No one questioned whether or not we had the gifts and talents *for* a particular commitment. No one asked if dispositions dovetailed with an involvement. Go for it!

When George and I reflect together we are moved by the compassion within our daughters' hearts and by their commitment to justice. On the side of the ledger labeled what we *do regret* is the sheer *quantity* of our involvements, and the tendency to jump from cause to cause. Cause, not people or place, was what we felt related to. Justice for farm workers one season, antiwar the next. Helping drug-addicted youngsters while being caught up in political campaigning. This messianic cause orientation caused confusion and chaos at home. It was easier to throw ourselves into a cause than to deal with the real-life family problems under our own roof. The young prophets we sent out into the big world on their own at age seventeen had to learn on their own that they were the exception, not the rule. Adjusting to "normal existence" and the need for acceptance by peers posed problems their parents might have helped them avoid had their parents not been so addicted to every cause that turned the corner of the street.

But when we share our misgivings with our daughters, the room erupts into a free-for-all. Their evaluations differ from ours: "Sitting around in groups talking about peace or praying about it was borrrring!" "The marches were wonderful!" We were energized because we felt we were making a *difference* in caring about the world!"

Our oldest daughter says she is appalled that we are wasting time second-guessing about how, as a family, we participated in social justice. "My friends *envy* what I experienced growing up! All they remember is a lot of suburban monotony. For us there was always someone or something to care about besides just us. Life was so alive for us *all the time!*"

"Yeah, Mom, we weren't sealed off from the rest of the world as if we lived in a mausoleum."

"You're still too busy nit-picking, Mom!" Another consoles me. "On the *really* important stuff you and dad had it right. On the rest. . . ."

Maybe they're right. For them, I guess, what counted was that we exuded *a kind of passion about the world.* That passion formed them more than particular projects or causes.

"Even about the church," another chimes in, "you two were either furious about something or head-over-heels in love with it. But you were never lukewarm . . ."

"And never obedient sheep!"

Endless laughter sails through the room, and I know suddenly in my heart that family is the greatest gift God and parents give to this earth.

Still, I must have my say. "But in your early twenties you felt everything we did was *wrong.*"

Our oldest smiles at me. "In my early thirties I've reversed my decision."

On that happy evening they forgot the resentment they sometimes feel for being the working poor because they combine mission with career. Causes at times became so important to them as college students that thinking about what their occupational or professional calling might be was a very weak second fiddle. This is, of course, the antithesis of the current trend to focus *only* on career preparation. Both extremes call for remedies. One younger parent I know puts it this way: "I wish I could undo *over-formation!* My son may drop out of college. He says he feels paralyzed every time the kids in the dorm talk about their future careers. All he can hear is me saying over and over, 'From those who have been given much, much will be expected.' He's petrified that God will disapprove of *any* choice he makes."

But our daughters were making an important point that evening. When formation is directly imposed, it may be resented or instigate fear. What our daughters seemed to be telling us was that the formation they valued came about from doing things *with* us—our sharing responsibility, our gradually relinquishing authority into their hands. Our caring about the world was contagious; it formed them.

What Jesus Teaches about Mission

Some lay believers readily perceive that their "webs of existence" have formed them, but they feel stymied about how to go about mission from and within these settings. Again the tenth chapter in Matthew's gospel reveals clues for solving this dilemma. Early on in the passage, Matthew reveals Jesus as giving his disciples the charge of proclaiming the reign of God, curing the sick, raising the dead, cleansing the lepers, and expelling demons. This appears to be the nub of the mission, and I imagine a few disciples muttering, "I hope he's going to explain how we go about accomplishing all that."

It certainly is reasonable to expect that Jesus is now going to talk about *how* to proclaim the reign of God, *how* to cure the sick, raise the dead, cleanse lepers, and expel demons. But that doesn't happen. Jesus seems to change the subject and get into "peripheral" issues—what to do if you are not accepted, what reactions to expect in families, whom you will meet on the road, and so forth. *How* to do the tasks with which disciples are charged seems to be forgotten. How strange.

One day while reflecting on this passage, I thought of the placement process at Weston. During their last year, students engage in this process in their search for ministry positions. During that process, we don't deal all that much with the actual ministry students will do. That is often settled before they participate in the placement process. We deal instead with the who, where, and what else factors.

Jesus in the placement process described in Matthew 10 talks about who—the "lost sheep of the house of Israel;" about settings —towns or villages you come to, houses where you will stay, shaking the dust from your feet if you're not accepted. Jesus describes a few "what else dynamics" that the disciples will inevitably run into if they engage in mission—encountering persecution but also encountering the Son of Man in the midst of the mission effort. Encountering being misunderstood as they go about their business

—being hated, family members turning against family members. It seems as if Jesus is determined to level with his disciples; he is determined to baptize them in *realism* regarding the mission journey.

But he doesn't tell them *how* to do the tasks he charges them with doing. There may be a few more clues in the passage that point in a helpful direction, however. A respectable hunch might be that they have learned how to do much of what they are supposed to do on mission *by accompanying Jesus day by day.* That reveals to us today that companionship with Jesus day in and day out (as Jesus is revealed to us in scripture) enables us to do tasks associated with mission. Jesus reminds the disciples that the Holy Spirit will be with them, especially during those times when they are most "up against it." And Jesus grants them remarkable freedom, telling them to shake the dust off their feet if mission isn't working out in a particular place. "Don't force the issue," he seems to be saying. "Be willing to let go and get on the road again."

Jesus relied on the strengths and talents that the disciples brought to the mission enterprise from the webs that had formed them. Didn't he tell them they would continue fishing? On mission, however, their fishing would not be for what lives in the sea. I like the continuity with their original callings found in this earlier passage on the call. For us today it might mean that we go on doing some of what we are already doing but *for a different purpose.* Sometimes that changes everything.

In Matthew 10 Jesus sends the disciples into familiar territory —Israel. They are to do mission within a place and culture they know, a culture with texture and flavor and mores they can use to the best advantage for the mission tasks he outlines but does not tell them how to do.

Application to Our Culture Today

The web of our existence is always within the larger web of a national culture. Each nation has a heritage that becomes part of and forms the smaller webs. In the intertwining of webs a dimension of one strand may conflict with a dimension from the other strand, calling for some fine-tuned discernment. But at other times the values found in a culture can enable the proclamation of gospel values. Three rock-bottomed North American values in which we lay people, especially the younger generation of Catholics, have been formed are:

- freedom of speech
- inclusivity (vigorously attacking discrimination is the only way a "melting pot" society can survive—the efforts of blacks and women to be included are almost necessitated by the type of society we live in)
- protection of individual conscience, which means in the United States legal protection for dissent

The *means* we utilize to accomplish mission will often be dynamics linked to our formation as North Americans—speaking up (exercising freedom of speech); feeling included and thus able to exercise *leadership within a given group;* lastly, what Joseph Pieper calls prudence: instantaneous wise decision-making (what develops from having a strong individuated conscience).

The Catholic Pro-Life Movement, for example, takes the *content* for its mission from a Catholic value system. But the *means* this movement has used to achieve its goals emerges from "place" —from values of freedom of speech, being included as citizens, and the protective laws regarding dissent and conscience.

How to activate gospel attitudes and values remains a challenge in our country because secular formation and education have paid limited attention to the insertion of other crucial moral ideals within the very real and public webs of existence in the United States. On the other hand, problems sometimes emerge due to a lack of understanding within the institutional church of how North American citizens internalize their civic heritage and how the inculturation of common civic values necessarily determines the *means* for accomplishing mission.

The Challenge of the Way We Live Our Lives

Among the challenges confronting us on mission is the *way* we live our lives as well as *what* we do with our lives.

Mission spirituality reflects social justice and shared ownership as values. But "Martha" is not the model of Christian adulthood. We are called to be contemplative, and avocations can help
in that development. Avocations inhibit stress, avocations can
evoke contemplation, avocations can heal and nourish the spirit,
avocations can help to shape vocations and our culture. As Christians we are called to choose *from* what our culture offers rather
than choosing anything and everything our culture offers. Although it is far easier to go along with whatever is prevalent in the
culture, choosing from the culture regarding both work and leisure
is the stance of mission spirituality.

Avocations and asceticisms provide balance for each other.

"I hate the word ascetical," a friend said to me recently.

Asceticism got its bad name because asceticisms were, at one
time, imposed in an authoritarian way. Vatican II, however, did
not do away with the need for asceticism because mission and
asceticism go hand in hand. It was Jesus—on mission, remember
—who spoke of foxes having dens but the Son of Man having no
place to lay down his head. On the other hand, we may be believers
who are always looking ahead at the crosses we think we're *supposed* to carry without realizing that it is the one we *are* carrying
that prevents us from embracing the ones we think we should be
carrying.

There's no need to wait until Lent to discover, through self-
reflection, what asceticisms you have already assumed. Perhaps
yours is living with an alcoholic, or the costs of college education,
or caring for aged parents, or single parenting, etc.

Few occupations exist without an ascetical dimension. Strange
as it may sound, identifying the asceticisms linked to your occupation can be spiritually freeing. Perhaps the ascetical dimension is
the conditions under which you work—the boring repetitive quality of your tasks, the physical toll, the risk and pressure. Or perhaps
it's the erosion of self-esteem that can come from working for a
tyrannical boss or the danger to one's ethical sensibility that comes
with allegiance to a company that "cuts corners" ethically. Sometimes surviving on the job takes all of one's effort or surviving
conditions at home takes all of one's energy. Then *asceticism* may
be the Christian witness of your life.

Accidental asceticism can invade our lives—the loss of a job or the onset of a sudden illness. For us last year it was a fire. Lay life means exposure to constant change. An attitude of "ascetical readiness" is essential. Pastoral leaders are invaluable when they enable lay believers to name and own the asceticisms that *already* exist in their lives rather than continually positing new and perhaps inappropriate ones for them. Choosing new crosses mandates knowing the ones we already bear.

If Christ at times calls us to assume the ascetical in our missions in life, Christ also gifts us with the freedom to liberate ourselves from inappropriate, damaging asceticism. When I entered my senior year in high school, I also moved out of the house. I could no longer go on bearing the cross of my father's alcoholism and my parents fighting about it. I became a live-in companion at night for an elderly woman. My *acting* rather than continuing to passively accept the co-dependency going on at home may have been the confrontation needed. Two years later my father stopped drinking. Shaking the dust from our feet is what Christ, in some situations, calls us to do.

Not all patterns for mission are alike; therefore, it is crucial that skilled guidance be available to lay believers, who often need an opportunity, individually or in groups, to name the patterns operative in their lives. Needed asceticisms that align themselves with a particular mission thrust can then be *chosen.*

To be fully Christian means to know how to celebrate life as well as how to bear the cross. We need to remember that we're human and remember to stay human. Plaster saints crumble when they step out into mission.

The week before our youngest daughter graduated from college, I overheard her father say to her on the phone, "You pick out one of the best restaurants in Manhattan for our dinner after graduation."

"Are you crazy?" I asked when he was off the phone. "Have you forgotten we're in hock for a wedding this month?"

At one of the best restaurants in Manhattan a week later, I nervously read the menu from right to left, the only one of the three of us following that directional signal. During the following week, amidst the flurry of the wedding preparations, a memory of the supper floated through my mind. Each time I saw George's face with the relaxed glow it had that evening. I took the image to prayer. There the insight came that our supper was a celebration of Tierney's graduation, but it was also a celebration of the end of helping to finance the education of four daughters. Fourteen years of ascetical practice had been lifted from a father's shoulders.

The feast for celebrating that milestone was worth every penny it cost.

The Connection Between Religious Existence and Religious Experience

Asceticism is a form of religious existence. Engaged in its challenge we seldom feel the dynamics we may associate with spiritual experience, with the presence of God.

When my mother, who had been living (by her own choice) as a widow, fell and broke her hip at age eighty-five, George and I, through informal consultation with our daughters, made a "family mission decision" to bring her to Boston to live with us. Caring physically for my aged mother evoked *religious existence more than religious experience.* Days were a marathon between work and home; sleep at night was consistently broken by her waking confused, upset, sometimes angry.

After three months, we returned to the local general practitioner who had seen my mother when she first arrived in Boston. When I heard the doctor say how much she had improved—her weight gain, her ability to remember with more acuity, the stabilization of her heart—tears filled my eyes. Helping her make her way back to the car with her walker, I was struck by how much *sheer survival* had characterized our own life at home those last few months. Hearing the value of it affirmed helped me realize the worth of that leaven "existence."

Sometimes religious existence can evolve into what we call "religious experience." By the fall of 1986 I was brooding about my mother again. She had become very frail, fallen and bruised herself, and contracted the flu. One weekend, through the generosity of a Weston student, we had a respite in the Berkshires. Early Friday afternoon I sought solitude in the backyard. For a while I gazed at a rarely seen, beautiful scarlet tanager. Then I walked under the trees and saw, felt, and smelled the red carpet the lawn had become.

Apples were everywhere, hundreds of them, as scarlet as the bird. Large, glistening apples extended from every bough. Overcome, I glanced toward the golden trees on Beartown Mountain and felt my spirit leap into those trees. As this happened I cried, "She is slipping out of my arms!" And from the mountain I heard, "Into mine. Can you let go? Can you trust that I love her?"

The super-abundant apple harvest I embraced as religious experience. I let God's fecundity sustain me the week Mom moved into the nursing home.

When mission stories are told in local communities they reveal the manifold destinies of the Christian faithful. They help us know that everyday life has extraordinary spiritual dimensions.

Witness to Mission

Vigorous, inclusive and collaborative pastoral leadership, and the opportunity for lay adults to share the kinds of mission in which they are involved, are what is needed more than anything else in the church today. One local community spent a year on this endeavor. Leaders designed gatherings around particular topics and invited people from the parish to share their own stories and to lead a reflection session in which others shared. Personal narratives were invited on the following:

- *Sheer survival*—the witness value of perseverance under exceptional stress.
- *Living out the call within one's calling*—sharing mission efforts made through callings lived out in the workplace
- *Calling beyond normal work setting*—the witness of outreach to those in hospitals and nursing homes
- *Call through communal service*—the witness of lay volunteers from a literacy program and from an ecumenical advocacy group for the homeless
- *Call exercised in global settings*—the reading of letters from a former parishioner now in the Peace Corps and from a lay volunteer in Central America
- *Call exercised in the civic community*—the witness of a parishioner who served as a delegate to a state political convention and of another who ran for elected office

Are we lay believers a passive people? The evidence that we are not might be found in the stories of those too busy to engage in parish activities. These stories are worth searching for. The witness of lives lived out in the webs of work, family, social justice, and civic and global activities need to be heard within our parish communities and associations.

Living Out the Call to Mission

Mission is witness. It is proclamation. It is apostolic. It does not necessitate climbing on a soapbox and preaching. Nor does it mean turning to a co-worker and asking, "Have you been saved?"

Mission sometimes is focused. Jesus is relying on us to set goals and then discover *how* to go about fulfilling them. When we do that, we not only become part of the church's mission within the world, but we also nudge the world and the reign of God into closer proximity.

Telling mission stories must happen in the parish family, the movement family, the diocesan family, the world-church family. Some narratives will be "work" stories. Some will be social justice advocacy stories. Some will be family stories. Some will be service stories. Some will be prophetic stories of confrontation. The stories are there. They need to be told *inside the church.* Only when they are told will all members of the church internalize as conviction that a world-caring consciousness is constitutive of Christian faith.

Spirituality for "On the Road"

A premise of mission spirituality is that God will unfold the meaning and intention needed if we embrace wholeheartedly our relationship to the world, energized by the call to discipleship and mission. Integral to mission spirituality is the need to reflect on one's lived experience in its particularity and in its connection to humankind beyond our own web. If we develop ways to pray contemplatively about our encounters with "earthly realities," the particular meanings and intentions necessary to persevere may be the grace we receive. Without this prayer our mission passion may overwhelm us, causing us to burn out or become messianic.

Lay spirituality emerges from a life lived "on the road"—publicly like Jesus' life of ministry and mission. Christian community, the Word, prayer and participation in sacraments are the necessary framework for mission spirituality. But living out this spirituality also means relinquishing dependency regarding any one particular sanctuary because one's spiritual life is one's whole life lived with passion and integrity as a "valid person in a robust world."

4

DISPOSITION FOR MISSION

When I ponder the twenty year span between the late 1960s and the late 1980s, I am somewhat startled by what we didn't know in the 1960s when we plunged ourselves forward into mission. Twenty years ago most lay believers, including ourselves, had no sense of the value and particularity of gifts and talents. *Consciousness and integration,* words more than ideas, were just beginning to infiltrate our everyday language. Spirituality, like vocation and calling, terms attached to priests and nuns, had no relevance to those of us, male and female, who thought of ourselves as "ordinary laymen." Religious experience, if recognized, was like frosting on the cake— an extra grace from God, not God revealing or leading one in particular direction. If someone in the mid-1960s had invited me "to reflect on my life experience," or if someone had asked me about the role of passion in my engagement of mission, I might have been intrigued and even drawn to respond, but I surely would have made an excuse, being far too busy with causes that flamed up one season and flickered out the next. Laying down one's life seldom meant fidelity to a particular people or issue in need over the long haul. Twenty years ago *formation, retreat, mission,* words that can be heard today in secular conversations, weren't part of religious conversation on the lay circuit. Last summer at a national church conference, participants listed church paradigms of the past and church paradigms of the present. Included in past paradigms were: the lay role is to assist the priest; theological image of God; co-dependence; religious education is for children; theological education is for a limited few; credibility as a minister is based on ordination; uniformity is an ideal; leadership as monarchy; God's will that clergy are men; the individual leader is a source of wisdom; celibate life-style is an essential of ministry; shepherd and sheep; conflict is bad but pain is good. Included in new paradigms since Vatican II: inclusivity; community; baptism is a source of our common ministry call; adult to adult; respect for individual life experience; holiness is a call to all; gospel paradigm for spirituality and mission; relational image of God; small faith communities; global awareness; wholistic religious education; ministry and matrimony are compatible; mutuality in ministerial leadership.

What of the future? Recently I heard a new graduate of a Catholic college explain to a neighbor that formation for mission is more than teaching about particular issues or urging lay adults to become involved in particular "causes"; formation for mission reflects on the life of faith as related *to the destiny of laying down one's life for others;* formation for mission takes into consideration the personal background, talents, callings, and ongoing life experience. It does this within the context of faith in God's call, in the gospel, and in a vision of the kingdom of God within a world context that is global and planetary. She then went on to explain liberation theology, another term unheard of twenty years ago, and to say that, yes, she did believe women should be ordained and that she would discern her call to the ordained priesthood were the ban to be lifted. Meanwhile she intended to attend law school.

This young woman is not worrying about whether the church will survive its present angst. She believes that the mission has a church, not that the church has a mission.

Today many of us have a better appreciation for the fact that we don't put aside our callings in order to engage in mission. Rooted in our gifts and talents, our callings are part of the strength we bring to the mission enterprise. Lay Christians are more and more coming to trust that the Holy Spirit invigorates their gifts and talents with an energizing power that enables mission. More and more lay Christians are coming to perceive a link between reflection and mission. They realize that a contemplative approach to life and faith not only vivifies our relationship with God but also our relationship with our world. They understand that unless we develop our God-created contemplative gifts, the full reality before us may not be *received.* In other words, we may not see our settings through God's eyes. Instead, we may drift into seeing our settings through the individualistic and competitive dynamics embedded in our culture, dynamics that tamper with the impulse for communal bonding and tempt us to "go it alone," to "get while the getting's good," to ridicule those involved in more than self-betterment.

On the other hand, motivated in part by the feminist movement in the church, more Christians are questioning an approach to reality that is purely rational with its tendency to short-change faith through its over-valuation of analysis. They also question an approach that skews in favor of the immediacy and feeling that dominate when subjective faith alone interprets reality.

Thirty years ago Catholic parents tended to over-form their children by assigning a one-size-fits-all "Christian disposition" on the kids when they were little instead of affirming, and trusting that God was affirming, the disposition that graced each one as she or he was.

There are many factors that influence formation for mission. While it is impossible to deal with all these factors within the covers of one book, it may be possible to trace significant patterns of at least one. I have selected *disposition* as a crucial element in formation, one until recently neglected. The advent of the Myers-Briggs and the Enneagram highlights the need for a clearer understanding of disposition. Gradually we have come to realize that our disposition may influence the kind of mission actions to which we are drawn and that one may lack the dispositional condition needed for a particular ministry or mission yet thrive in another ministry or mission because of dispositional factors.

Being Disposed Toward the World

What is disposition? How does it shape who we are as persons? as persons who are Catholic Christians on mission?

Knowing something about how our dispositions operate may shed light on the link between self-and-world, both the immediate world of our own lives and our universe-home. Our reflection will gradually encompass how disposition through the prism of religious experience and passion is energized for mission.

Disposition is what we bring to our ordinary life experience day after day when we bring ourselves into that experience. In the

Phenomenology of Feeling Stephan Strasser explores the dispositional phenomena of the heart: direct feelings, binding ties, attitudes, convictions, comportment and passion.

According to Strasser, disposition is the way in which you or I
are *"disposed toward the world."* Disposition is an essential dimension of being human—of being in the world. Day after day as
we live life "in the world," interiorly a meld occurs. We, so to
speak, integrate "being-in-a-mood" and *"acts* of striving, knowing,
evaluating and feeling which are directed to the world and the
environment."[1]

According to Strasser, the feelings and actions we direct toward the world emerge out of our disposition and shape our experiences. These experiences *in turn* affect our disposition.

> . . . all that "pushes toward" us in our becoming aware of the
> world, and in our intimacy with the world, can move us and
> resonate in our innermost center. Stirring, shaming, exalting
> events, successes, defeats—all have their dispositional reverber-
> ations . . . ultimately everything lived through and experienced
> condenses itself into a . . . being-in-a-mood.[2]

The example Strasser gives is the way we might be after the
conscious grief over the death of a relative has passed. Day after day
we may no longer bring the relative to mind but a *"sad mood"*
characterizes our disposition. It is the *"residue of what we have
(consciously) lived through."*[3]

What connection is there between our disposition and our
spiritual orientation toward life?

Without my realizing it, my spiritual outlook often shapes my
disposition and vice versa. We are not talking here about a deliber-
ately cultivated spiritual life but about a deep faith that has been
internalized. We may only take note of this faith occasionally, but
it may be internalized within us in ways that shape our disposition.
Consequently, any serious consideration of the spiritual life necessarily includes reflection on disposition even though, day by day,
we may scarcely be aware of our disposition. I may live today and
tomorrow without giving much recognition to the "feeling of I and
the world together," as Strasser puts it, but how I am "disposed

toward the world" establishes the ground-work for how I perceive and act in the world.[4]

Directed Feelings and Disposition

In the past decade within the field of spirituality, as well as traditionally within the field of psychology, there has been an emphasis on the significance *of expressing feelings* as they are felt, even in prayer. This is not altogether new wisdom. Friedrich von Hugel once put it this way in a letter to a friend:

> Try more and more *at the moment itself,* without any delay or evasion, without any fixed form, as simply and spontaneously as possible, to cry out to God. . . . The all-important point is to make (the petitions) *at the time* and *with the pain* well mixed up with the prayer. . . .[5]

In the pre-conciliar school that taught many of us, whatever one was feeling did not matter to God; obeying the will of God was what mattered. In some ways I handed this down, my daughters remind me. "Put a smile in your voice; no one likes to hear a whine," was one of my favorite admonitions. More than one child in a good Catholic home felt discomfort with his or her own feelings, because the *value* of feelings was discounted. When feelings are repressed, desires often follow suit. Motivation dissipates.

Because I was disabled in that regard, therapy was inevitable. I will always remember an hour in therapy when our family was about to buy a dog. The therapist kept asking me what kind of dog I wanted, and I kept replying whatever kind of dog would make everyone else happy. The therapist kept repeating the question. I listed each kind of dog everyone else in the family wanted. She pressed for what *I* wanted. Suddenly I felt panic because I knew I wanted a dog, too, but I could not uncover within myself the particular kind of dog I wanted. Feeling did burst through at that moment, however, and I shouted, "I'm sick and tired of always having to reconcile *what everyone else in the world wants!*"

Like many other Catholic women, it had become part of *my disposition to repress my feelings.*

The process of therapy often enables the living of life at a deeper level of faith. We foster the sin of pride if we think that because we are Christians we don't need therapy. Therapy can be a humbling, painful, freeing experience directly related to one's spiritual life because it strips us of pretensions and allows us to be more naked before our God.

The recent popularity of the Myers-Briggs and the Enneagram, mentioned earlier, points out the value of being able to distinguish between disposition and directed feelings. But the value of feelings, because we live in a culture with sophistication regarding psychology, may be more familiar to us.

Is there a difference between a fresh feeling engendered by a particular event and one's overall disposition? Strasser thinks there is. Both are significant to formation, but disposition is that *interior soil from which directed feelings sometimes shoot up* like plants from nature's soil.

Repressed feelings may need to be dealt with before one is free to pursue a calling or engage in mission. But noticing my basic disposition and affirming or dealing with that disposition can be as valuable as dealing with repressed feelings.

In the pre-conciliar church formation was often an attempt to engender a *particular disposition for all* instead of working to discover the particular disposition of the particular person within the formation process. Encouraging a like disposition made community life easier to control. One's disposition evoked a personal identity, and vibrant, individuated personalities were considered a problem. Today most pastoral leaders realize that a one-size-fits-all, put-a-smile-in-your-voice, Christian dispositional mode seldom suits the needs of mission.

We have been considering two dynamics with differences we don't always take the time to distinguish: directed feelings and basic disposition. Both are significant to how we are formed.

Binding Ties

It is not an exaggeration to say that functioning as a Christian adult rests on how our spiritual processes and our feeling processes are interwoven. Though we seldom sense it consciously, we live that integration *dispositionally,* for disposition is the "nourishing ground" for our *intentions*. Unlike specific religious experiences and direct feelings, disposition points in no particular direction. It "lives the All-Encompassing without being able to grasp it."[6]

Let's look at a very simple example of this. Let's say I am a morning person. I wake one morning earlier than usual. A glance at the clock tells me I can roll over. But I notice the bright spring sun showering through the window. A sense of anticipation floods through me. I forget to roll over. As though I wanted to embrace the world, I spring from the bed. I'm not aware of wanting to embrace the world—something just propels me up.

Whenever the heart-spirit dynamic is activated, *a binding tie comes into existence through our sense of attachment*. What has "grown close to the heart" has animating power, engendering feelings of wonder, acts of creating, and yearning for participation. We are not talking here about a *conscious* act of binding oneself—of making a commitment or entering into a covenant. We are talking about something more foundational, individual concrete realities that attract us to the point of *attachment* without a deliberate realization that this is happening. (If we sense a binding tie being *imposed* on us by others, interior conflicts often emerge.)

Many of us have a binding tie with the sun. When it is missing for days on end and the rain pours and the heavens are gray, our dispositions often alter, at least temporarily. When we speak of a binding tie, we are talking about a binding within our own interior being that is not "sought, willed, or devised but 'grows organically' ... letting the world and the environment resonate in oneself (with) the character of an attraction...." Within our disposition the I becomes a we. "The other (the sun) has become 'a part of me.' "[7]

This same kind of "we" sense happens in mission when we sense a binding tie with the homeless or the black people oppressed in South Africa, or with our brothers and sisters in Central America or with the elderly, or with a calling like music or medicine or making machines.

On the other hand, when a traumatic event happens to us, it may seem as if most of our binding ties have been severed. When we are in despair, all sense of binding tie is lost. We feel isolated and may crave those times the disposition of our hearts enabled "the continuity, productivity, wholeness and relative stability of normal lived experience."[8]

Generativity grows from the innumerable binding ties within us linking us to the world and the people in it. Mission is the fruit of generativity evoked by strong binding ties. And it is through "binding ties" that *callings* emerge in our lives. The interwoven spirit and heart dynamic leads to our being disposed toward flowers or fixing cars or helping people in need. Binding ties often emerge without moral preaching from parental figures trying to impose them; parental figures, on the other hand, are wise if they notice their emergence.

Attitudes and Convictions

As we develop into adults we don't react with fresh emotion to every event and encounter. Repetitions occur. An event is repeated. Most of us don't stop at each juncture and quiz ourselves by asking, "How should I feel?" Our disposition "anticipates" life. Our disposition, in other words, *prepares* our feelings. Consequently, when an event happens, on the dispositional level we just feel.

Being pre-disposed is another way of speaking about *attitudes.* Attitudes help me respond automatically. I couldn't live life otherwise. But there is a danger to this. How we become *formed* on the dispositional level often reveals how our attitudes are formed. In regard to mission, if we engage in prophetic action before we have developed strong, internalized *convictions,* then the action is grounded in the shallow soil of attitudes. Within the church it is not uncommon to let our attitudes be shaped in a second-hand fashion; we may go along with the convictions of a ministerial leader without any awareness of our own convictions. This too is shallow soil.

Attitudes, on the other hand, often give rise to *convictions.* Convictions are similar to attitudes, but convictions differ in one important respect. Within our dispositions convictions are more embedded, more lasting. They are coupled with what Strasser calls a *spiritual fixing.* Convictions have an "underpinning" we may not be able to articulate but one that provides *a depth* lacking in attitudes. A person without convictions is often considered superficial.

Religious faith and participation in church community can play a significant role in solidifying attitudes into convictions. A calling often awakens convictions in us that encourage us to take a mission stance in our workplace or to donate our talents beyond the workplace. On the other hand, addictions to individualism and consumerism may be linked to placing value on ambition and on rewards. Thereby hangs the danger of work that is not a calling.

Comportment

Within the dispositions of persons who are fully adult we find a rich variety of integrated feelings, binding ties, attitudes, and convictions. These shape the way "I comport myself." Comportment reveals how I have been formed, i.e. how I express "who I am" *in and to the world.*[9] Comportment is what makes us reliable as well as predictable to others. My comportment in the world helps others to know what to expect of me. It is the way in which I "gradually accustom (myself) to the environment and the world."[10] Our comportment often depends on the "world-picture" we have: how we envision the world and ourselves in it.

"If religious reality becomes All for me then I am religiously disposed. If I see in all things only one terrible danger, then I find myself in a panic disposition."[11]

Basic comportment, the fruit of my disposition, is the "*total style*" of the way I am in the world. If my total style is *power-seeking,* for example, then my world-picture is one in which I see myself using the world for my own gain. My style is to minimize my responsibility and maximize my authority. Intimacy is sought for the pleasure it brings to me.

If my basic comportment is *service* I may focus on the sufferings of the world; I may maximize responsibility and minimize authority. I may be constantly aware of the intimacy needs of others and neglect my own.

If my basic comportment is *acquisitional,* I may be responsible toward my family and work tirelessly at my job to acquire all the things I feel I need to be content with life, but I may believe that the world begins and ends with my own circle of friends and interests and ambition.

The basic comportment of the world-dreaming pilgrim reveals a binding tie with the world and usually differs from the basic comportment of the person who wants to own the world or wants North Americans to own the world.

In our culture, basic comportment is seldom explicitly imposed by external forces; it emerges from within each person. That's a lesson we do well to learn as Christians. Like other parental figures, it took me a long time to learn this lesson. I felt I had to clear the path of stone and briar, I had to fertilize and water, if my daughters were to comport themselves as Christian adults when they grew up. I left nothing for the Holy Spirit to do! It never dawned on me that the exposure and the example our daughters were receiving was the best formative process of all.

We don't trade in our dispositions in order to get faith or to grow in faith or to do mission. We may, however, want to ask ourselves, "Have I internalized my faith, enabling it to reveal itself in my comportment, my way of being-in-the-world?" Disposition, we have seen, is "all of a piece"; it is one fabric. Basic comportment is an exterior manifestation of disposition, of what has been internalized.

Catholic believers sometimes reveal two very different kinds of spiritual disposition. Some believers (priests, sisters, brothers and lay adults) have an internal set of doctrinal and folk *beliefs* which they try to impose *onto* their experience. Other believers have an internalized *faith* dynamic *through which* they filter their experiences of life, noticing and claiming what, in an experience, reveals God's presence or power or love, including corrective love. The difference between believers operating out of these two dispositional dynamics may be the cause of some of the polarization in the church at the present time.

If, after a traumatic life experience, we try to manipulate our feelings and our interpretations to fit our internalized beliefs instead of continuing to let our feelings emerge *followed by* a synthesis of feeling and interpretation from our internalized Christian faith, we are hard at work trying to *manufacture* our disposition rather than trusting it.

Passion and Religious Experience

What is the role of religious experience in forming that internalized faith dynamic that shapes our disposition and comportment? Passion may be one fruit of religious experiences if the experiences have been integrated into our "total style." With that passion-energized integration comes a gathering of all one's interior power, exercised in living out life. This stance is a contrast to comportment that is motivated by duty or by obedience to a remote, impersonal God.

Authentic religious experiences can create a sense of passion that both heightens the meaning of our experiences while protecting us from being entrapped by any *particular* experience. We sense a spiritual meaning to life that moves us beyond the immediate. Energized by passion, we find ourselves free to embrace mission. Passion and mission become *forward mobility.* No longer caught up in our culture's penchant for upward mobility, we more freely accept an ascetical dimension for the sake of mission. No longer entrapped by a sea of worry because downward mobility does not always characterize our Christian life, we are fully engaged in moving forward.

In her 1989 Madeleva Lecture in Spirituality, *Passionate Women: Two Medieval Mystics,* Elizabeth Dreyer defines passion as "an intense form of affectivity, especially of love and desire between God and the human person. In addition to the descriptor 'intense,' one thinks of 'strong,' 'vehement,' 'enthusiastic,' 'ardent,' 'zealous.' . . . Further, I will posit that passion is a mysterious impulse toward human wholeness and freedom. The passionate experience has the potential to open up one's personality, to lead one toward fuller self-knowledge, and to contribute to a new self. Passion functions to organize every aspect of an individual's life, allowing no compromise."

Lay women and lay men in many diverse church settings are discovering through religious experience the freedom to be the "same as myself," energized by a passion that enables life to be lived for others through mission. When they find themselves suppressing this forward mobility, or "breakthrough" as Rosemary Haughton puts it, at work, in the family, or within the church, they sometimes begin to feel that they are doing violence *to the formation God is enabling.* Often spiritual guidance with someone skilled in discernment is needed in these situations.

The call to be "the same as myself" comes from God ("Be not like the hypocrites"), yet it can lead to self-centeredness or a feeling of self-importance. Neither slavish uniformity nor rugged individualism is spiritually mature. What is called for is the integration of faith *with* disposition to engender authentic comportment, energized by passion. In other words, my disposition and passion remain *my* disposition ánd passion, yet they become transformed by God for mission.

When the dispositional level is in this process of formation, one begins to notice transformations in the *exercise of intimacy, responsibility, and authority*. The interpenetration of heart/spirit and the deepening of particular binding ties invigorates intimacy as it is experienced and as it is expressed. Because the passionate dimensions of self are strengthened, struggle may increase. But this is accompanied by a greater appreciation for intimacy, especially intimacy with God.

Assuming responsibility is no longer performing duties for others in particular places at particular times; it has become *who I am* in the visible unfolding of my binding tie with the world. Responsibility becomes an alignment of attitudes, convictions and comportment, in action, rather than an inventory of tasks accomplished or to be accomplished. Responsibility is energized by the evocation of passionate feelings, the gathering of interior powers. Directed feelings may still erupt but they are now part and parcel of my attitudes and convictions rather than disconnected and enigmatic.

What is perhaps most noticeable is the transformation of my sense of authority. Authority now has a substantial inner base. Authority is not grasped defensively; it is held confidently. Authority depends less on the approval of those in whom I have invested a greater authority; it depends more on my own ability to live with the authority within. God's authority is perceived as encompassing a mutuality that bears the fruit of mission. *Authority over myself,* rather than my authority over others or the authority of others over me, is paramount.

Passion and Calling

How does the formation just described affect call (to discipleship, ministry, mission) lived out through callings?

If I have not yet responded to work-callings, the transformation that is forming who I am as a believing person may influence the callings to which I respond. If I am already established in the world of work, the transformation may cause a crisis unless my work and my transformation are partners. But all of this happens within the realities of who I am and how callings are operative in this place and culture.

Let's compare, for example, a calling within the creative arts with a calling within a technological enterprise.

Creative acts emerge from the dispositional level. Without the engagement of a heart-spirit interpenetration, binding tie dynamics, and passionate comportment, there is no creativity. Most creative acts that are the work of any artist are "unbidden, uncalled-for, even unexpected. They are gratuitous."[12] For the artist (the writer, the painter, the actor) the proximity between work (the exterior result) and self (the interior disposition) must be immediate, the encounter intimate.

Contrast this with the way Strasser describes the work of an engineer or technician, "The secret of technical success . . . consists in keeping the . . . way free from all exuberance of feeling . . . all passionateness is shifted . . . to the goal. The employment of the means and instruments must follow soberly and factually—but only in order the more intensely to shape the enjoyment"[13] when the goal is reached. Feeling must be suppressed, love put on hold, all the interior dynamics that not only invigorate but also actually create the result for the artist must be suppressed when the technician goes about his or her work.

I will always remember the MIT student who came each Friday afternoon the first year I was a Catholic chaplain on campus. He came for counseling regarding a relationship. It was not a relationship with a woman friend or a parental figure that was causing his stress. The relationship was with his *machine,* as he put it, and it clearly was a love-hate relationship, *one he could never express while working on his machine.*

Another student was stymied by ethical imperatives of her faith and church. "All the work decisions made in technology that are significant are made by a group. I feel powerless as it is futile to push a different ethical stance. The common mind-set is so strong. My voice is just ignored."

The complexities noted above mandate much greater attention to theology related to the actual situations of lay adults engaged in mission through callings as well as more welcome attention to reflections *from* lay adults to this enterprise.

Passion and Spiritual Identity

The role of prayer is to nourish the *spiritual maturing* of the heart-spirit interpenetration. Men and women are capable of making idols of an incredible range of entities. We can all be carried away and believe that this or that is "the sole possible way of access to satisfaction. . . . Pleasure, cruelty, power (can) become forms of . . . transcending experience. The total style . . . can also display the characteristics of superficiality, vanity, inauthenticity. . . ."[14] There are "legitimate and illegitimate" modes of passionate comportment, and even religious goals can become victims of passion that is fanatical. Passion can be dangerous to oneself as well as to others, but passion can also be engendered and sustained for a good. The latter is more likely to happen if we consistently bring our life experience to God in prayer, and if we realize the dangers as well as the potential of passion.

Passion is the *disposition* of "prophets, heroes and saints with their passionate will . . . their passionate longing . . . their passionate profession (of faith), their passionate struggle for salvation."[15]

Passion about life prevents desolation from engulfing us. Passion in the very best sense is "distinguished by consistency, perseverance, composure, and awareness of a goal. One who is passionate is also able to govern self; he (or she) is disciplined in many respects in order to dedicate self all the more unreservedly (to the) absolute value."[16]

According to Strasser "passion is always rooted in . . . a drive toward that which is beyond self."[17] Passion that is the fruit of *religious experience* strengthens our desires, intensifies our will, enables us to sacrifice, and bestows the gift of sensitivity and compassion.

Struggle may not subside. The process of growing *with* God "does not always happen uniformly and harmoniously." Responsibilities will not vanish. Indeed our passion will find its expression in our active and challenging lives. But intimacy, responsibility, and authority are newly experienced in a way that transcends fears and pettiness and parochialism. Infused with passion they are donated in service to the persons and the dimensions of the world that evoke binding ties for us. Often these binding ties are broadened and become more inclusive of persons and places and concerns we may previously have shunned. In addition, because I have become individuated, individualism is no longer an addiction. My personal identity, my spiritual identity, and my communal identity not only inform one another; they have become one.

There is no deep sense of calling without passion. There is no true response to call without passion. And there is no sense of mission without passion.

Within our culture and church we see people of like passions bonding together for the common good. To participate in mission we may bond with others locally, nationally or internationally, others who have the same or similar callings. Or we may find ourselves providing a particular witness within a group with diverse callings. There are countless instances of people bonding together to carry out a mission that betters our country or world. MADD (Mothers Against Drunk Driving) is one. Solidarity in Poland is another. The Union of Concerned Scientists, whose mission is reducing the risk of nuclear war, is a third. The folks who gathered at the North American Conference on Christianity and Ecology, a fourth. The one thousand representatives of twenty-five thousand Hispanics who came to III Ecuentro in Washington D.C. in 1985, a fifth. One can be vigorously involved *with others in the ongoing challenges of one's culture* and be prophetic.

Part of formation for adult life is identifying one's callings, assisted often by mentors. Society can lend a competitive edge to callings, but callings by nature are not competitive. Freedom of assembly is a value within our culture, enabling the bonding together with others to happen without fear of reprisal. Uniting with others of good will beyond the borders of our church, a significant mandate of Vatican II, is one way many Catholic lay adults engage in mission. At times this provides a selective yet prophetic counter-cultural stance for believers who do not feel drawn to a prophetic counter-cultural stance that alienates them completely from their culture. Through individual efforts in the workplace, through mutual efforts in the home, and through communal efforts in the civic and public arena, passion energizes their mission thrust.

Without the discipline of ongoing reflection and prayer, passion can lead to self-righteousness and arrogance. Without the discipline of ongoing reflection and prayer, the customs and habits of our society and secular culture can erode the formation of Christian values.

A number of topics suggesting questions and reflection have emerged in the preceding text:

1. *Destiny and goals.* Do I have a sense of my destiny as a Catholic Christian? How is the call to mission part of my destiny? What goals have I set regarding my destiny? How have I been able or unable to activate these goals?
2. *Callings and work.* Am I able to live out my calling within the workplace? Am I able to distinguish between work and avocations or do I make work of my avocations? Is my work a calling or just a job? What's the difference? How have I been able to assume responsibility for mission in my workplace?
3. *Religious experience and integration.* Am I able to contemplate my everyday life and identify experiences where God has become manifest in encounters and events? Do I bring my everyday life to prayer to help it become integrated with deeper levels of who I am as a person? Have I discovered the paschal mystery of Jesus' death and resurrection enfleshed in my life?
4. *Disposition.* Am I aware of the binding ties I have with the world? What are my convictions? How do they align themselves with my callings and my attempts to engage in mission? Do I repress directed feelings? Or do I let them overwhelm me? Can I deal with them? Where in my life do I sense passion? How do prayer and religious experience engender this passion? Does my disposition align itself to where and how I feel called to lay down my life for the sake of others?

The Synod on the Laity, including the national consultations that took place before the gathering in Rome, has drawn to the surface issues significant to lay life that are pertinent to the church in the diverse cultures where the church exists all over the world. An issue like the rise of Islam may be more significant in some cultures than in others. In the United States no reflection with the laity on the laity will be complete without some theological reflection and insight on the impact of individualism or the impact of higher education on the lay Catholic populace or the impact of secular values that emerge in our settings.

According to the Pontifical Council on the Laity in its statement *On Formation of the Laity:*

> Formation occurs in *specific* social, economic, political and cultural contexts. It cannot be achieved in a full and effective way unless the presuppositions about life that underlie these contexts be identified, understood, and critically examined on the basis of the values of Christian faith. Persons being formed thus need to be able to take a reflective stance toward the society in which they live, to grasp *how they have embodied its values in their lives,* and to begin to understand how they may change themselves and their society by retaining, developing and transforming in the light of the faith all that is good in each context. (Emphasis mine.)

In order to probe the "presuppositions about life that underlie these contexts" (social, economic, political and cultural) it is essential to look first at the *power of place* in our formation. From that vantage, we will also consider a phenomenological foundation for a *spiritual* relationship with place, including the place we call planet earth. Because lay women and men are identified within the church *by setting,* i.e. world, any consideration of their calling and mission is incomplete without taking into account binding ties between people and place.

PART FOUR

1

PLACES: FLAVOR/TEXTURE/MORES/OWNERSHIP

Places Invite Relationships

Formation by place for my children differed from the formation by place I experienced as a child. When our youngest daughter started school, our family had lived for two years in an inner-city neighborhood. After her first afternoon of kindergarten, she stomped into the house and shouted at me, her voice rich with anger. "It wasn't like you promised at all! You kept sayin' the kids would be different. But they're all black-white-'n'-Puerto Rican, just like me!"

She railed on: "There were no Chinese! No Indians! No Eskimos!"

"Eskimos! I never promised Eskimos."

"But you kept saying the kids would be *different*. Instead, except for two kids from Italy who don't speak English, they're all black-white-'n'-Puerto Rican just like me!"

Inner-city place had shaped her perception. But her being in that place was the result of a decision made by her father and me. Had we remained in the small New Hampshire city where we lived prior to our move to the inner city, her identity would not have been formed the way place and experience formed it there. For her, at five years old, there truly was "no Jew, nor Gentile . . . male nor female. . . ."

We are formed by places—by their texture and flavor, by their "shoulds," by the relationship established between us and many particular places. This element of formation will now be our consideration because *where* Christians live as children and as adults is a significant factor in formation.

Some places of memory attract us. We are drawn to their generativity in reverie again and again. Some places of memory we avoid. Even a mention of them evokes feelings of dread or fear. Relationality happens between places and ourselves. We affect each other. Sometimes a place is in charge of us. Sometimes we take charge of a place. Sometimes we negotiate back and forth.

We are shaped by the particularity of the places where we live in our growing up years, but as adults who are Christians we are called to shape the places where we live as adults. That mandate was proclaimed with a strength at Vatican Council II.

One's faith is not meant to be a gloss over self or an element "beside" self. Our church experience is one powerful element within our total life experience, which is what forms most of us to be the kind of Catholic adults we've come to be. A revelation of spiritual identity—who I am in relation to God—can gradually become more apparent when we travel back in time and, through fresh eyes, see the formative dimensions *of place* in our lives. These dimensions help to disclose who I am as a person whose faith is indivisible from the me I am.

Deeper self-understanding comes from our noticing as an adult the perspectives that the place where we were born formed within. Peggy Sue, in the movie *Peggy Sue Got Married,* years into adulthood returned to high school and discovered things about herself by being a teenager again, one with a mature adult perspective. When in reflection or prayer, we return to childhood as the adults we are today, we notice things we were unaware of as children, we are attracted to what we may have overlooked before, we discover on a more profound level the reality of the place that formed us. The people who were part of that place influenced that formation.

Flavor and Texture of Place

Real people are formed by real places. But what makes a place real?

The flavor and texture of a place make it real. The mores (beliefs, behaviors, attitudes) of its people make it real. The kind of ownership operative within a place makes it real.

The flavor and texture of the place that formed me in western Massachusetts was ethnicity and a textile mill's working class environment. I grew up in a town brimming with the duplexes and triple-deckers of first and second generation Polish, French and Irish immigrants. I lived on the same street in that same town until I left home during high school. (Our daughters lived in five "places" before leaving home.) There were Yankees in my home town as well as ethnic groups. They lived on Main Street with its spacious lawns and its large, brick single-family houses. When my aunt and uncle moved into that vicinity, they were branded Yankee Catholics by many of the parishioners in their Irish Catholic parish across town. To be a Yankee Catholic was to be, in some sense, a pariah.

In the town where I grew up your ethnic identity was intertwined with your personal identity. If you lived in the section called New City you were Polish. If you lived by the textile mills, you were French. Place fused with ethnicity to reveal more than place and ethnicity; it revealed something about the *person* you actually were. To move to the place called Main Street was frowned upon. You had split your person from your people. Who would you be now?

When I moved to a different place, a college twenty miles away, I left a vivid, technicolor world for a pastel world—everything seemed pale, everyone seemed alike. We are shaped by the particularity of place where we live in our growing-up years, and the change in particularities that moving away brings about can be felt as a loss.

Never mind that the college twenty miles away was the state university where a good half of the population probably came from home towns identical to mine. We second and third generations, the paler generations, left behind the first generation. Many of us who were Catholics were only too happy to become Yankee Catholics.

Even before the days of ecumenism, it wasn't a sin to feel like a Yankee Catholic. Yet the process of becoming one affected your spirit fully as much as the sins you recited in the confessional. When Lent arrived, we Catholic freshmen straggled down to St. Bridgid's, awed by the realization that we'd offer months, not weeks, to the confessor when we admitted the lapse since our last confessions.

Leaving my technicolor ethnic world meant I became a particular other kind of Catholic than I might have become had I not left. But leaving revealed more to me about the place where I grew up than staying there ever would have.

One of the names for where I now live near Boston is the Massachusetts Eighth District. According to Robert L. Turner in *Street Smart and Worldly Wise,* "The Eighth (District) is tremendously heterogenous in its composition, but tremendously homogenous when it votes. . . . The Eighth has several of the highest crime neighborhoods in the state, and is probably home to more Nobel Prize winners than any other district in the country. . . . It contains by far the most college graduates, yet ranks only fifth in the percentage of its residents who have completed high school."[1] As the smallest geographically, it is also the most densely populated. It is by far the most Asian district in the commonwealth. The texture of Mass. 8th is *diversity.*

Its flavor is politics. I don't mean political in the sense of reflection and discourse in a refined way about policy and international event. The flavor is politics—fighting to win, going the long haul for your candidate. For example, Tip O'Neill years ago became the representative of Mass. 8th only after a long and bitter primary fight between Irish and Italian factions. As Robert L. Turner puts it, "in the Eighth the diverse elements more often than not seem to push each other in . . . innovative, progressive and activist directions."[2]

From May to November in 1986, every morning on the way to work George and I were greeted by women and men standing in the streets waving large posters for candidates for the September primary and the November election. Six months of daily political hoopla evoked a flavor that affected my perception of citizenship, that helped me realize that in other places where we've lived I had felt "inside" the process of politics for a week prior to a national election. By fall in 1986 talk about politics and sitting at the supper table had become synonymous.

Even my mother, who came to Mass. 8th at age eighty-five, caught the flavor. One day that summer she came home from her adult day care center with the news that she had danced that day with "young Kennedy who's runnin' for Congress." Early in the fall she said, "You should come to Windsor House and see the nice snapshot on the bulletin board of young Kennedy and me dancing a jig."

When I followed her bidding there was no nice snapshot—there was an 8" by 10" political flyer with a large picture on the cover of my mother and the candidate dancing a jig over "Kennedy for Congress." Joe Kennedy, helped by my mother, did win the election.

Only in the Mass. 8th—as they say.

The Mass. 8th primary helped me to understand the place where I had been living for almost a decade. In the past I had lived in places where so little happened and where there was so little to do that *boredom* was the flavor of that place. I had lived in places where too much happened. The first summer we lived in the inner city neighborhood, there were five separate murders within a block of our house. *Fear* was the flavor of that place. The election in Mass. 8th revealed to me that it is a place where people have a fighting spirit, where some people have roots in the past and others seem to have moved in yesterday. It also helped me to understand something about a state I've lived in most of my life, summarized well by Ralph Whitehead, a journalism professor at the University of Massachusetts at Amherst, "The traditional culture, which is largely Irish-Catholic, believes in extremely high standards for private behavior, but has compassionate 'live and let live' standards for public behavior. The modernist culture, largely mainstream Protestant, has exceedingly high standards for public behavior, but has a 'live and let live' standard for private behavior."[3]

The texture and flavor of a place affect the formation of its people. Understanding "local place," including region and state, can help develop a greater awareness of one's culture and society and one's *call* to participation in that as an adult Catholic.

Reflecting on place to notice how it has formed and is forming us does not have to be done in an analytical way. Intuition and discovery are the tools needed to notice the subtle entities that make the texture and flavor of a place. The purpose of engagement in this reflection is to discern how you are *already* formed by place. The decisions we make *affect* how we are formed but we fool ourselves if we believe that we form ourselves. It is part of wisdom to realize that, *often without our being conscious of the process, we are being formed.*

Mores—Shoulds—Religious Values

Few of us who are Catholic adults have grown up without "shoulds" instilled in us. As adults we may not realize how many "shoulds" reside within us, yet we live them out day after day. In the aftermath of Vatican II we may have become conscious of particular *church* "shoulds" in a striking way and debated about them—"shoulds" like eating meat on Friday or not practicing birth control. In this respect Vatican II was a "consciousness-raising" event, one deserving our gratitude.

At the end of the last sentence I sneaked in a "should." Did you catch it?

We may be aware of "church shoulds," yet we may be much less aware of the "shoulds" that have crept into us from the places where we grew up or now live and work. These have great strength in forming us. Developing awareness about these "shoulds," called *mores* by sociologists, is a necessary component of any Christian adult formation program.

According to Webster, mores (pronounced more-ays) are the "fixed morally binding customs of a particular group." Webster also indicates that habits and manners are called mores.

Sometimes I notice the mores in a place other than my own more easily than I recognize the mores of the place where I live. That's because the latter have become part of me through osmosis. When we go to a new place, we bring along the mores from the place where we live. Sometimes it calls for fancy footwork to avoid tripping over our shoulds as we react to the shoulds of the place we have come to visit. If we don't recognize that we are bringing with us our own shoulds, we double our chances of tripping over them.

For example, a while ago I presented a day-long workshop for Catholics involved in ministry in a diocese in Florida. If possible, I like to localize some of the material I present as people seem to participate more readily with what is familiar. To launch this segment of the program, I passed around a clipping from a newspaper with a picture of a local teenage beauty queen wearing a dress that revealed a naked V to the navel. While the clipping was making the rounds, I read a letter to the editor that deplored the style of the dress the adolescent beauty queen was wearing. Then I went on about pressures on females and the challenge of Catholic values versus secular culture. Suddenly a woman, well into maturity, shouted at me, "Don't foist your Puritan values on us who live in Florida."

Rattled, I muttered something about thinking we shared common Catholic values, but by then the room was in an uproar, most of it directed at me. "That dress isn't any worse than what kids see day in and day out on the beach!" "Let's not reinvent the Legion of Decency." "You'd never see a dress like that up north because New Englanders are too uptight about themselves." I took a risk related to mores and it flew right back in my face.

As this story illustrates, all the "fixed morally binding customs" found among believers in any particular region are not likely to have emerged from their religious faith, tradition, or local church. The *culture* of their place generously contributes its shoulds. An everyday interior reinforcement of those shoulds occurs because mores are part and parcel of *ordinary interaction*. This gives mores a power. Eventually the cultural mores of our region may infiltrate our religious values. For example, the economy surrounding a military base may depend on that military base. Eventually, it can become difficult for the believers in that region to be actively engaged in peacemaking efforts because military mores have formed many people in that region.

Part of the trauma of late adolescence and early adulthood is the process of sorting out the mores instilled in childhood from the values one wants as an adult. That transition has been food for innumerable novels, plays and movies. And, indeed, the process has a dramatic edge because *feelings and mores fuse,* as my example from Florida reveals.

Distinguishing between the mores of the place where we live and the religious values we embrace can be—indeed, should be—a lifelong process. For example, if peace and reconciliation are strong ethical values within myself, then I need to beware of any kind of patriotism in my region that fosters an "us against them" kind of mentality. If I believe that religious faith is an important value for a viable society, then I need to beware of attempts through advertising, media, and lifestyles that make secularism an idol. If the conviction that God loves all peoples who inhabit this earth is a spiritual value to me, then I need to beware of mores that denigrate certain groups of people.

The argument here is not between having mores *or* having religious values. We can hardly avoid having *both* if we interact with the place where we live and if we were raised in or converted to a faith system. So the contest is between *some* of our mores and *some* of our religious values.

No society exists without mores. Mores are like a second skin and many are not related to values. If Leslie visits Tierney in Manhattan and leaves the window open by the fire escape, Tierney may slam it shut and shout, "In Vermont you can open all the windows you want, but no one in New York opens a window by a fire escape!"

We always have more shoulds in our life than we have religious values. Some mores may better reflect our values than others. And some, like racism, sexism, or militarism, may reflect a value system in a given place that does *not* cohere with Christian values. The aim of good formation is *to weed out mores that don't cohere with one's religious values.* Jesus, as portrayed in the gospels, responded to those who challenged him about healing on the sabbath by saying (put in contemporary context), "Hold on a minute—you are trying to pass on mores you have absorbed as if each were a revelation from God or a literal inflexible teaching of the torah."

In my own life, if I have never taken the time and effort to distinguish between my religious/ethical values and my mores, if I am interiorly tolerating mores and values that are opposites, then I am setting up *interior conflict* within myself. This conflict often leads to feelings of free-floating anxiety or semi-depression or undefined guilt. I am not sure who I am.

Unless we have some awareness of the mores that shape our identity, we are apt to be victimized by them, the equating "cleanliness with godliness" syndrome. In the settings that are the web of lay life—the secular workplace, clubs, civic committees and political parties—we can engage in mission by identifying where mores don't mesh with the overall purposes stated by those gathered in that place, i.e. cheating, cutting corners or putting out a shoddy product. We can only do that if we have been *reflective about our own values.*

Our local culture (or socio-economic class) invests a "rightness" in these mores. That sense of rightness is the basis for their appeal. If we go along with that rightness we can become victims of consumer manipulation and political propagandists. Some commentators in the last national presidential election felt that the pledge of allegiance was used in that way by a political party.

The description I've presented on mores has been cautionary. Beware of the way shoulds from the *place* where you live can infiltrate your authentic religious values to weaken and compromise them. The aim of good formation is to reverse the process, *to develop my spiritual values until, in an almost effortless way, they influence related mores,* i.e. to live as a person of peace if world peace is a value, to live as a person of faith in all respects if faith is a value. In this way we connect and weave together our value system regarding the world and the way we live out intimacy, responsibility, and authority day after day after day.

All this is not meant to deny that many of us have received a kind of excellence in the formation of our mores by the place and the parental figures it was our blessing to have in childhood. Children often pick up religious values from the customs and habits of their parents, a way that is often more effective than sitting a child down to give him or her a moral lesson. The latter quickly turns off the ears, mind and heart!

My mother and father, opposites in many ways, shared a deeply held spiritual value. They made it one of their consistent mores over the years. All the "shoulds" that affected relationships with every person and group beyond our threshold had their substance in "Love your neighbor as you love yourself."

"Milton Cohen is a Jew but I want him as one of my pallbearers," my father often said. "Milton teaches more about how to be a Christian than half the pillars of the church over at the parish." My formation regarding Jewish people, in a town with few Jews, was shaped by remarks like this.

Neither of my parents ever said directly to me: "Love your neighbor as you love yourself." It was always taught through mores. My dad would say things like: "When you're out for a walk before seven in the morning or after seven in the evening, always greet with a word the strangers you meet. People are apt to feel lonelier at those times." (And in those days in the place where I grew up, it was safe to greet the stranger.) My mother, as I said earlier, was one of thirteen children, and occasionally she would murmur to me when I was a teenager, "I can't quite figure out why I'm the only one who's on speaking terms with all twelve of them."

Black people were total strangers to my mother until she was eighty-five years old and came to live with us. One day on returning from the adult day care center she said, "Lots and lots of Negroes came to our place today. They're going to stay a while! I didn't think they could come to Windsor House."

"Black people have rights too, Mom," I responded.

"Don't call them black people, dear. They don't like it. But you know, it's strange being in a room with a Negro."

For about a week Mom seemed quieter than usual. Then she came home one day all smiles. "Those Negro people really can sing! The two things they like to do best are the two things I like to do best—sing and pray!"

When my mother entered a nursing home she was placed in a three-bed unit with one roommate—a beautiful black woman, made feeble and mute by Lou Gehrig's disease. Mom took to Viola immediately and made sure the rest of us took to her as well. "Give Viola a kiss too; it makes her feel better," Mom urged us every time we entered the room. After three months together Viola was moved to a maximum care level. My mother cried when she told me Viola had left. "We were such good friends. She was so dear to me."

The way our spiritual values infiltrate our mores influences the way we witness to our faith in all the varied places we choose to go. Our lives will probably come to a close, however, in a place we'd choose not to be. My mother is happy in the nursing home and radiates that happiness to others. She has made more friends in her eighty-seventh and eighty-eighth years on earth than many younger people make in a decade. That gift for friendship was not formed within her four years ago when she moved from a place where she had spent most of her life to a strange, new place. That gift for friendship is the harvest of a lifetime of loving others. I may have preferred that she love me *as a mother* in other ways, but I would never deny that she has a gift for loving, a gift exercised in earlier years, a gift rooted in spiritual values that formed the mores that day after day characterized her life.

Our well-being, psychic and spiritual, is at stake in the contest between our spiritual values and our mores.

Owning Place

When our granddaughter Nicole was four she took up squatter's rights that Christmas in our apartment between a large old sea captain's chest and the window seat in the living room. Each morning before breakfast I would find Nicole in her pajamas squeezed into that narrow isthmus, inching her bottom up to sit on the sea captain's chest in what, to us, looked like an awkward and uncomfortable position for play. During the day she exercised the territorial imperative that goes with owning a place. Anyone who put an object on the chest or window seat got scolded. Then one morning, in a massive effort, she abandoned the sea captain's chest and moved everything from the window seat to a corner in the dining room.

Children have a nomadic spirit. They can let go of place. Because the fantasy dimension of the child's personality is so ripe, the child can make of one place another kind of place, one that suits whatever momentary desire emerges in the heart. The doll house, the tree house, the jungle gym and the sheet over a table all become particular "places" that seem alive through the child's power to imagine.

We adults, who often labor to feel at home in a place, frequently struggle in our souls if we are called to relinquish a place we feel has become our own. (Ownership and security are likely to become synonymous in our perceptions.)

As Christian adults we are not meant to be nomadic spiritually, though we may sometimes feel like that, physically and spiritually. We are pilgrims. The idea of pilgrim implies spiritual development *simultaneous* to journey. The pilgrim, ready to move on when sensing a call, deepens and integrates spiritual substance *through* the journey. Being "on the road," moving from place to place, is meant to *enhance* spirituality, not diminish it.

At the heart of lay spirituality is pilgrim spirituality. In our culture, however, the territorial imperative of owning one's own home has the strength of a fixed morally binding custom. At times this has spawned two-acre lot zoning. In some communities owning your own place becomes identical with isolating yourself from others. On the other hand, what used to be perceived as a transitory place, the small rental apartment (often where neighbors are too close for comfort), is taking on permanency for young families. In addition, rental costs have escalated. According to David Schwartz and Richard Ferlauto, "Families with incomes under $10,000 experienced a 4 percent decline in real income from 1976 to 1986 and an increase in real rental costs from 48 percent of income to 58 percent."[4]

Our family has experienced both modes of living space. As our daughters were growing up, we first built a house in a rural area with a farm nearby. Then we moved to another state, bought a large, comfortable bungalow in a residential area of a medium-sized city. From there we moved to the inner city. When we moved to the Berkshires, we lived in an old house with barns in the back yard near a village center until the school where George and I worked closed.

"What do you want to do with your life?" George asked me at that time. "I've gone for the jobs I've wanted and you've always packed up and moved with me. You choose this time, and I'll pack up and move with you."

I chose to study theology in preparation for ministry, and he packed up and followed. That same year our twins followed their older sister and started college. Rather than buy a house near Boston, we thought we would wait. While we waited we nibbled at the equity we gained from selling our house in the Berkshires. By the time I finished school housing costs had skyrocketed, so we continued to rent.

For ten years we owned no property. Separating ourselves from the middle class territorial imperative of owning one's home was a strange experience. Sometimes we felt a freedom we had not experienced since early in our marriage. Sometimes the risk we were taking troubled us and evoked tension. Sometimes we felt fear.

There were times, always at night, when we would ride through neighborhoods and notice, in home after home, the intimate glow of lamps that spoke of a kind of "at home" feeling we did not have. A yearning would fill my heart and bring tears to my eyes.

In December 1984 George's mother died, and in January 1985 my mother broke her hip and came to live with us. The fear of leaving me with a part-time job and a high rent, if he should die suddenly, motivated George to raise the issue of home ownership again. That spring we bought a two-family house we could afford. It is back in the Berkshires, two and a half hours away from where we work. Because we can't commute five hours a day, we have kept the apartment we rent near Boston. Sometimes we use one of the apartments in the Berkshires, and sometimes we rent both of the apartments depending on our own financial situation. We feel fortunate to be able to do that.

Financially, not owning a home for ten years was a disaster. Spiritually, it was edifying as they say. It helped us to perceive how embedded in our culture are the mores about owning—not only one's home but also one's street and neighborhood and club and school and church. We've come to feel that *owning is a much stronger value in the United States than sharing.*

We bought a house two and half hours away from where we work because we cannot afford to do otherwise. When we moved to Boston, two-family houses sold for $60,000. Now it is hard to find one for under $200,000.

This revolution, one that is forming North America to be a class society in a radical way, took over the country with nary an outcry from churches or Christian adults, even though it is a reality that creates homelessness. Home owners, who carried mortgages with relatively small payments, gained financially and may not have been generatively concerned enough to warn the younger Americans and poorer Americans who are the ones most victimized by the fact that "in 1973 the typical 30-year-old paid 21 percent of his or her income for payments on the average house. Today those payments by a 30 year-old employee are over 44 percent of income."[5]

As this happened churches on the local level seemed to look the other way, relinquishing *their* generativity responsibilities. When churches in the United States focus on narrow issues and avoid what is going on in the "mainstream," they evoke the impression that mainstream policies and mores *don't affect justice issues* and future generations of every socio-economic class. In spite of the churches' valiant effort to help the homeless, the rich have become richer in the United States and the poor have become poorer. This might not be true if Christians had been as active about mission in the halls of Congress and the corridors of corporations as they have been in soup kitchens and shelters. That the leading association in the United States for Political Action Committee fund-raising is the realtors' PAC is a fact that churches may need to scrutinize.

When we moved to the inner city, I went with a Lady Bountiful attitude, excited by all I would be able to do for minority people. It didn't take long to discover that I would do very little *for* them; they paradoxically would do much for me. Primary in that was teaching me what *community* really means. Community for the people we lived with was a basic need for sheer survival. They welcomed us into their community—a privileged placement, one we needed in order to reflect on our own lives and on all that we owned in contrast to the little they could call their own.

Ownership is always a *moral* question.

Sustaining quality family life has, for centuries, been a Christian value. Family creates stability and contributes to the common good of the whole society. Home, closely identified with family, evoked almost sacred overtones when the workplace became separate from the home place. Home was no longer the small commonwealth of daily work as well as domesticity that provided modeling for the greater commonwealth of the state. Home became the domain of mother and children, needing valuation if family was to stay intact now that father was away from home for all the day. As time passed *ownership of home* developed a quasi-religious value connotation.

I defended home ownership, if you remember, when a vowed religious challenged me about it. It *is* simplistic to leap-frog from the way we value owning a house to the way we tolerate fiercely competitive multinational ownership. I am not saying that home ownership or any particular kind of ownership is right or wrong. I would say it depends primarily on the *intent and scale* of the ownership. Is it an end in itself and therefore a value, or is it a means to another value, i.e. family life? For the Christian adult *that* end should relate to his or her Christian value system and determine the scope and limits of owning material goods.

The post-conciliar church has gone beyond a narrow perception of avoiding occasions of sin as well as sin itself. For the mission-oriented Catholic lay adult the whole self needs to be developed into a stance of *moral maturity*. This means being conscious of our experience and of the values we bring to that experience, including how we value ownership of the places in our lives. In order to do this the mores of the upper and middle classes must not be casually embraced or rejected or judged by church leaders and ethicists. *Formation by place* always has socio-economic overtones. It deserves respect and greater reflection and discernment within the church.

Shared Places

In order to heighten our awareness of the power of place in our lives, we might want to take the time to contemplate meaningful places of the past. One way to do this is to become quiet and gaze at a non-distracting vista and then simply ask God to reveal a place that formed you in the past. One day when I did that I initially saw and sensed a great deal of varying shades of green on trees, broken by a frequent expanse of similarly tinted grass. Then I saw a narrow river where I skipped from rock to rock and later crossed a small bridge. Suddenly I was on my back in a pool—an expansive, gorgeous pool. And I then recognized where my memory had taken me. The pool was in a large park, developed privately by a family, then donated to the city next to the town where I was raised.

I was in the pool alone, floating on my back from one end to the other as I used to do when swimming lessons were over. Then the reverie shifted to a small bridge where I was standing with a young man. We were both seventeen—meeting for the first time on that bridge, shyly and slyly flirting with one another, unaware that the bridge encounter would lead, as of this date, to thirty-nine more years of intimate encounter.

Then we were both in the playground of this public park with our daughters, watching them climb jungle gyms and ride swings and see-saws. I saw us celebrating summer birthdays in the park, at the picnic tables, with his family as well as mine and ours. And as our daughters grew in age, I saw us paddling canoes with them at the pond in the park. I saw my father, hand in hand, with two of our daughters climbing onto the miniature train they all loved so much to ride on with grandpa.

Finally, I saw us with our own granddaughter between us walking down toward the same train her mother had enjoyed with my father.

As the reverie ended I saw all of us, the four generations, feeding the ducks at the pond formed by the river crossed by a bridge where the two who were to become one found one another.

The memory of the park left me with a feeling of gratitude too deep to express to myself or God. So I just stayed quietly with the thankful feeling for a while. Later, I felt awed by the discovery that one place had linked us from generation to generation as it drew us closer to one another.

We can still go to that place—we share it with one another and with many, many others, yet in memory and reality it is ours as well. I cannot go back to the house where I grew up. We cannot go back to the home where we first established our own family. These places are owned by others now, and we would enter them feeling like voyeurs or tourists. We have gone back to the parishes where we worshiped, but there is no one parish where all the generations came together. Also each parish church has been renovated so it is no longer a place that belongs to us or unites us.

In an uncanny way the park is much the same today as it was during every yesterday I remembered. In a way, it's a symbol that embraces the span of my entire life. The shared green-space of God's good creation rather than any particular building or room is the place that has the power to do that.

2

PLACE AND SPIRITUALITY

Contemplating Our Connection to Place

Cultures can help or hinder spirituality and the living of the Christian life. In one culture the *natural* attributes for spirituality may be enhanced; in another they may be denigrated. The North American culture tolerates a great range of diversity, enabling a variety of spiritualities to come into creation. Our culture also values action —quick thinking, fast pace, utilitarianism, achievement, competition. Because of this, North Americans may need to pay more attention to the "building blocks" of spirituality itself, including a deeper awareness of the *existence* of an interior life, one that cannot be just psychologically explained, yet one that has natural components, like reverie, that contribute to the way we "exercise" ourselves spiritually. In addition, the way we are intimate, the way we take responsibility, and the way we use authority often mirror our interior self.

This book is an attempt to disclose a spiritual foundation for the development of mission within lay adult Catholics. Moral maturity is essential, of course, to any mission enterprise, but moral maturity emerges from a spiritual foundation, a *felt* connection and commitment to God, to others and to the earth we all inhabit. In a culture where even connectedness within family is fragmented, where a lack of commitment on a civic level encourages us to ignore corruption, poverty, violence, and environmental poisoning, the ability to care about the connection to *place* can pose problems.

Another difficulty in discussing spirituality for mission in the world relates to what we mean by world. In common discourse of late there is a tendency to declare allegiance to either the natural earth which we inhabit or the world of nations and varied cultures, societies, and political tensions. On the other hand, the rise of

225

environmental concerns has helped us become more conscious of connections between both worlds.

Perspectives for the Christian's relationship to planetary earth emerge from three theological concepts: the first, the most traditional, is found in the Old Testament. Humans, through the Genesis stories, are called to be stewards of the earth God has created. The second, found in some patristic writings and in the Greek Orthodox tradition, posits women and men in partnership with the earth God has created. The third, of more recent vintage, is found in creation-type spiritualities and views humans as dependent on the vitality of the earth.

Put too simply, in the first, stewardship, humans are greater, in value if not in size, than the earth. In the second, partnership, both earth and humans seem equal in value. In the third, dependence, the earth seems greater in value than any of its individual inhabitants.[1]

We have looked at how place can affect the formation of values and mores. It is now time to reflect on *consciousness* of place and then at possible intrinsic spiritual dynamics awakened when we explore different kinds of places, natural places. A spiritual foundation, based on how we experience the space God has created, might reveal that we who are created by God are intended by God to be drawn into relationship with God's creation. Our experiencing awe, reverence, and love for particular places in nature may provide evidence for that. The authority implicit in stewardship, the responsibility implicit in partnership, and the intimacy implicit in dependency, underscored by spiritual dynamics inherent in our relationship with natural places, may help us understand with greater clarity our spiritual birthright for mission. Within this framework baptism does not deliver us *from* the world but, building on natural connections, roots us more deeply within it.

An initial step in this regard is to grasp how *sense of place* has been historically understood in our country. The consciousness of citizens in earlier times in the United States concerning sense of place may influence today our perceptions and values regarding place.

North America and a Sense of Place

A few summers ago, while visiting my daughter Kerry in Omaha, Nebraska, I was startled to see photographs showing Indian teepees on the outskirts of Omaha. The photos, in a library exhibit, were taken at the turn of *this* century. In the United States a consciousness of place could not help but be a *developing* consciousness because the totality of the place called the United States has only gradually unfolded for all but native Americans. American history shows that "Until Henry David Thoreau in the middle of the 19th century, America had no great literature of place and scarcely even the beginnings of such a tradition. Here is an extraordinary cultural phenomenon. . . ."[2]

According to Frederick Turner, before Thoreau, "searching for some authentic sense of place, some *assent* to the land, (one) becomes a kind of wilderness wanderer, lost in a thicket of resistance . . . the real world was always elsewhere."[3] For other than native Americans that "elsewhere" was Europe, the home of most immigrants. For example, in *Landscapes of the Sacred* Belden Lane reveals the impact of continental French spirituality on early French settlers in North America.

Without a native sense of place that evokes *reverence,* a limitless permission *to alter place* may be generated. This effect is felt even today. On a global level, we North Americans have projected a stance of limitless permission, not to conquer, but to alter place through technology or political manipulation. When efforts were directed at third world development, our motivation may have sometimes been generous, but altering place was part of our American soul and often seen as the *only* way to accomplish goals.

Without a sense of *spiritual* connection to place it is easy to deface place, even if that place is the whole world. Native Americans, on the other hand, have revealed a gift for savoring place as it is in its createdness. Native Americans have a "sense of place." Within their traditions is a conviction that "the land itself (is) a living thing, and its various features—caves, groves, mountains, rivers—lie under the protection of numerous guardian spirits."[4]

Thoreau was the literary pioneer to express sense of place to compatriots. Thoreau, "driven deep into the American earth," took "*imaginative* possession of his portion of it."[5] From this came his book *Walden.* Not initially a commercial success, it became a book that, "like a pebble tossed into his pond, widened from the intensely local to the national and even the international . . . he had succeeded in re-creating in his own time, the ancient numinous *sense of place.*"[6]

Other regionalists followed like Mark Twain who "came upon the vast treasure of the Mississippi, buried in his memory,"[7] and Willa Cather who roamed before she fell "in love with the Southwest, and as always, love had inspired imagination."[8]

In earlier times in New England, Puritans had fenced off wilderness, clung to covenant and village life, and perceived in the new world natural vistas terror as well as majesty. In later years, as Belden Lane points out, here and there the individual mystic or community like the Shakers would exercise religious imagination in interpreting America's landscape.

In our own time, a visual artist, Georgia O'Keefe, experienced a response akin to Willa Cather's for the southwest where she transplanted herself from New York City: "I've been sleeping on the roof this week. . . . I like to see the sky when I wake and I like the air—and I like seeing all over my world with the rise of the sun. . . . Now I've told you something about my world because I think it is good."[9] Considered an eccentric for her dedication to place, O'Keefe herself noted the spiritual intensity she experienced: "When I stand alone with the earth and sky (I feel) something in me going off in every direction into the unknown infinity. . . ."[10]

A sense of intimacy regarding place, according to Turner, allows "people to participate emotionally in their place of living . . . these works in their places remind us to remember. And the end of that remembering is to know again that *we do not live in some existential vacuum—and never had.*"[11]

For the Christian adult the challenge is to participate emotionally and spiritually in the place where one lives without making ownership of place an idol.

For Catholics in the nineteenth century the mill town, the urban ghetto, and the local church were often home. The immigrants' struggle to maintain a toehold in their new culture meant a passage toward upward mobility through education, a passage accomplished by the offspring of second and third generations. By the 1980s the American Catholic Church had been somewhat "gentrified" by the spreading affluence of its members.

Since World War II, and with remarkable swiftness over the last generation, the 52 million members of America's largest denomination have become more affluent, better educated and are wielding more power in the professions and corporate board rooms. . . . *One out of every three Catholics now lives in the suburbs.*[12]

No longer with an eye turned back toward Europe, American Catholics live today with a *familiarity* about their own place in the American place which, paradoxically, may inhibit their *sense of relationship to world place.* Not feeling awe and reverence for natural place may result in surrendering place to utilitarian values. Utilitarianism, in turn, always silences whispers of caring intimacy between world and self.

Rapidity of change also impedes our forming a realistic relationship with the world. What world? The world is being altered every minute of every day. Keeping up with new names for old countries becomes a task. This hardly encourages contemplation and spiritual bonding with our planet. When we lack a strongly internalized generative stance toward the world, it is easy to buy into the images of the world others sell—the globe as market place or the earth as vacation paradise for those able to afford the airfare.

To develop the spiritual fibre that links us with our earth and its peoples, North American Catholics in particular may need to perceive in a more striking fashion their church as a world-church community composed of companions in faith who live out that faith in cultures of great variety and vibrancy on planet earth.

Naturally Contemplative Spiritual Dynamics

But is it possible to develop spiritual intimacy with something as immense as the planet earth? Our guide for discovering an answer to this question, Gaston Bachelard, the French phenomenologist (1894–1962), believed in that possibility. By helping us to remember the experiences we have already had in familiar places, places that evoke *a kind of immensity,* Bachelard reveals that an interior foundation for relationship to place has *already* been forged. Naming this dynamic enables greater consciousness about our relationship with the world.

Bachelard reveals that the most common of experiences are sometimes contemplative. This becomes more apparent when we consider familiar, if often neglected, human dimensions:

- engaging in reverie
- discovering images
- daydreaming

Contemplation, whether we are contemplating a beloved friend, God, or the universe, makes use of inner resources that come with who we are as humans. In other words, our *capacity* for spirituality comes from our createdness by God. Reverie, image-making, and daydreaming may be neglected or trivialized in our culture but they are valuable components of any contemporary Christian spirituality.

Reverie

Day after day, for too many days during any given week, I say to myself, "Oh, it's that late already!" or "I'll never get this done by noon." In reverie, on the other hand, "The hours leave us with no jolt."

Bachelard perceived that in reverie "we gain gentleness of living. Gentleness, slowness, peace, such is the motto of reverie. . . ." Bachelard called this *anima*. A precursor of what is now called feminine spirituality, Bachelard felt that experiencing reverie for "any human being, man or woman . . . is one of the feminine states of the soul." Reverie is ". . . the great tranquility of the intimate feminine being."[13]

Through reverie we often experience a sense of well-being and integration because, as Bachelard puts it, "Reverie teaches me *to be the same as myself*. . . ."[14]

During reverie our consciousness seems to expand. "The soul is no longer stuck in a corner of the world."[15] We begin to believe again in the possibility of a harmonious existence *because we are feeling that harmony within*. This concrete experience of myself being in harmony heightens my hope for universal harmony. "Ah! The gentle fluency of the reverie which helps us pour ourselves into the world, into the well-being of the world. . . ."[16]

Reverie, the state perhaps most easily recognized as contemplative, is akin to repose. Recently I came across a set of snapshots taken when Nicole was a tiny baby. In many of them she is sound asleep on her grandfather's chest. In the photos he is in different chairs, indicating varying times of day. Yet the image in each photo is identical: Nicole cuddled into sleep on her grandfather's chest. Across her grandfather's face, there is peace of soul and heart. She is in the land of dreams, he is in the land of reverie.

Images

"A whole essay might well be written on the danger of thinking without images."[17] Images are part of ourselves, part of our everyday lives. Artists, especially poets, are mentors, so to speak, who help us to notice more carefully the images that come to us. But no artist, no poet, can make us *receptive* to an image. That is up to us. And if we aren't receptive to an image at the moment it appears, we may forget it through the distractions surrounding it.

In Catholic tradition image and symbol have had a place of prominence. Following Vatican II, *changing* the images and symbols within church buildings might have been preferable to doing away with them. The loss of image-making capacities can lessen what we have to offer others and planet earth.

Attitudes toward place, like images, are seldom neutral. Contemporary Catholic affirmation of the value of the world has to contend with traditions based on *contempto mundi,* rejecting the value of the world. Activating our potential for *intimacy with the world* depends not only on our own experiences with the world, but also on the *valuation* we put on these experiences. This in turn depends on images we have of the world and on images we have of ourselves. In other words, as Catholics we may need tutoring in how to value our global world while as North Americans we may have to learn how to value the world without having to own it.

Paying attention to how we relate to the known world today is *spiritually as well as ethically significant.*

How do we pay attention? One way is by noticing the images that come to us, noticing how we are when we daydream, affirming times of reverie. In other words, if we limit our connection to the world to what we popularly call "head trips"—intellectual analysis, rational thinking, abstractions—we have not only halved our resources for knowing our world, but also dismissed those dimensions necessary for an *intimate* relationship with the world. Intuitive thinkers, ones who value reverie and are at home with images, are often rooted in a reality based on more than rationality.

Intimacy is the seedbed for images. Jesus' sense of deep intimacy with Abba bore fruit in images. Jesus embraced the poetic image, revealing God to us as the one who searches for lost sheep, perceiving himself as a mother hen who longs to shelter her young, the kingdom as a mustard seed. If we doubt the power of images we need only remind ourselves of the power of the material images Jesus revealed.

Jesus deepened the sense of the kingdom of God for his hearers through images, and through images we can deepen our sense of the world created by God as the setting for that kingdom called into being by God.

To develop that kind of spiritual intimacy we need to slow down and really see the spaces we inhabit; we need to perceive how they affect us, and how we respond to them. In other words, we need to welcome images that emerge within us, savor them and let them unfold into new images. We may also want to remember images from a particular time or place in the past. To do this, we need to take time for "reverie."

Some people keep a record of images that emerge each day, perceiving them as links to the unconscious and/or the Holy Spirit.[18] People who do this may have a profound sense now and then that we are made in the *image* and likeness of our creator God. Getting to know ourselves as image makers deepens our knowing who we are as a faith people.

Daydreaming, Original Contemplation

Daydreaming is the third ordinary human activity linked to contemplation.

When we daydream we experience a sense of infinity and a sense of being elsewhere. So for Bachelard, "Daydream is original contemplation."[19] In Bachelard's view our ability to daydream, as well as our capacity for reverie and image-making, creates affective intimacy with the world. If the modes he suggests surprise us, it is probably because we have had in our lives too many parental figures convinced that reverie, imagination, and daydreaming lure us *away* from knowing and understanding the world.

Bachelard reminds us that we do not dream with "taught ideas." *We dream with images that emerge from experience and memory.* We are speaking of a valid kind of knowing, a kind of "knowing" that does not come from analysis and rational thinking. The latter is the kind of knowing that considers the world as an *object*. If we know the world only as an object, then we can easily perceive the world as a thing to be manipulated or militarized. Decades ago, when less was known about the world, when we had never seen the world from outside of itself, we may have actually felt, through modes like daydreaming, an intimacy with the world more fully realized than we do now. Now the world, particularly in the west, is considered by some as *one object in an inventory of objects.*

The dreamer, according to Bachelard, is a contemplating *subject* in relation to the world as *subject.* The dreamer has the capacity of perceiving the world in its authentic reality (as one would another person) because perceiving the world as a subject allows feeling to enter the relationship.

Life becomes a spiritual adventure when the believer values and welcomes "images and ideas, contemplation and experience *at the same time.*"[20] Images may lead us into daydream; images may come to us in daydream moments. Reverie may lead to daydreaming or daydreaming may come to a close with a sense of reverie.

One of the few blessings of being an only child is the natural way one becomes contemplative from experiencing so much solitude. Because I was an only child, sitting and staring out the window was never considered a sin when our children were growing up. Some parents seem to worry if a child has a spare minute, and they may bless the television set for filling any void in the child's life, yet Bachelard urges us to let the child be bored. Bored, he or she may begin to dream.

And the dream, according to Bachelard, "coordinates life, prepares beliefs for a lifetime."[21] He quotes the well-known French Catholic writer, Julien Green:

> It is a bizarre disposition of mine to believe a thing only if I have dreamed it. By believing, I do not mean simply possessing a certainty but retaining it within oneself in such a way that the being finds itself *modified* by it.[22]

Spirituality is not possessing certainty about matters of faith like the resurrection of Jesus, for example, but *appropriating* these, through memory and imagination, until they begin to alter one's own being. By creating hope where there was doubt or desolation, the spiritual power evoked refashions us within. Without the gifts of reverie, image-making and daydreaming, prayer and worship may stay superficial.

The House, the Intimacy of Confined Space

When the challenges of life exhaust or frighten us, "we comfort ourselves by reliving memories of protection."[23] Adults, single or married, eventually feel the pull to establish a home, for home is the place that has come to symbolize protective intimacy. "The house is a space that is supposed to condense and defend intimacy."[24]

I remember returning by train from Boston to my hometown for Thanksgiving vacation during my first year of teaching. In spite of home having ambivalent meaning for me as a child, as the Holyoke range of mountains appeared on the horizon, as I saw my beloved Mount Tom, the mountain visible from my bedroom as a child, tears wet my face. I felt what Bachelard describes. "From all over, coming from all objects, an intimacy lays siege to us."[25] I was coming home.

Within a home, the simplest and most routine of activities happen but daydreams may accompany these household activities. The dreaming and the simplicity of the activity actually help to create the intimacy that inhabits the house. What many might dismiss as trivial, Bachelard sees as formative, as preparation for adult life. "If I were asked to name the chief benefit of a house, I should say: The house shelters daydreaming, the house protects the dreamer, the house allows one to dream in peace."[26] Part of the intimacy a house provides is intimacy with self, and daydreaming, an activity that is often characteristic of self-intimacy; these possess "values that . . . mark humanity in its depth . . . for daydreaming . . . derives pleasures from *its own being.*"[27]

Why is something that derives pleasure "from its own being" of value or significance? Without a formation that provides this, we may always look *outside* ourselves for cues to fulfillment. This can lead to compulsive activity. We are, then, outer-directed rather than inner-(being) directed. Eventually, within the person whose focus is only on the active life, who does not engage in reverie or know how to daydream, stress erupts. Life becomes broken into isolated compartments, "fragmenting outside us and within us." The lack of a sense of being "rejects us to the exterior of things; thus we are always outside. We are always *opposite* things, opposite the world, opposite other people with their mottled humanity."[28] *Competing becomes compulsive.* Unfamiliar with our interior self, we "hide our depths," having no way to articulate them.

A life in which activity or work is interrupted only for relaxation or "fitness exercise" is *reactive;* a life that alternates work with reverie is *restorative.* Or as Bachelard puts it elsewhere, "A communication of being develops . . . between the dreamer and his (or her) world."[29] We are drawn *to another place.*

For the child, the intimacy of home is the most familiar, most formative intimacy in the child's life. How then can the child dare to leave home? According to Bachelard, dreaming and reverie animate the nerves of the future. The *dream* enables the going forth to meet the world. Your daydreams pushed you out of the nest just as mine did.

We are confronted here by a marvelous paradox. The formative intimacy of home protects the daydreaming. But through the daydream comes the call to leave the intimacy of the home. Conversely, Bachelard sees "a dynamic rivalry between house and universe" which he explores and symbolizes by portraying a house buffeted by a hurricane. We cling to the protection of the house, yet it is this very house that prepares us for the hurricanes of the world. "Come what may the house helps us to say: I will be an inhabitant of the world, in spite of the world."[30]

Intimacy with Immensity

For children formation for mission starts with home and day-dreaming. Home forms us as persons, gives us the sense of *being the same as myself.* Home helps us to learn how to discern values and mores, to discover spiritual intimacy. Daydreaming can shape the desire to become a pilgrim as it is often the contemplative link within us between ourselves and an image of God's kingdom. Church and home are both significant in shaping how we come *to envision the world and God as well as the world with God, and God with the world.*

Without meaning, purpose, and spiritual vitality, our immense world may continue to make noise. But if we don't learn how to live on intimate terms with it, our immense world may become simply and solely a noise.

Intimate immensity. How can one be intimate with immense space? Bachelard handles this idea with grace.

Within ourselves there is an analogous interior immensity; consequently we can experience intimacy with the immensity of our earth. This striking insight synthesizes self and our created world, both enabled by the giver of all true gifts. Bachelard reveals noteworthy insights about the kinds of natural space that evoke contemplative spirituality and mirror the interior places within us.

The Desert and the Night

The persistence in spiritual imagery of the desert and the night is not fanciful; this imagery reflects elements that are integral to who we are as God-created persons within a God-created universe. The immensity of the desert mirrors the immensity within ourselves. The immensity of night awakens us to "the desire for confrontation" with "the infinite universe."

Jesus was driven into the desert by the Spirit. The desert experience, one that is always an experience of open, desolate space, reveals the open and infinite depth of interior "space." What is natural and *exterior* to us, what awes us, is akin to what is natural and *interior.* Jesus experienced, in the desert, a process that battered him just as our spiritual as well as physical desert experiences batter us. Yet it was in the desert that Jesus first articulated his faith and his destiny, and he did this through confrontation with evil. And it was in the desert that he experienced the angels ministering to him.

The image of the desert, as spiritual literature for ages has testified, draws us into an encounter with the *"inner intensity"* evoked by who we are as solitary persons affixed to the contingent and vulnerable human condition. At some time, each of us becomes "a dream-haunted traveler" within a desert.

In the months before my mother moved into a nursing home, entering her room felt like stepping into the desert. Everything seemed dry—her skin, the air, the bedclothes. She had failed greatly, her body seemed almost lifeless, her disposition was unusually harsh. Each time I opened the door, the *desert wandering I felt interiorly* during those weeks intensified.

Bachelard suggests that through the experience of "wandering," with no exit, no solace, no finality in sight, *the depth of our inner space becomes known to us.* Strangely, the "interiorization of the desert does not correspond to a sense of inner emptiness." In desert-wandering, one finally comes to realize an *adherence to an inner substance.* Before that discovery is made, however, one may feel as if one's spirit had vanished. "I was a desert within a desert."[31]

The *immensity of night* is different from the immensity of the desert. The immensity of night, the darkness with the stars, the darkness without the stars, reveals a paradox. Night heightens for us the discrepancy between small and large. We may, experiencing the dark night, feel minuscule, yet there is perhaps no time when we feel so related to the farthest star in space. Georgia O'Keefe treasured that experience. "My life is very pleasant this year—one of the events was a particularly brilliant star."[32]

The night is dark, yet only in the night can we see what the light of day blinds us to—the moon, the stars, those signs that there *is* a universe beyond our earth. In the darkness that is the immensity of night, we cannot see our own hand before our own face, yet, in spite of that hiddenness, we can see the hand of the universe and sense it drawing us into a world without end.

When we feel most acutely the smallness of ourselves, we sense most acutely that we and the immensity that is the universe are "two wedded creatures ... united in the dialogue of their own solitude."[33] In this intimacy we may come to "sense the concordance of world immensity with intimate depth of being."[34] It may feel like a loving parental figure bending over a child.

As Edith Stein said, "The night takes away the use of our senses, it impedes our movements, paralyzes our faculties; it condemns us to solitude and makes our own selves shadowy and ghostlike. It is a foretaste of death. And this not only has a natural, but also a psychological and spiritual significance. . . . Before we try to grasp what this is we have to realize that even the cosmic night has a double aspect. The dark and uncanny night has as its contrast the gentle, magic night, flooded by the soft light of the moon. . . . All that is hard, sharp or crude is now softened and smoothed; features which in the clear daylight never appear are here revealed; voices, too, are heard which the noise of the day tends to drown. All this has its effects also in the psychological and spiritual spheres. . . . The spirit . . . can be drawn into the deep relationships of its own being and life. . . . And there is a deep and grateful rest in the peace of the night."[35]

The Forest

When we enter a forest, we soon know that its space is not the same as the space from which we have come. After a while, even if a touch of anxiety descends, we feel pulled, "going deeper and deeper into a limitless world. Soon, if we do not know where we are going, we no longer know where we are."

Even though the forest is large in scale, *enclosure is felt*. Within the forest there is a sense of "presence." Experiencing the forest, for Bachelard, is experiencing the "presence of immediate immensity, of the immediate immensity of its depth." In the deep forest there is immense silence, yet "The quiet trembles and shudders."[36]

Though psychically an illusion, forests seem imbued "with the mystery of . . . space prolonged indefinitely."[37] The forest engenders inner peace. "In the forest, I am my entire self. Everything is possible in my heart just as it is in its hiding places in ravines."[38] Deep in the woods of the forest I know I am in a place I did not create. I know it is a world created by no other human. It is "other."

A meadow is also "other." To both I can say, "You are not me." Yet my relationship with the forest differs from my relationship with the green and flowered meadow. The forest is always a "before-me, before-us" kind of other while the meadow is a "with-me, with-us" kind of other. That's why I may feel awe and aloneness while treading through a forest, yet experience a sense of companionship, even if I am solitary, when I walk through a meadow.

Certain forests evoke a hidden grandeur, yet we do not back away. We inhabit. We let ourselves be intimate with this immense non-I. We may experience what Jules Supervielle perceives: the forest as a mirror of our interior life: we are "sensitive inhabitants of the forests of ourselves."[39]

Interior Change

We may think we go on a vacation by the ocean to relax and rest our bodies, but we actually want to be "in an absolute elsewhere that bars the way to the forces that hold us imprisoned in the 'here.' "[40] When we choose sand and sea we are choosing a natural setting in which we are powerless. We may be persons who strive day in and day out to be assertive beings, not letting ourselves be outdone or done in by any other creature, even the pet dog, but when we step from that immense stretch of sand into that limitless sea, we relinquish every nudge to control.

In other words we do not so much "change place, we change our nature."[41] What we savor is not so much the place to which we've changed, but the *nature of ourselves that has changed.* We may acknowledge the beauty of *that* change far less than we acknowledge the beauty of the place that is a change from our familiar place. Yet the change we sense within is why we are drawn again and again to a place like the ocean. What we do with our leisure reveals, often, who we are spiritually.

When the oppressiveness of life makes us feel desolate, instead of bending low under its brutalizing force, we may need to "come away" at least interiorly, and imagine a place of natural immensity where we have experienced interior healing through change.

"Space, vast space, is the friend of being."[42] We seek the vistas

Bachelard describes—the forest, the night, the desert, the ocean—
for what happens to us when we contemplate them, not for what
happens to them because we contemplate them. The place continues to exist in its being as God created it.

If vast space is a *friend* of being, we, out of our intimacy with
this friend, have the responsibility of protecting it and what it
traditionally symbolizes. These "places" are the great shared spaces
of our earth; ownership is not mine, not yours, *it is ours and God's.*
The intimacy may be felt personally, but the authority and responsibility to protect it derive from mutuality with that immensity and
with one another and with God.

Responsibility for Shared Space

Immense space, God-created and evocative of intimacy within
human peoples, is a spiritual treasure too valuable to be destroyed
or scarred. We need these vistas to sense "the marvels God has
wrought," to know our God is the creator God and to know that
God's creativity always surpasses our own. We need these spaces to
know ourselves, to know the immensity of our interiority. We need
to continue to let God own them through mutual responsibility
with others. We have come dangerously close to believing we own
for ourselves, not for the sake of our children, even the heavens—a
new colonialism. This self-indulgent attitude may persist so long as
the coming generation is perceived as solely the responsibility of
natural parents and not of *all the adults* in a given culture.

Within ourselves contraries are reconciled, healing correspon-
dences are made, when season by season we experience the vastness
of nature and sense our own dignity which is so often diminished
by the mechanized, computerized, dehumanized workplaces we
inhabit.

The "inner immensity (we experience when we encounter the
immensity of space) . . . gives meaning (to) the visible world."[43]
Without that meaning, we might categorize the physical matter
before our eyes in a totally utilitarian way as developers often do or
in a purely objective way as geologists do. An affirmation of *spiritual* connectedness is crucial for the survival to the world.

For peace and for justice, for the sake of the commonwealth of

God, we are called to perceive this world as a shared home for all of humankind. This sense of intimacy emerges from within us because it originates *from our engagement* with place, not from the place itself. Engaged, our spirit surrenders to God the prerogative traditionally associated with God—*the power to initiate and to put closure on human history.*

3

THE WORLD-DREAMING PILGRIM AND PRAYER

The world as a shared home: others can close their doors to the world; for Christians the world is a shared home. No amount of preaching or teaching can fix that perception within the believer. To be believed and embraced calls for conversion in how we see the world.

When we find ourselves naming within ourselves the world as our shared home, rivalry between mine and yours disappears. We *move into relationship,* into living on intimate terms with the universe that houses us. Momentary insights are not lasting relationships, however. Our spiritual journey moves forward when we embrace the realization that this universe home was created by a vast and loving power beyond ourselves and belongs to the one who created it. The only claim we make is that our universe-home is a world *given* to us and a world enhanced by a *giving from us.* The created world is generative to us. A relationship imbued with generativity becomes our response to the world.

The house-world rivalry Bachelard cites cannot be underestimated, however. If the world is not a welcoming place, we may lose all desire to enter it. We may stay in our enclaves—our homes, our safe suburban towns, our condominium complex, our country clubs, our church communities that decry the neo-paganism of the world without moving into the world to convert it. We may confine ourselves to our private, domesticated homes rather than our universe-home and become as small in spirit and narrow in virtue as the enclave we inhabit.

Christians willing to explore the world may begin with a new experience of God-created space and discover that the world can be a welcoming place. Eventually they may find that they not only care about the world but they also act on that caring no matter where they live. If we are these believers, then we may find ourselves being led to contemplate our global universe. Through this we discover that in "dreaming on the universe, one is always *departing; one lives in the elsewhere.*"[1]

We are beginning to be pilgrims. It is as if an "exchange of being"[2] has been initiated between the interior immensity of self and the exterior immensity of the world. The world is acknowledged, through our experience, in its own reality. My ownership of the world succumbs to a sense of shared ownership—with nature, with others like and unlike myself, with God. *The world as shared home becomes internalized within.*

Laurie Forfa, director of nursing at a hospital, has this kind of consciousness of our world. In an article defending letter-writing, she tells about writing to Li Peng, the acting prime minister of the People's Republic of China, one to Hastings Kazmuzu Banda, president of Malwai, and one to Turgut Ozal, prime minister of Turkey. Each letter was on behalf of a specific prisoner of conscience as part of Amnesty International. Ms. Forfa goes on to describe other ways she is involved with life beyond the small town in a rural part of New England where she lives.

> I write to Sens. Edward Kennedy and John Kerry and Congressman Silvio Conte about apartheid in South Africa, the building of a memorial for Vietnam nurses, funding for nursing education and programs to deal with homelessness and hunger. I've sent letters to state (representatives) about the Massachusetts health care bill and the controversial struggle over upgrading the educational requirements for entry into nursing practice.

She also dreams of a better life for poor people in the south.

> I still send letters of friendship every month to the two Mississippi families with whom I'm matched through the Box Project, a family-to-family anti-poverty program. My words (along with boxes of food, clothing and household goods) join those of nearly 2,000 BP helpers across the country, some of whom have been mailing their letters since the mid-'60s.[3]

Ms. Forfa also sends letters of hope and encouragement to Mikhail and Elena and Polina, a refusenik family in Leningrad.

And the tradition is being handed down. Her daughter Allison has pen pals in England, Israel, and the state of Washington.

Mission depends on internalizing the world as a shared home as Laurie Forfa has done. Such a process within a church community can help to form us to be a people of peace and justice. We become world-dreaming pilgrims who do not "regard the world as an object." We become companions of the world, absorbed in contemplating the companion.[4] "The dreamer believes that between self and the world there is an exchange of looks as in the double look from the loved man to the loved woman."[5]

If we do not see *the peoples of the world* as well as the universe in any meaningful way *within the context in which they live their lives,* we may not relate to them as *people.* An instance of this in my own life concerns South Africa. For a long time I had seen glimpses of the situation there on the nightly news. I had read articles and Winnie Mandela's autobiography. But it wasn't until PBS did a full-scale series on South Africa, showing the history of the peoples there, that I saw the historical and everyday life *context* of the black people in their struggle. Only then was my heart deeply moved. Only then did I feel *related* to the people who had for years "entered" my living room on the nightly news.

Shared Space

How we live, as well as the decisions we make as a citizenry, affect how others live in cultures the world over. Few of us are naive enough to believe that the way citizens live in highly developed nations will alone alleviate the plight of those in poverty-stricken nations. But how we live affects how we perceive the world we live in and how we care about that world.

When we move out and reach outward to others, we are also called to move inward and explore our interior world of meaning and depth. A part of the process of becoming world-dreaming pilgrims, whether done alone or with others, is to contemplate the meaning of shared space in one's life. One way to initiate this is to identify the "shared spaces" that one savors. For example, there are few manifestations of shared space that I savor as much as I do a train; a journey by train actually provides a kind of spiritual experience for me.

Trains are unique in that they are "moving spaces." A car or airplane can never be that kind of space because a car or plane is standardized and seldom varies enough to establish singularity. But a filled train has flavor and texture, it evokes its own set of mores, and it invites relationship. There is a need in me to ride a train, preferably long distance, almost every season of the year. The reason is not to get from *here* to *there*. It is the sheer contentment of sharing space.

One of the blessings of sharing a train is walking through a darkened coach car late at night. As I walk past the sleeping bodies sprawled side by side, I feel awe.

That little child in the neat sailor suit, hugging his teddy bear as he sleeps beside the wizened old man with the toothless mouth and shabby clothes . . . that young woman with the pale face and the mousy hair half-hidden by a beret . . . that tiny lady in the calico dress snoring gently beside the tall, thin, black youth with a pic stuck in the back of his Afro: where else in America can we find the aged and the frail, the athletic and the disabled, the black and the white, the down-and-outer and the well-to-do, close enough to touch one another yet sleeping through the night? Where else besides on this fast-moving place called a train do we experience this intimate proximity among remarkably different people—without fear of mugging, murder and rape?

As I walk slowly down the darkened aisle my heart is moved by my sleeping companions and by the fact that the vulnerability of this night in this neighborhood does not invite violence. The weak and the strong are in the same "place," both literally and figuratively, owned by the moving place called a train, a place that has become trusted space. Deep within I sense the promise of justice, harmony, and peace to be found in the commonwealth of God.

Places That Own Us

Beds are places we let own us. We surrender to them in a spirit of trust. If we didn't, we wouldn't fall asleep. Falling asleep is an act of surrender which comes from letting a place own me, metaphorically of course.

I know a man who lets farm soil own him. For years he has

been a city dweller but each spring he feels an urge to drive out to the country and take a piece of black, moist, midwestern farm earth in his hands, raise it to his nose to smell it, then let it fall through his fingers. In a sense he surrenders to that place where he is crouched down. He lets it, momentarily, own him. He claims that the spring event each year is a spiritual experience. He grew up in farm country.

Some folks are owned by a cabin in the woods, others by a street corner where they hang out.

Places We Resist

It can be interesting to contemplate space where we resist surrender. In a hospital strangers sleep side by side, but a hospital is resisted space. For a year, two days a week, I was a chaplain in a large university hospital with six buildings. The pattern of initial resistance and eventual surrender by most patients to this place intrigued me. Some came to a sense of surrender out of a defeatist attitude: "There is nothing I can do about the place so I might as well let it have me." The care and attention others received was a welcome or new experience for them, one that converted suspicion and resistance into trust.

During that whole year, within one group of patients I found a great resistance to surrender through their entire stay. It was as if they were saying, "If I can't own this place, I certainly won't let it own me. We'll fight a tug-of-war to the end." Each of these resisters was a successful professional or business man; all were white and often affluent; most were in mid-life. They may have been unable to admit that others "own this place" and I am at their mercy. Years of strategy to avoid ever being at another's mercy had hardened them into making surrender of self a taboo. One of these resisters kept repeating to me and to himself, "Before you know it I'll be back at the office."

"You never left the office," I wanted to reply. "There's only one place that owns you, and that's the workplace." Later, with a pang, the realization of how enfeebled, physically and spiritually, this patient was would come to me, allowing some of the compassion I felt for the other patients trickle into my resistance toward him.

It is essential to react to hospitals, of course, when they abuse or take advantage of us as patients. On the other hand, hospitals are for healing. Healing implies some kind of mutuality, some kind of letting go of control and handing it over to others or to God. Sad to say some of us try to own, *by controlling,* every place we enter—the home we live in, the office or shop we work in, the tennis court or bowling alley we go to for recreation, the barber shop or beauty salon where we let our hair be cut (watching nervously in the mirror that reflects the frown on our face). No matter how affluent we might be we are more to be pitied than envied, for our darkest desire is the desire of the despot—to own the whole world.

Loss of Place

What do we experience when we're forced to lose a place that has meaning for us?

Eight months after moving to Boston, we received a note from our landlady, a recent widow, telling us that she wanted a married son to live with her, so would we please vacate our apartment by the beginning of the next month. After the disappointment wore off, I felt lonely and vulnerable. Our response to that loss was mild compared to how we felt in early February 1987, ironically on the feast of the Purification, when a fire blazed through the apartment above us before dawn. At first we were in shock. When Kerry arrived, without advance warning the next day from Albany, I blazed at her, "Why did you come? It's no big deal! We told you all we had was water damage!"

"Mom, you've lost your home."

"It's just an apartment we *rent.*"

"Mom, you've lost your *home!*"

She knew what I could not, in shock, admit until later when I fell into the grip of *reactive* emotions—fear, anger, grief at the sudden loss of familiar home space.

Our apartment was totally soaked. By law in Massachusetts when an electrical fire happens, electricity cannot be turned on until the whole system is replaced. Consequently, there was no light or heat in the apartment for weeks. After work, George and I would rush out to the apartment to "clean up." What that meant essentially was discovering by dim light more loss. After a half-hour, dispositions would plummet. One of us would say, "I'll sit in the car and wait for you."

We felt the loss because that rented space had become *valorized* by our living in it for six years. Without our realizing it, over time we had invested part of ourselves in it and in the objects that had become familiar to us. For a time, no amount of considering how others were in a worse predicament could stop those strong emotions from overwhelming us. Gradually we found ourselves becoming more sensitive to others who suffer loss, especially the homeless and those who suffer a loss similar to ours but without the insurance that allowed us to live in the very supportive and protective temporary shelter we had. We also became aware of people with no major trauma but who lead water-damaged lives. One day in prayer an image of a friend appeared. And I sensed for the first time that her vocation seems to be that of reaching out to people with water-damaged lives. In the whole scheme of ministries and mission in the church right now, she, too, isn't appreciated. My friend *notices* while the rest of us go our way without sensing the suffering that's there from being worn down by small, daily losses, from mildewed dreams, from disappointments dampening the spirit. My friend notices the *context* of people's lives.

Developing a sense of the context of people's lives sometimes unfolds when we develop a deeper sensitivity to our own feelings about places we share, places that own us, places we resist, and places we lose.

Contemplating World and Prayer

Children are naturally contemplative. That is why their imaginations are so creative. They let themselves be drawn by what attracts them.

The first time after the fire that our granddaughter Nicole came to visit us, she seemed awed by the view from our high-rise temporary quarters. We contemplated together the river shimmering in the moonlight and the lights of the city stretched before us. Nicole then went to bed in the next room. In the morning when Leslie awakened, Nicole was missing from her bed. In panic Leslie looked in the bathtub, searched in the closet. No Nicole. When she opened the drapes, there was Nicole asleep by the window. In the night or at dawn she had obviously awakened and slipped under the drapes to see again the immensity of the world that the window invited.

We can sometimes learn from children because the ability to *contemplate* the world begins by becoming entranced by what is *beyond* us. Immensity in nature attracts and awes adults as well as children; from its ability to magnetize us, we can sense how God draws us. Our spiritual intimacy with the world may emerge from a sense of intimacy with God, or it can lead to a sense of intimacy with God.

Letting Reverie Digest Reality

Some places draw us into reverie and let us see and listen to how God envisions the world.

A quiet pond is an invitation to reverie. By still water, "the dreamer *adheres to the repose of the world.*"[6] We who are so intimate with the clamor of the world can there discover the world in repose. By still water, "the universe has lost all function of *against.*" Opposition ceases to be recognized. I begin to feel "nothing more *against*" me. In this union the spirit meditates. There is a "forgetfulness of self which descends to the depths of being."[7]

Near still water, gazing at the trees reflected in the pond, we learn a simple lesson for imaging the world: within the water, "the colors of the *reflected* world are tenderer, softer . . . those colors born by the reflections belong to an idealized universe." In that reflection we may hear God urge us to always go a little beyond the real in order to know all that the real can be.[8]

In "Our Task Is To Create Worlds" (*Commonweal,* June 2, 1989) Emil Antonucci speaks of crossing the bridge over the East River between Brooklyn and Manhattan when he was an adolescent. As he walked he watched a patch of reflecting, golden light move across the water. "It suddenly struck me that the entire river surface was, at once, both dark *and* radiant, depending on one's angle of vision, but clearly both. I still don't know the 'meaning' of that image, but I have never lost the feeling of its power: the reconciliation of contradiction, the embodiment of both appearance and inner reality. God around us, within us. . . ."

Throughout the centuries some Christians in every culture have been able to be attentive to those locked in suffering and pain because they have the capacity to see "the embodiment of both appearance and inner reality." The reflection of the shore in the still water, the doubling of worlds, is in a sense the vocation of the Christian, for the Christian can never shy away from the *reality* of the world but is also called to dream of the *potential* for God's kingdom within that reality. When we experience that "two in one" we begin to feel free to embrace the *cost* of helping God transform the reality of the world into a commonwealth of peace and justice.

When we stand apart from the world of work and treat ourselves to the world of nature and silence, we sometimes sense the intertwining of our faith and our destiny. This phenomenon may account for the renaissance of the retreat house. When retreatants go to Campion Retreat Center, for example, a place not far from the city of Boston, they inhabit the small prayer room and the forest behind the retreat house—space that is enclosure and space that has immensity. Both evoke interior harmony. That sensibility may be one reason why, in a large survey of Catholic adolescents, a sizable number, without solicitation, cited a retreat house experience when queried about their faith.[9]

At Eastern Point Retreat House in Gloucester, retreatants sit in repose in the evening before the fireplace; during the day they walk down to a nearby still pond. Both places evoke intimacy with God through reverie.

Bachelard notes, "To be warm is a way of dreaming for the body." Before the fire, as we become warm, "the well-being of the world invades us from all directions."[10] We "experience an expanding cosmos of repose. . . . Our being is no longer chained . . . is no longer obliged to make strong affirmations, decisions . . . before the hearth, the dreamer is alternately soul and body, body and soul."[11]

Throughout the ages, millennium after millennium, men and

women sat before a fire in the evening, letting the warmth before them become warmth within them, *letting reverie digest the reality of the day.* Central heating and television offer an entirely different experience, one that represents progress perhaps but with a consequent loss of a humble but precious human means for integration, an end of the day process for *"letting myself become the same as myself."*

> In front of the fireplace, a dreamer experiences a reverie which *deepens.* Dreaming before the fire . . . one knows a sort of stable reverie . . . of integration. Then the images have roots. In following them, we adhere to the world; we take root in the world.[12]

In order for that to happen we need those times when reverie digests reality. In reveries like those described before the fire or by a still pond, we "melt into the world." We become, in a sense, "reconciled to the glory of abolishing (self) without, however, dying."[13]

Those times when we have been drawn into a sense of intimacy by a natural phenomenon, like a forest or an ocean, awaken us to the realization that *we are already formed with a capacity for intimacy with the world.* From this can unfold *the responsibility and authority to preserve this world.* For Christians the intimacy the world in its immensity evokes calls us "to pour ourselves into the world."[14] Lay Christian believers, in particular, can pray, "Give us this day our daily . . . hunger for the world."

Bringing the World into Prayer

If the mission we embrace is peacemaking, we need those times when we feel "nothing against us." If the mission we embrace is enhancing justice, we need those times when we let reverie digest the reality of an unjust world. Whatever our mission, we need those times when we experience "being the same as myself." We need to know that we are more than the endeavors in which we are engaged in the workplace or the civic place.

American missionaries from Latin America, from Africa, from Asia, often come to the two retreat houses mentioned earlier. There they are renewed by the expansion-of-being evoked by the immensity of nature and the immensity of God. This renews their commitment to embark again, sometimes to new third world settings, which will, in turn, form them again. While on retreat they dream, but they see *the peoples of the world, not themselves at the center of their dreams.*

There are places that have already and unwittingly formed us; the Christian pilgrim is called to understand this early formation and to build on it by reaching out to other places, new places, and inviting these places to form him or her. This is the vocation of missionaries, and all of us are called in one way or another to be on mission. To be on mission calls for an adulthood in which we no longer have to be at the center of our daydreams.

Through reverie, images, and world-dreaming we experience "a subjective, clarifying force"[15] that may activate the heart while opening the mind. That becomes more likely when prayer becomes part of our life.

Vatican II was a call to Catholic Christians to "open up to the world." The earth was finally recognized within the church as "valorized space," as a place of inherent value. Before Vatican II, the world was looked upon as a kind of rented apartment, a temporary setting with little or no value. It took the trauma of world wars and holocausts, it seems, for us to begin to realize, as my daughter Kerry put it, "This is your *home!*" It may not be permanent but it does have *value.* The aftermath of the war, and Vatican II, helped Catholic believers perceive not only that the world is our home, but that it is a home too many humans are brutalizing, too many humans are despoiling.

In order to become generative regarding the peoples of the world we begin by valuing the world, by acknowledging the ways in which it is generative to us, the ways it mentors us. This deepens our acceptance of the world as *shared space, owned by all peoples* rather than by particular, privileged nations. By seeing the spiritual value of the earth and world, we begin to care about those with whom we share this earth and world.

We are talking here about *a spiritual foundation for mission.* Without such a foundation we run the risk of doing mission the way networks report the news of the world—in an isolated, sporadic, fragmentary fashion.

The modern age in which we live may need what Bachelard

urged—the development of a "psychology of the universe" to complement the established psychology of the individual person. That does not mean that nations would disappear. But in the age of the greenhouse effect, of nuclear might and potential madness, nations are called to collaborate with the globe as shared space. We all experience "shared space" at times in our life, some of us more frequently than others. It is not a Martian proposition. But it may call for new perspectives in spirituality.

Medieval models of spirituality are inadequate for our age because the medieval vision was necessarily based on a limited worldview. The only way to lessen resistance and really *receive* the immensity of the world is to let it transform the intensity of our interior being—to let it heal us of parochialism and self-absorption. To do this we need to discover formative ways to unite the outside cosmos with the inside cosmos of who we are.

A modern spirituality teaches us how to live *emotionally* and *spiritually* with the place we call world. It converts those of us "who have everything but this doesn't seem to mean anything" into a people who have less perhaps but who find meaning in more. It converts us into a people who perceive the world as more than chaos, more than marketplace, more than vacation place. This spirituality, matched to modern times and perceptions of space, welcomes "images and ideas, contemplation and experience at the same time."[16] This spirituality resonates with the signs of our times without flagellating us with guilt. This spirituality reveals to us a sense of destiny that, if embraced, thrusts us forward to accomplish mission.

But that destiny can only be embraced if it is rooted in love— rooted in the love of God, rooted in love for friends and family, rooted in love for the world which means *its peoples*. To transform love into mission means to be free enough and secure enough within the above relationships to let this love *inspire imagination.*

Prayer can happen when a person experiences reverie, contemplates an image, surrenders to a daydream, *and desires to have this time be a time of companionship with God.*

Words do not create prayer. Prayer is created by the heart. A little parable from life illustrates this.

My husband and I finish eating dinner. We sit at the table for a while watching the purple finches, the nuthatch, the pine siskind, and the turtledove feeding on our small back balcony. Occasionally I point. Then he points. Neither of us speaks for the twenty minutes we spend gazing at the birds. Finally as the last finch leaves her perch, we stir, smile at each other, touch hands, and rise from the table.

Were we communicating with each other?

Someone watching us might say no. We'd both say yes. In fact, we might say it was the best communication between us of the day. We might even admit that our communication in silence by the window had healed a hurtful communication that had taken place earlier in the day.

In a similar way, your contemplating the world, and your desiring God to be present contemplating with you, could be the best communication between you and God of this day, or this week. It could be in silence, accompanied by your pointing to an aspect of the world and God pointing to an aspect of the world, letting the world be your silent bonding place. Elements of reverie and imagination can be found in some of the most profound prayer experiences. An example from my prayer comes to mind, a prayer that happened fifteen years ago yet is as fresh as yesterday because of the power of image.

For several years I had corresponded with a man living in India, a man I had never met. We had exchanged pictures of family; he had asked me to write to his wife when she was expecting their first child to tell her what happens in childbirth as she was too shy to ask relatives. Sometimes in his letters he would describe the poverty in India or the destructive force of a great flood. I would take this suffering to prayer and convert it, there, to worry and futility. One day, however, I just sat with God and saw with my inner eye a map of India and the sea around it. Relinquishing thought, I stayed with the image of the map. Gradually the triangular shape of the country evolved into the shape of a heart. The suffering of this heart was sensed as blood flowing into the sea. This image touched depths within me, depths of sorrow and desire for solace for the people of India, in a way that no prior prayer had done.

Did the image bear fruit in action? It did because the image was a "subjective, clarifying force." To experience it I had to *stop thinking* and stay with the intimacy that the contemplation evoked.

Through contemplation even a small incident or simple symbol from nature can be invested with immensity because "the contemplative attitude is such a great human value that it confers immensity upon an impression."[17]

The prayer led me to feel a deep desire to be more generative toward the world, to give some response to the needs of the world. At first I felt almost despondent at the end of the prayer with the image, but I stayed with the image, and gradually other images came that helped me to see how I could enflesh that desire in responsibilities I could assume closer to home. A strong sense came that our policies in the United States often affect people in third world countries, and I began, through pressure on legislators, to try to affect those policies *here*. And I discovered that I could relate more directly to third world peoples here. After the prayer I started teaching reading to students from Africa.

Even as I write this a memory emerges from that experience. One day on campus word came that one of my students' mother had died. I rushed to her basement room in the dorm where Wanjera was surrounded by students from Africa and black students from the United States. In a wail, Wanjera opened her arms to me as she called my name. For four hours, I held Wanjera as we kept vigil with her. Through the narrow basement window the sun grew dim. Twilight melted into a darkness that embraced us in our shared grief.

Images of Our Universe-Home

Photography and film, graphics and televisions, have converted this century into an age of images. This fact needs more attention in the church where we may at times forget the power of images. In daily life an image-centered age may help us to nurture images that come to us in prayer and those that are gifts to us from poets and prophets. With this in mind it is fitting to close this chapter with three images that evoked for me global intimacy. One of the images came to me in prayer; the other two were brought to prayer.

The first, an *image of grass,* is from a Swedish poet, Arthur Lundkvist:

Grass
    carries away the rain on its millions
    of backs,
    holds back the soil with its
    millions of toes

    . . . .
The grass
    answers each menace by growing.
    Grass loves the world as much
    as itself.
    Grass is happy, whether times
    are hard or not.
    . . . grass wanders
    on its feet.

When I brought into my prayer the way this poet images grass, along with Bachelard's insight that the poet "puts the bent-bending being *on its feet*,"[18] I sensed Jesus—Jesus in the gospels over and over putting "bent-bending" people on their feet. Then I sensed people of faith from all over the world as God's grass—carrying away the rain that falls on the just and the unjust, holding God's good soil, answering each menace by growing, loving the world as much as they love themselves, happy whether times are hard or not, wandering as pilgrims on their feet.

The second image of our universe-home came to me on retreat. The chaos and terror, the militarization and sufferings of the world, as I brooded over them on that retreat, brought a kind of paralysis into my prayer. Then one night in the darkness of the chapel I saw our planet as it has been pictured from space. All at once, I sensed it as the lost sheep of the universe. This sudden, perceptive image opened my heart. Tears came, and I let the sorrow pent up for months flow. Later I sensed the strength to beg God to search for this lost sheep—to help us restore it, to enable this within the fold of God's embrace.

The last universe-home image is that of a nest. It is from Bachelard's chapter "Nests" in *Poetics of Space*. According to Bachelard, "A nest . . . is a precarious thing, and yet it sets us to *daydreaming of security*."[19]

Twigs and grass and bits of twine do not by themselves make a nest. From these materials the bird makes a home. How does the bird, "a worker without tools," shape the mound of twigs, grass and bits of vine into a circle called a nest? "In reality," says Jules Michelet, "a bird's tool is its own body, that is, its breast, with which it presses and tightens its material until they have become absolutely pliant, well-blended and adapted. . . ."[20]

This "house (is) built by and for the body, taking form from the inside . . . in an intimacy that works physically."[21] Later Bachelard says, "The world is a nest, and an immense power holds the inhabitants of the world in this nest."[22] After reading this, I brought the image to prayer where I saw what the birds do in shaping the nest as what Christians are called to do within the world-nest upheld by the power of God. From the *inside,* from the intimacy of a known world of work and family and friendship and civic commitment, Christians imitate the bird by shaping our world from the materials given.

"The house is the bird's very person; it is its form and its most immediate effort, I shall even say its suffering. The result is only obtained by constantly repeated pressure of the breast. There is not one of these blades of grass that, in order to make it curve and hold the curve, has not been pressed on countless times by the bird's heart, surely with difficulty."[23]

The nest is shaped by the fidelity of the bird to the task, a task "which make a surface originally bristling and composite into one that is smooth and soft."[24]

Mission is never accomplished by positioning oneself outside the reality of the world and judging it. Mission is accomplished by believers who dare to be inside the world, acknowledging from that perspective that the surface is diverse, complex, and bristling. Mission is the constant, circling pressure of Christians and others of good will, from within the world, until the surface is smooth and soft, a nest, a fit habitation for humankind. The purpose of church is to enable and strengthen these world-dreaming pilgrims as they shape the world, from the inside, with the materials at hand and with the pressure of hearts that must *love* this world to respond to the call of mission.

4

MISSION THROUGH LAY WITNESS
AND PROCLAMATION

Tell What You Have Seen

After the death of Jesus, Mary Magdalene could hardly separate herself from the place of Jesus' burial. She rushed toward the tomb as early as the light of dawn would allow. In John's account, we see her rush to Peter, then rush back to stay by the tomb. Overcome with grief and weeping, she still searches—bending over, looking inside, sharing straight from the heart when she is questioned: "They have taken my Lord away. I don't know where they have laid him!" Then the gardener questions as the angels did. Her grief-stricken heart is bold, "Tell me where you have put him—I will go."

Go to Jesus, go to Jesus—the beat of her heart that morning contrasted with those who were drifting away or lost in doubt. Finally, Mary Magdalene, her heart frantic with loss and desire, heard the call of her name, and she—recognized by Jesus—recognizes Jesus. In this narrative we find that tutoring follows recognition: The relationship I have with the one I am going to, says Jesus, is the relationship you and the others have as well. Go—go find the others—go tell them what you have seen. Mary Magdalene is called, tutored, commissioned.

Mary Magdalene teaches an incomparable lesson about the foundation for Christian mission—that it is to be rooted in the passion of love for Christ.

In the time between Gethsemane and Golgotha, we see in scripture a community falling apart. Just one betrayer within that community was needed for it to happen. Then, as Evelyn Underhill puts it, "those whose courage and fidelity failed at the first withering touch of the passion" scattered. After the death of Jesus, Thomas was lost in anger and doubt; Cleopas and his companion leave the city; even Peter and John at the tomb seem to be solving a problem—a missing body—more than grieving the loss of the one whose life had given meaning to their lives.

Mary Magdalene refused to let her heart go into the dark chamber of hidden self-pity, of martyred hurt. She refused to stay in the upper room with the others at the wake-without-a-body. Nor did she hurry away from the city to make a shrine out of the fact that she had been left behind.

Mary Magdalene didn't lean on the community or ask Peter's permission; she separated herself from the others and obeyed the love still vibrant in her heart for the one who had healed her and brought her to where she was that sorrowful week. Foolish love, her companions may have thought.

What is remarkable about Mary Magdalene is that she *grieved on her feet,* feet that were compelled to be on the move. A symbol of fidelity, she teaches us a great lesson today: to have a heart that remains fixed on the holy one even if the holy one seems missing from our lives—a heart that reveals itself to those who ask questions about the search.

Two on the Road to Emmaus

In John's gospel we also meet two who are rushing away from the tomb. What was the spiritual experience of Cleopas and his companion on the day they took that road toward Emmaus? It begins by meeting a stranger. Their knowing what the stranger doesn't seem to know puts them, initially, at an advantage. Speaking in general terms about the one from whom they are distancing themselves, Cleopas and his friend don't reveal how deeply each feels personally about the one who died on the cross. Instead it is the stranger who reveals what he feels about them—"so slow to believe!" They tutored him about the events of the past week, and now he tutors them about the whole context of scripture that led to the events concerning the prophet in whom many had placed their hopes.

On reaching Emmaus, Cleopas and his companion offer hospitality to the stranger who took the bread, said the blessing, broke the bread and handed it to them as recognition broke through.

Then the one who was no longer a stranger vanished. Reflecting on their experience, remembering their own reactions along the road ("our hearts burning within us"), helped them to see that what led to the recognition could not be separated from the sudden sight that came to them at supper. What their ears heard on the road, and what their eyes eventually saw, came together as one experience of risen life.

The Experience of the Doubter

The Thomas we meet in John's account was as resistant and rigid as rock. No leaving Jerusalem. No searching for the missing body of Jesus. Above all, no believing on the witness of what others had experienced. Thomas demanded his own experience.

"Give me your hand," Jesus says to him. What Cleopas *saw* in order to believe, what Mary *heard* in order to believe, Thomas must *touch*. Thomas must touch the wounds made by nails and the wound made by piercing spear. Overwhelming evidence, overwhelming acknowledgement: "My Lord and my God!"

Jesus responds with just a touch of tutoring about those who never see and those who never hear and those who never touch—yet they believe. The tutoring of Jesus in the story of Thomas is a consolation to those of us who believe without the evidence of sight, hearing or touch. It is also a lesson for us about mission. The story of Thomas is cautionary: many will not believe on our evidence—especially those whom we may want most *to* believe, relatives and close friends.

Diverse Religious Experience

In the narratives from scripture described above this proclamation comes to us through three *different* spiritual experiences. These narratives absorb our attention because they reveal how varied are the ways Jesus is encountered. The images within the stories are diverse: two together on a road; one alone who refuses to stop searching; one in the midst of community who refuses to be at one with the community; a stranger, bread, a gardener, wounds. Jesus comes and commissions a woman, then the community—

but he does not commission the ones with whom he breaks bread. He accepts hands held out in the hospitality of shelter and food. He refuses the hand of the one who reaches out to touch him. He reaches with his hand *for* the hand of the doubting one to enable the touch that turns desolation into consolation.

We savor the encounters with risen life recounted to us by the evangelists, but do we let ourselves be challenged by the diversity within them? Have they taught us to savor the religious experiences of the people in our own faith communities? In our church do we relish the *varieties* of religious experiences as much as we savor the variety of gifts and talents? Do we perceive that diverse faith experience is part of the gifts and talents lay believers donate to the upbuilding of the church? Do we even *listen* to those who tell tales that differ from our own or do we call these nonsense as some of the early disciples did?

When Jesus urged Mary Magdalene to tell what she had seen, it may have been because others would be tutored in faith by her proclaiming her experience. The command was to share first what she had seen *within the community of faith led by Jesus.* Within the church today small group gatherings encourage that kind of sharing, but what pulpit in today's church lets a woman like Mary Magdalene and a layman like Cleopas share their experiences of risen life? share their encounters in mission? Mission within the world will limp along until two modes of lay "voice" are heard with clarity *within the church.* One is the witness of the stories of spiritual vitality that lay believers experience in their ongoing life. The other is the proclamation of mission life recounted by lay adults.

Two Ways That Lay Voice Must Be Heard Within the Church

As a 1989 project of the Spirituality Task Force of the National Association for Lay Ministry, fifteen lay Catholics were interviewed in depth by a research team. What was striking was the number who were startled, amazed and delighted that someone within the church was finally asking them about their relationship with God. As one man put it, "I've been in the church for sixty-six years, and nobody has ever been the least bit interested in my relationship with God." It was profoundly moving to hear in these stories of faith so much evidence of God working in people's lives, evidence that if proclaimed would tutor others in faith.

I have been tutored in the past year by a voice of a lay woman who has not been inside a church for many, many months. About six months before my mother entered Neville Manor in Cambridge, I brought home a large picture of Jesus and the cross. My mother said to me, "Who's that fella? Some saint?"

I was stunned that my mother could, in her senility, fail to recognize Jesus. Mary was the next to go. That frightened me. Was my mother now too old for any kind of religious experience?

One afternoon when I went to visit my mother in the nursing home, she was quite excited. "I'm going to see my mother!" she said, her face aglow. "My mother wants to see me. I just sensed it so strong today. All of a sudden like, she called to me."

Everytime I went to see my mother for the next two weeks, all she wanted to tell me about was going to see her mother. Her anticipation was palpable. But she had questions: "How can we get to Northampton? How far is Northampton from here?"

One night she asked, "How old am I?"

"Eighty-eight," I replied.

"Well, if I'm eighty-eight years old, my mother must be awfully old. Maybe she doesn't live in Northampton anymore."

The following afternoon she said, "I've figured it out. My mother's in heaven. She's calling me from heaven."

Very quietly I said, "Do you want to visit her there?"

"No! Not yet." My mother sighed. "But you know, when you're at your very weakest like I am, the one you want to turn to more than anyone else is your mother. So I turn to her and I say, 'Dear Mamma, I love you so much!' And she says back to me, 'I love you, too.' "

Later my mother told me that she's glad she has a daughter she can talk to about her mother in heaven. I'm glad I have a vehicle so others can hear the story of my grandmother and my mother because it is a story that evangelizes and a story that tutors about the spiritual life. But knowing that so few lay voices have any amplifiers within the church for telling the stories of their encounters with God is agony for me.

Is my mother's story the story of an encounter with God? Is it a religious experience? To me, it's God, in the gentlest, most loving way, guiding my mother, through her mother, home.

Like Cleopas, like Mary Magdalene, like Thomas, like my mother, all of us are called to tell the stories of our encounters with God if any hope for substantial mission is to become a reality in the church. Mission today needs what it needed in gospel communities—variety of witnesses who share their experiences of God and of mission. Mission needs the firm foundation of spiritual depth; this foundation is built by the proclamation of those of us who have experienced God and engaged in mission, even if your story is about a stranger and mine is about a gardener and another's is about a mother. Or if your story is about seeing, and my story is about hearing, and another's is about touching. Or if your story is about being tutored after breaking bread, and my story is about being tutored after being called by name, and another's is about going home to Northampton and discovering that home is where heaven is. The movements toward God and from God that stir our hearts and our communities of faith are *always more significant than the symbols we use to express them.*

This lesson is revealed to us in the Pauline epistles, especially in the struggle concerning inclusivity. Could the early church be variegated or did the symbolization represented by circumcision and by abstaining from particular foods have to be imposed on all? Community won out over conformity then as it must now.

Even earlier we find, in the Pentecost experience, the descent of the Holy Spirit engendering a *variety* of spoken languages. Later centralization in the church abrogated the vernacular tongues for the language of Rome. One might say with the restoration of the vernacular through Vatican Council II, Pentecost was restored within the church.

The core of our faith is belief in God through Christ expressed all over the world in a variety of languages and cultures as the sign that the Holy Spirit is alive within the church. The upheaval and uprooting within the post-conciliar church may be a sign that the New Testament is being proclaimed and challenging anew—that the silent have started to speak, giving a witness that reveals that Christ and the Holy Spirit are not owned by a particular few, indeed are owned by none.

The second "voice" that must be heard is *lay voice through stories of faith transformed into mission.* The lay man mentioned above, who has never had an opportunity to talk about his relationship with God in the church, is a retired accountant who donates his efforts, full-time, toward running a center for those in need. His mission story has also never been told within the church.

Woundedness will continue to afflict the church so long as manifestations of the Holy Spirit found in the spirituality and the mission of lay believers remain barred from full inclusion.

Who Are We in the Missions of Our Very Real Lives?

What would a process look like today if it mirrored the witness and proclamation given in the earliest Christian communities? What would we hear if our lay sisters and lay brothers like our lay sister Mary Magdalene and our lay brother Cleopas proclaimed what they had seen and heard to the gathered community? What would happen if mission witness, proclaimed by lay pilgrims, was perceived as essential to the warp and woof of the church as the eucharist is?

We would hear stories about mission within work settings. We would hear narratives about the reality of family life that might reveal for the first time that mission endurance is what Christian family life is all about. We would hear witness that might convince us that lay engagement in political leadership can be lived out as call expressed through calling. We would begin to understand and appreciate the ways in which we witness by the way in which we "comport" ourselves within the world.

By pondering stories I have heard these past three years, some through secular media, I perceived two primary dynamics to the process of mission: witness within the world and proclamation within the church. Because the latter is seldom encouraged, we know far less than we should about the mission engagement of lay women and lay men. The Synod on the Laity might have been redundant had mission in the world, a powerful call of Vatican Council II, been implemented. If the *proclamation phase* of lay mission finds its way into the church within the next two decades, we won't be talking about yet another synod on the laity in 2007.

The following stories only scratch the surface regarding the narratives available for proclamation and the settings available for mission engagement. They are mentioned as a stimulus for a longer inventory and creative ways to encourage proclamation in local, diocesan, and world church settings.

Richard Fratianne, on Mission in Medicine

The story of Richard Fratianne is the story of growth in spiritual consciousness leading to focused engagement in mission. Dr. Fratianne, director of the Burn Center at Cleveland General Hospital, participated in a cursillo weekend that became a *revelation* through which he learned "that a personal and loving relationship with God was possible!" Richard also discovered that sustaining this relationship required learning how to live a life of prayer. In prayer he experienced "God pouring out . . . transforming love and I began to realize that I could be a channel of his love to others."[1]

A call to envision a deeper, broader sense of mission destiny led to a *mission goal:* helping each patient feel lovable. At first Richard found himself "frightened and overwhelmed by the prospect . . . because the patients needed so much and I had so little to give. It was apparent that the only way that I could help them feel lovable was to love them as Jesus loved them." Enlisting the team that was under his direction to treat each patient as a whole person, Richard's mission began to bear the fruit. He discovered that "an ambiance of love and compassion truly transforms (the patients). For some it is their first experience of a sense of dignity and a sense of value and self-worth." Richard Fratianne takes little credit for the transformations his mission has enabled. "Almost surprisingly, I saw the power of the Spirit begin to work as the members (of the staff) became united into a team . . . began to live those values with each other and with the patients. As this occurred, I noticed that the atmosphere in the unit changed from one characterized by pain, agony, fear, anger and guilt to an atmosphere of peace, joy, faith, patience and hope. These changes occurred in all of us—staff, patients and families. We began to live compassion without pity; love without sentimentality."[2]

To achieve his mission, Richard Fratianne first had to become a good doctor. As he points out, "I have learned two things: first, to be a Christian physician I must be the best physician I can possibly be because if I am incompetent as a surgeon anything else I do is fraudulent. The second is that as I orient myself to try in my halting and oftentimes clumsy way to open the channels of God's transforming love, I have witnessed miracles."[3]

Richard Fratianne had to take the risk of letting himself be "formed" by the professional standards and criteria of what has become a secular endeavor—medicine. Only by doing *this* wholeheartedly yet prudently was he being faithful to his call and his giftedness and his God. Dr. Fratianne participated in the church's mission to the world through his vocations of husband, father, and doctor. Following his religious experience on the cursillo weekend, his *intimacy with God deepened* and he heard a further call from God. He then *expanded his realm of responsibility and authority* to develop a process that would heal the patients spiritually as well as physically. Richard's calling was transformed into mission in a particular way, one related to the setting where his expertise and commitment *already* were engaged.

Dr. Richard Fratianne has had the rare experience of offering *proclamation* to the church community concerning his mission within the world. At the NCCB Bishops' Committee on the Laity's Conference on *Faith, Society, and the Future,* held at Notre Dame, Richard shared his mission story. He has given witness to his faith and mission since then in other settings, i.e. directing a retreat for the priests of the diocese of Cleveland. Richard's mission story highlights the *interdependence of individuation and community as formation for mission.* The cursillo weekend was a communal process. The teamwork at the hospital was collaborative. Richard, however, was called to medicine and engaged in studies as an individual.

Callixta Belomo Essana, Economist on Mission

A small glimpse of the strength inherent in lay mission stories was heard in 1987 at *The Synod on the Vocation and Mission of the Laity in the Church and in the World* in Rome. For example, the mission settings shared by Callixta Belomo Essana of Cameroun, an economist, are impressive: Chad in 1978 for the Swiss Technical Cooperation, Benin in 1981 and 1983 during FAO missions, Senegal in 1984 and 1985 as part of UNESCO, in France during studies from 1979 to 1983. Callixta Belomo Essana has also donated service to the church as secretary for Young Catholic Students in school, in the Catholic Rural Movement, and as a member of the Pan-African Commission and of the World Council of the International Movement of Catholic Agriculture and Rural Youth. She perceives her path as a Christian as a permanent catechumenate. In addition to relating her ministry and mission activities, she realistically noted that her path has been "strewn with: difficulties in the family; difficulties in the professional milieu; problems with apostolic groups; personal doubts, overclouding and hesitation; discouragement and, at times, revolt; bitterness because of my weaknesses, my powerlessness."[4]

Nonetheless, she goes on. "In the strength of the Spirit of Christ, I remain, I try to remain in an intimate relation with God, in fraternal communion within the church, sharing the life situation of the women of my time, at the heart of a world that has become a great village. That is why I turn my eyes also toward the other women of all milieux and of the whole world. My family life, my life in a neighborhood of the city of Yaounde, my professional position and my apostolic commitment bring me close to other women in their joys, their sufferings, their hopes, their questioning, their doubts, their revolts against society and/or the church."[5]

Stories like Callixta's help me to sense the sweep of the changes, the turnabout of perceptions, initiated by the Holy Spirit through and since Vatican Council II. They also reveal that the responsibilities and authority one assumes in mission *emerge from intimacy with a loved God and a loved people.* As an origination for ministry and mission, this felt intimacy cannot help, at times, but confront a stance that perceives responsibilities and authority as granted from above through ecclesiastical office. It has always been thus in the church.

Mario Cuomo, on Mission in Government

Sometimes the proclamation stage of a mission story can challenge the political establishment. Sometimes it can challenge

the institutional church. In the life of Mario Cuomo we see the
development of a calling. Mario Cuomo became a lawyer. That
calling took on a stronger mission edge when he ran for elective
office. After becoming governor of New York, Mario Cuomo kept
a diary. By publishing his diary, Governor Cuomo publicly revealed the power of faith in his life. Later he ran into opposition
from the hierarchy in New York concerning his public stance on
abortion. To respond to this challenge he shared his moral convictions in an address delivered at Notre Dame University.

Governor Cuomo's becoming a lawyer I see as call lived out
through a calling. His becoming an elected leader in New York I
see as a call broadening and deepening into a more intensely active
mission witness. His diaries and his address at Notre Dame I see as
proclamation that unfolded *from a mission rooted in a calling.*

Laying Down One's Life on Mission:
Tommy Gill, Mission on the Job

Following one's calling does not usually lead to loss of one's
life, but in some work settings that possibility is more apparent
than most of us take the time to think about.

The last of three front page stories about Catholic lay believers
(not identified as such) during the winter of 1988 in the *Boston
Globe* was the story of Tommy Gill. This Vietnam vet and a seventeen year veteran of the Boston police department was killed by a
train on the afternoon of February 10 while searching for a laundry
bag containing fourteen guns that had been stolen from a home
near the railway tracks. As the *Globe* reported it, "The impact . . .
threw Gill 74 feet and apparently killed him instantly."

In a letter to Tommy Gill's widow, Ann, Boston police com-
missioner Francis Roche said, "Your husband was a person who
understood leadership, but, more important, provided leadership
during his life. Everyone around him seemed to perform better and
become better persons. . . . I have never seen such an impact . . . on
police officers before . . . during his short time he planted many
seeds that will ensure his values live forever." Like many of us,
Tommy's formation for his calling came from his home and
neighborhood. Both his father and his father-in-law were Boston

police officers. Perhaps the best accolade from a fellow officer Tommy received after his death relates to formation: "I hope one day my son can become the kind of man Tommy Gill was."[6]

Christa McAuliffe, on Mission in Space

The mission of one lay believer may be disturbing to other lay believers. I felt a great deal of anger after the Challenger explosion. Part of it emerged from the difficulty I have in perceiving value in the space program, especially in a world that suffers from famine and homelessness. More of it stemmed, I feel, in reaction to the horror of Christa's family, especially her children, witnessing her death.

A few days after the Challenger explosion I was facilitating a women's weekend retreat with a friend, Jeanne Trainor. On Saturday afternoon Jeanne and I found ourselves reflecting together on Christa's death and also found ourselves with different perspectives. Rather than judging Christa, Jeanne felt awed by her passion and courage, her ability to risk all for what she believed. If we had not reflected together, I might have stayed on the judgmental level regarding Christa's mission. Dialogue with Jeanne drew me into pondering the meaning of her sacrifice.

Later, I had to admit that in Christa McAuliffe we saw not only a brave and uniquely adventurous woman, but also a rare instance of the proclamation dimension of mission. From the start of her initiation into the space program, Christa's public witness of her binding tie with children merged with her binding tie with the space exploration. Citizens across the country were attracted to Christa, not because she was a teacher who was chosen to venture into space, but because her calling as a teacher came across as remarkably genuine. Christa united the passion she felt for her calling as a teacher with a technological enterprise where, as Strasser reminded us earlier, passion can be posited only on the final goal. In all the weeks of preparation for the space flight, one never sensed in Christa a self-serving attitude or the impersonal and objective persona one sometimes sees in some space-travelers. Christa's calling as a teacher unfolded and embraced the new call to travel in space. She would not forsake her passion for teaching and children for the prestige attached to being the "first teacher in space." In other words, Christa would not give up "being the same as myself" when her calling as a teacher became a mission. Her tragic death does not invalidate the lesson of that proclamation, one that technologists should take to heart. When they do, religious values may begin to alter the mores and decision of the technological establishment.

Christa McAuliffe was more than a "world-dreaming pilgrim." She was a "universe-dreaming pilgrim."

Mission in Family Settings

Sometimes our mission is to bear the tragedies that happen in family life. During that time no more can be expected.

Two weeks before the story of Tommy Gill in the *Boston Globe* the front page headlines were about a different kind of story, one that is no less tragic: "Family tragedy: Brothers' love ends in violent death." The story was about Phil and Mark, two brothers from East Boston. The brothers who were like two close friends had remarkably different dispositions and personalities. For years Phil had carried Mark out of bars where Mark had instigated brawls. "Phil was the calming force in Mark's life, trying constantly to steer him to the straight and narrow, but it was a path Mark (an ex-offender) would never fully walk."

On the morning of Mark's funeral, Phil "clutched tightly to the metal handle on the wooden casket and carried his brother for the last time—into St. Joseph-St. Lazarus Church for his funeral Mass. . . . No one, not even his closest confidants, expected that the brother who was his keeper would also be his killer. Yesterday that same brother carried and kissed his coffin and read scripture at his funeral."

Three days earlier, when Mark's uncontrollable temper erupted and he lunged for a woman friend of Phil's, Phil picked up a kitchen knife. "Mark was stabbed once: his lung was punctured. Police and emergency medical crews found Phil cradling his brother in his arms when they arrived."

As Phil says, "There were a lot of bad guys who wanted to do a lot of bad things with (Mark). God knows, and with the help of God everyone will know, I was never one of them."[7]

When one's mission reality is family it can take more courage to "tell it like it is," especially in a public forum, than when one's mission reality is the marketplace. Because more intense intimacy dynamics are at stake, in the past the church, rather than relating some of the truth found in family life, tended to rely on rhetoric that, in turn, made parents feel guilty. More courage in proclaiming the reality of mission in family is needed. Therese Saulnier has that kind of courage by sharing her journal story of feeding one of her babies in the middle of the night:

Three a.m. Sitting on the couch with my feet propped against the edge of the coffee table, I wonder if I should try my hand at hypnotism . . . I have become a stranger to myself in these few weeks; one who considers violence and abandonment; who is capable of hating so passionately the life I have proclaimed to be my joy; and then the cramps of revulsion set in as I think of who I have become. . . . There is no walking away for me. There is, right now, only care. Care that must be given tonight, tomorrow, and the days beyond. Care that is gift and burden.

Little one, I see that you need me for your survival. You will die if left alone. You need me to be patient for a while, until you can sort out things for yourself. You need to see love and delight in my eyes, just as surely as you need the milk from my breasts. . . . I imagine the question "Can you be trusted?" in your eyes. A question that scares me more than all the tabulated chores I'll ever be required to perform for you in the next eighteen years. Who will aid me? Who will instruct and comfort and nurture me? I begin to cry because I know the answer: no one. Not the partner I chose to share my life. He draws back into a role we swore we would be free of and I do not know how to demand he act differently. I feel the desolation of loneliness overwhelm me and I feel guilt for my wants. . . .

Moving to place my daughter into her bassinet, where she finally sleeps, I whisper a prayer that she will sleep for more than a couple of hours. . . .

I am exhausted, yet I feel I have retrieved a cord that connects me to life. There is an energy I can tap into that links and flows through all creation, and a wisdom that reveals the mysteries. It occurs to me that this is God's work, and I have gained a little understanding of it tonight.[8]

Mission in the Workplace

In many work settings, Christians in management positions bring values into the workplace. At an ecumenical meeting, *Frontiers: A National Consultation on Theological Education of Laity,* held in California in May 1987, I remember a nurse describing her journey from direct nursing care to teaching nursing courses to another form of leadership within the profession. There she had the opportunity to influence the mission stance of a large hospital by serving on its board of directors. Within that placement, her endurance was tested as she argued to keep a sense of altruistic service, a spirit of *caritas,* within the mission of an institution that, like many of its counterparts, was tempted to put primary emphasis on profit. Her mission was to affect the mission of the workplace where she had first exercised her calling.

The April 1989 issue of *Chicago Studies* describes the mission of businessman Joseph Sullivan, CEO of Sullivan and Proops, a Chicago investment firm. The companies owned by Sullivan and Proops are managed from a value-stance—for example: encouraging management to enhance the dignity already inherent within workers; delegation of authority and responsibility; providing full knowledge of the company's performance to employees; enabling employees to develop to their full potential; an Employee Assistance Program designed to help workers to deal with personal problems such as substance abuse; encouragement of civic involvement at all levels. Despite industry losses currently, Sullivan and Proops has maintained profitable levels for four consecutive years.

The pseudo-rivalry between lay ministers and laity in the marketplace will quickly evaporate when proclamations such as those described above become part of the way we "do church."

Mission in National Settings:
Joan Cooney, Lech Walesa, Cory Aquino

When Joan Cooney received the annual Christophers Award in 1989, she recounted how, as a college student, Fr. James Keller, founder of the Christophers, had inspired her toward mission through media. Little did she know then that her efforts, eventually culminating in *The Children's Workshop,* would help to form millions of America's children through the consistently acclaimed television program, *Sesame Street.* This is but one example of mission within a national setting.

It is incredible that Mother Teresa, great woman that she is, is still so singularly cited as an example of ministry and mission for lay adults by preachers in the church. Why do we never hear Joan Cooney's story or Lech Walesa's stirring story of service to a people that culminates in the incredible liberation of Hungary, Czechoslovakia, East Germany and Rumania as well as of Poland? This flesh and blood steel worker, a union organizer imprisoned for his public witness to his conviction, a husband, a father, and a Catholic layman is a model that believers can relate to. Without Lech Walesa, truly God's pilgrim on mission, the hope and promise of peace would not have become vibrant.

In both Poland and the Philippines the liberators and leaders are Catholic lay adults, but if you want to read about their mission, look in secular papers and magazines. In spite of their very apparent public witness to deep faith, you find few stories about the missions of Lech Walesa and Cory Aquino in church media. This slighting not only demeans these two valiant lay leaders, but it also is dangerous, for shunning the stories suggests to many clerical and lay believers that Lech Walesa and Cory Aquino are only secular political figures, not lay Catholics with courageous missions.

In Cory Aquino, a great lay woman of the church, we see again the transformation of calling into mission. After the death of Mrs. Aquino's husband, her vocation as a mother did not cease but she broadened her *responsibility.* Cory Aquino became the liberator of all of her people. Worldwide, people were awed that this petite, feminine woman of faith could lead her people, through a peaceful revolution, to freedom. Following that unique event in recent history, Cory Aquino assumed greater *authority* as well as responsibility by becoming the elected leader of her land. One instance of public reflection on this process and its meaning (the proclamation phase) occurred in a secular setting, Harvard University, where President Aquino delivered a major address on peaceful revolution.

Mission effort comes in many sizes and shapes and evokes various hues, yet as lay brothers and sisters—Richard, Lech, Callixta Mario, Cory, Therese, Tommy, Phillip, Joseph, Joan, and

Christa—reveal, mission is *consistently generative.* Faith in God and in a God-loved world and its peoples motivates mission. When mission is alive and well, justice or healing or love or liberation is enhanced. The commonwealth of God is glimpsed.

Mission is accomplished within a world that is global, secular, relational and God's. Mission enables others to see that it is God's role, not that of any particular nation, people, or person, to put closure on history. Mission enables others to see that it is our role as human adults to give sober witness to the call to care about those who are workers, or imprisoned, or homeless, or sick, or illiterate, or children. The posterity of a society is not neglected. An ancient variation of "Give us this day our daily bread" in the Lord's Prayer is "Give us this day our bread for the morrow." Women and men engaged in mission are bread for the morrow of others.

Because life circumstances and callings differ it is impossible to come up with a *formula* for doing mission which all lay believers can follow. Example teaches how to do mission. It is a parabolic process. The gospel shows Jesus revealing God's mission through parables—God's mission of seeking, God's mission of welcoming the prodigal one. The formation potential for mission can always be created anew because it emerges from the lives of those engaged in mission. That is why we must hear *within the church* their stories. Mission-minded families will breed mission-minded families whether the families are natural families or families of friends who in faith worship together.

Comportment as Mission

Sometimes dramatic mission stories in a lay believer's life stand forth less than the overall *way* the man or woman comports himself or herself, challenging the church to find ways for the witness of comportment in the public proclamation of mission. Our closing narrative, which reveals this dimension of lay mission life, is another story told on the front page of the *Boston Globe* early in 1988, the year of the Synod on the Laity. In this secular newspaper the format for the story was liturgical—the prayers of the faithful from a funeral mass.

The front-page headline was entitled: *A FIGHTER—In death,*

editor leaves legacy bursting with life. Between the headlines was a picture of Sarah Droney McGurrin, former prize-winning reporter and editor of the *Waltham News Tribune.* At age thirty-one Sarah Droney McGurrin had contracted a virus that eventually hospitalized her and caused her to lapse into a coma from which she never returned. On New Year's day, her son Christopher was born in an induced vaginal delivery. Six days later Sarah Droney McGurrin died.

For the life of Sarah, who brought excitement and vitality to everything she did. For this let us pray.

Sarah's mother, who had lost her husband in 1984, offered the first prayer. Mrs. Droney, as active as Sarah, had once sought a Democratic nomination for Congress. After the funeral, she spoke about her husband and her daughter. "Sarah and her father were 'kindred spirits.' " Sarah's father had been a veteran *Boston Herald* newsman.

For editors and reporters, that they may always bring to the news business the dedication, the élan, and the jaundiced eye that are the marks of the professional—qualities that Sarah learned from her father Jim and sought to impart to those working in her newsroom. For this, let us pray.

At 5:30 A.M. Sarah had been at her desk at the *Tribune* where she had become the first woman managing editor. Sarah "directed her staff with shouts across the room, a cup of coffee . . . in one hand and a telephone in the other."

As one reporter put it, "You had to like her, even if she was giving you hell. We wanted to please her, and we were applying her standards to our work."

This young lay Catholic woman, who took the trolley to her graduation from Boston College in her cap and gown, who brought her dog Jazebo home from an animal hospital by sled because the 1978 blizzard had closed all roads to cars, who rode to her wedding at Immaculate Conception Church in a horse and buggy (followed by an Irish bagpiper), would often end a work week by cooking Mexican food for staff members. "She'd be cooking," recalls her assistant managing editor, "and she'd be on the phone with fifteen reporters telling them what to do."

Sarah Droney McGurrin had passion for her mission.

For Sarah's family and friends, present and absent, whose

*support and love have made this impossible burden bearable, that
their grief will be replaced with hope. For this, let us pray.*

Most of all Sarah "liked to spend time with her husband."
Avid Celtic fans, Sarah brought a thermos of ice chips to the games
"so she could keep her throat from getting sore from all her
yelling."

*In thanksgiving for the life of Christopher James. For this, let
us pray.*

Sarah loved her niece and nephew, and looked forward with
great anticipation to the birth of her baby. Christopher lives with
his father and grandparents. Christopher, the first grandchild in the
McGurrin family, will have ten aunts and uncles in addition to his
dad and grandparents to help him get to know his mother, Sarah
Droney McGurrin.[9]

We are a people, once called "saints and sinners." From
Richard Fratianne to Therese Saulnier to Lech Walesa to Callixta
Mario Cuomo to Cory Aquino to Christa McAuliffe to Tommy
Gill to Joseph Sullivan to Joan Cooney to the brothers Mark and
Phil to Sarah Droney McGurrin, who at age thirty-one edited a
newspaper and anticipated her first baby, we are a people. We are a
world-wide people on mission. Passion is the comportment we
bring to that mission, whether the mission is developing management policies from a value system, rehabilitating burn patients so
they know they are lovable, uniting workers into a union, governing the people of a state, governing the people of a nation, forging a
new path for teachers and children, forming children through television programming, searching for evidence in a crime, protecting
a blood brother, or tracking down the truth for a newspaper.
Whether recognized or not, we are a people called to mission by
our God. We are a people who hear that call and live it out with our
lives. We are a people entitled to proclaim—to tell what we have
seen—within our church as well as within the world our mission is
transforming.

NOTES

Introduction

1. Robert C. Broderick, M.A., *The Catholic Layman's Book of Etiquette.* St. Paul: Catechetical Guild Educational Society, 1957.
2. David C. Leege, "Who Is a True Catholic? Social Boundaries on the Church," *Notre Dame Study of Catholic Parish Life,* Report #12, March 1988.
3. David O'Brien, "Catholic Social Teaching: Remembrance and Commitment," p. 234, *New Catholic World,* Sept./Oct. 1986 (my italics).

(Part One) Chapter 1

1. Erik Erikson, *Insight and Responsibility.* New York: W.W. Norton, 1964, p. 95.
2. Ibid.
3. *Boston Globe,* June 29, 1986, p. 25.
4. Ibid.
5. *Apostolic Regions of the United States: 1971,* Glenmary Research Center, Atlanta, Georgia.
6. Maria Harris has summarized how lay is commonly defined: "not in clerical orders (Oxford), not in holy orders; not of the clergy; not clerical; not ecclesiastical" (Webster), "relating to members of religious house that are occupied chiefly with domestic or manual work" (Webster) and continues "not of or from a particular profession, not having special training or knowledge, unprofessional, common ordinary." Funk and Wagnalls, besides agreeing with these, adds, "inexperienced, ignorant, and uncultivated," and concludes with the information that "in cards a lay hand is one with few or no trumps." "Questioning Lay Ministry," Maria Harris, presentation, *Authors Series,* Paulist Community, Boston, Mass.
7. See Virginia Sullivan Finn, "Laity: Mission and Ministry," in *Vatican II—The Unfinished Agenda,* ed. Lucien Richard, O.M.I., New York: Paulist Press, 1987.
8. George Wilson, S.J., "Who Hates Process?" *Human Development,* Sept. 1986, Vol. 7, No. 2, 20.
9. Conferences sponsored by the NCCB Bishops' Committee on the

277

Laity include: *Conference on Sharing Ministry Responsibly, American Catholic Spirituality, Work, Faith, and Society,* and *Shared Responsibility in Diocesan Pastoral Councils.*

10. Bishop Raymond Lucker, *Vocations of the Laity—Linking Church and World.* National Conference of Catholic Bishops Assembly. Collegeville, Minnesota, July 9–16, 1985.

(Part One) Chapter 2

1. John Calvin, *New Testament Commentaries XI* (my italics).
2. William Bouwsma, "Christian Adulthood," in *Psychology and Religion: A Reader,* ed. Margaret Gorman. Paulist Press, 1985, p. 3.
3. Ibid. p. 87.
4. *Adulthood: Essays,* ed. Erik Erikson. New York: Norton, 1978.
5. Ibid. p. 192.
6. Ibid. p. 195.
7. Sandra Schneiders, *Woman and the Word.* New York: Paulist Press, 1986, pp. 58–59.
8. Ibid.
9. Georgia Masters Keightley, "Women's Issues Are Laity Issues," *America,* August 6–13, 1988, p. 79. See also *The Honours System.* London: Alleson & Busby, 1985.
10. USCC Adult Education Conference Proceedings, 1985.
11. Gerald O'Collins, *Fundamental Theology.* New York: Paulist Press, 1981, pp. 35–42.
12. Ibid.
13. Ibid.
14. According to Ann Bedford Ulanov, a Jungian Christian psychotherapist, the spiritual malaise the above questions raise is the result of too much "reliance on reasoning and the outer forms of religion." What happens is what Ulanov calls a "leanness of experience" when the *inner connection to the reality represented by our religious symbols* is lost. If our secular culture, with its emphasis on external achievement and consumerism, evokes this leanness, this feeling empty inside, and we turn to church to find meaning yet we discover even there a focus on the importance of form, one that makes the mass a performance rather than a communal, participatory ritual, then that inner connection to the reality of God may be jeopardized. See Gorman, op. cit.

(Part One) Chapter 3

1. For further information about the project of the NALM Spirituality Task Force write to NALM, 1125 W. Baseline Rd., Suite 2-67, Mesa, AZ 85210. The association has received funding to explore in greater depth lay religious experience in the "web of life" and to develop a handbook for parish use.
2. See Sandra Schneiders' *Response* in "Spirituality in Theological Education," in *Theological Education* (Autumn 1987), Vol. XXIV, #1.
3. Wilfred Sheed, *Frank and Marie—A Memoir with Parents.* New York: Simon and Schuster, 1985, p. 11.
4. Cynthia Ozick, *Art and Ardor.* New York: Alfred A. Knopf, 1983, p. 13.
5. Ibid.
6. Dean Hoge, *Future of Catholic Leadership—Responses to the Priest Shortage.* Kansas City: Sheed and Ward, 1987, p. 30.
7. Ibid.
8. M.-D. Chenu, *Vatican II Revisited,* ed. Alberic Stackpole. Minneapolis: Winston Press, 1986, p. 20.
9. Op. cit., Archbishop Dereck Worlock, p. 248.
10. Jay Dolan, *The American Catholic Experience.* Garden City: Doubleday, 1985, p. 427.
11. Ibid. p. 426.
12. Chenu, op. cit. p. 167.
13. *Called and Gifted,* National Conference of Catholic Bishops, 1980.

(Part One) Chapter 4

1. Joseph P. Whelan S.J., *The Spirituality of Friedrich Von Hugel.* New York: Newman Press, 1971, p. 219.
2. Ibid. p. 212.
3. Harvey Cox, *Religion in the Secular City,* p. 210.
4. Pierre Babin, *Communications Media and Spirituality, The Way* Supplement, Number 57, Autumn 1986, p. 51.
5. Friedrich von Hugel, *Eternal Life: A Study of its Implications and Applications.* Edinburgh, 1912, p. 253.
6. Whelan, op. cit. p. 36.
7. Cardinal Pironio, *The Formation of the Laity: Twelve Theses.* Vatican City: Pontifical Council for the Laity, 1987, p. 12.

8. Rosemary Haughton, *The Passionate God.* Minneapolis: Winston Press, 1978, p. 197.
9. Ibid. p. 245.
10. Pironio, op. cit. p. 9.

(Part Two) Chapter 1

1. Recent research reveals that perpetrators of sexual abuse on children often image themselves as peers of the children, as feeling themselves to be the same age as the child.
2. Gaston Bachelard, *The Poetics of Space.* Boston: Beacon Press, 1958, p. 188.
3. As quoted in Beldon C. Lane, *Landscapes of the Sacred.* New York: Paulist Press, 1988, p. 4.
4. Linda Brani Cateura, *Growing Up Italian.* New York: William Morrow, 1987, p. 100.

(Part Two) Chapter 2

1. Morton Kelsey and Barbara Kelsey, *Sacrament of Sexuality.* Warwick, NY: Amity House, 1982, pp. 278–279.
2. "Spiritale Vinculum": Joseph H. Lynch, p. 197.
3. Ibid. p. 182.
4. Ibid.

(Part Two) Chapter 3

1. Judith Goenner, Letter to the Editor, *Woman's Day* magazine, Sept. 1987.

(Part Two) Chapter 4

1. Lanford Wilson, *Angels Fall,* from *The Burns Mantle Theater Yearbook: Best Plays of 1982–1983.* New York: Dodd, Mead & Company, 1983.
2. *Boston Sunday Globe,* "Minimum-wage jobs enable survival, but little else," March 29, 1987, p. 39.
3. Ibid. p. 29.

(Part Three) Chapter 1

1. Thomas Flanagan, *The Tenants of Time.* New York: E. D. Dutton, 1988, p. 444.
2. *Partners in the Mystery of Redemption—A Pastoral Response to Women's Concerns for Church and Society.* First draft, NCCB, Spring 1988.
3. Dean Hoge, *Future of Catholic Leadership.* Kansas City: Sheed and Ward, 1987, p. 128.
4. Andrew Greeley and William McManus, *Catholic Contributions.* Kansas City: Sheed and Ward, 1988, pp. 106–107.
5. Ibid. p. 40.
6. Ibid. p. 38.
7. Ibid. p. 18.
8. Ibid. p. 65.
9. Robert Kinast, Summary of NCCB Consultative Process for Synod on the Laity, 1987.
10. James Fowler, *Becoming Adult, Becoming Christian—Adult Development and Christian Faith.* San Francisco: Harper and Row, 1984, p. 81.
11. Kinast, op. cit.
12. Friedrich von Hugel in *The Spirituality of Friedrich von Hugel,* Joseph Whalen S.J., ed. New York: Newman Press, 1971, p. 246.
13. Ibid. p. 213.

(Part Three) Chapter 2

1. From a review of *Middle America Individualism* by Herbert Gans. New York: The Free Press, 1988. Review by Steven Kelman, *New York Times Sunday Book Review,* August 7, 1988.

(Part Three) Chapter 4

1. Stephen Strasser, *The Phenomenology of Feeling.* Pittsburgh: Duquesne University Press, 1977, p. 184 (italics mine).
2. Ibid. p. 185.
3. Ibid. Italics mine.
4. Ibid. p. 186.
5. Douglas V. Steere, *Spiritual Counsels and Letters of Baron Friedrich von Hugel.* London: Darton, Longman & Todd, 1964.

6. Strasser, op. cit. pp. 190–191.
7. Ibid. pp. 194–199.
8. Ibid. p. 200.
9. Ibid. p. 278.
10. Ibid.
11. Ibid. p. 190.
12. "Goodness Knows Nothing of Beauty," *Harpers,* April 1987, p. 43.
13. Strasser, op. cit. p. 253.
14. Ibid. p. 293.
15. Ibid.
16. Ibid. p. 295.
17. Ibid.

(Part Four) Chapter 1

1. Robert Turner, "Street Smart and Worldly Wise." *Boston Sunday Globe Magazine.*
2. Ibid.
3. "Public Life, Private Ethics," Robert A. Jordan, *Boston Globe,* November 14, 1987.
4. David C. Schwartz and Richard Ferlauto, "Helping solve the housing crisis", reprinted from *The Christian Science Monitor, The Berkshire Eagle,* September 3, 1988.
5. Ibid.

(Part Four) Chapter 2

1. L. Berger, "Catholics in America," *New York Times Sunday Magazine,* August 23, 1987.
2. Fredrick Turner in "Literature Lost in the Thickets." *New York Times Book Review,* Sunday, Feb. 15, 1987.
3. Ibid.
4. Ibid.
5. Ibid.
6. Ibid.
7. Ibid.
8. Ibid.
9. Georgia O'Keefe in letter to Henry McBride 7/19/48 in *Georgia O'Keefe Art and Letters* by Jack Cowart and Juan Hamilton, National Gallery of Art, Washington, D.C., 1987.
10. Ibid., letter to William Howard Schubart, 7/25/52.

11. Turner, op. cit.
12. See Footnote 1.
13. As a philosopher, Bachelard wrote thirteen volumes "in which scientific competence went hand in hand with philosophical acumen" (Gilson, p. viii). Although he wrote books with titles like "The Experience of Space in Contemporary Psychics," we need not feel intimidated. The two books useful for our reflection are *The Poetics of Space,* Boston: Beacon Press, 1967, and *The Poetics of Reverie,* Boston: Beacon Press, 1971. For convenience Sp. will refer to *The Poetics of Space* and Rev. to *The Poetics of Reverie.* Here p. 192 Rev, quoting Henri Bosco.
14. Ibid. p. 19.
15. Ibid. p. 193.
16. Ibid.
17. Elizabeth Drew quoting Coleridge, *Poetry, A Modern Guide to Its Understanding and Enjoyment.* New York: Dell, 1959.
18. See Ira Progoff *The Practice of Process Meditation.* New York: Dialogue House Library, 1980.
19. See p. 184 Sp.
20. See p. 210 Rev.
21. See p. 160 Rev.
22. Ibid.
23. See p. 6 Sp.
24. See p. 48 Sp.
25. See p. 6 Sp.
26. Ibid.
27. Ibid. Emphasis mine
28. See p. 162 Rev.
29. See p. 163 Rev.
30. See pp. 46–47 Sp.
31. Quoting Henri Bosco, p. 205 Sp.
32. O'Keefe op. cit. (to Russell Vernon Hunter, 1933).
33. See p. 189 Sp.
34. See p. 140 Rev.
35. Hilda C. Graef, *The Scholar and the Cross.* Westminster, MD: The Newman Press, 1955. p. 212.
36. See p. 187 Sp.
37. Quoting Marcault and Therese Brasse; see p. 185 Sp.
38. Quoting Rene Menard; see p. 187 Sp.
39. Ibid. Quoting Supervielle.
40. See p. 207 Sp.
41. See p. 206 Sp.

42. See p. 208 Sp.
43. See p. 210 Sp.

(Part Four) Chapter 3

1. Gaston Bachelard, *The Poetics of Reverie.* Boston: Beacon Press, 1971, p. 177. Rev. following citation.
2. Ibid. p. 181.
3. "Still Writing," Laurie Forfa, *The Berkshire Eagle,* Saturday, April 23, 1988.
4. See Rev. p. 185.
5. Ibid.
6. See Rev. p. 196.
7. Ibid.
8. See Rev. p. 198.
9. National Catholic Education Association (NCEA) study of adolescent faith.
10. See Rev. p. 193.
11. Ibid.
12. See Rev. p. 196.
13. See Rev. p. 203 quoting Jacques Andiberti.
14. See Rev. p. 193.
15. See Rev. p. 183.
16. See Rev. p. 211.
17. Gaston Bachelard, *Poetics of Space* (Sp.) p. 211. Boston: Beacon Press.
18. Ibid.
19. See Sp. p. 102.
20. See Sp. p. 100.
21. See Sp. p. 101.
22. See Sp. p. 104.
23. See Sp. p. 101.
24. See Sp. p. 102.

(Part Four) Chapter 4

1. *New Catholic World,* May—June 1984, pp. 130–132.
2. Ibid.
3. Ibid.
4. "Woman and Her Christian Mission," *Lay Voices at the Synod.* Vatican City: Pontifical Council for the Laity, 1988.

5. Ibid.
6. Boston Globe, p. 1, February 11, 1988; p. 36, February 14, 1988.
7. Boston Globe, p. 1, January 31, 1988.
8. Therese Saulnier, "The Labor after Creation," *Sacred Dimensions of Women's Experience,* ed. Elizabeth Dodson Gray. Wellesley: Roundtable Press, 1988, pp. 71–76.
9. Boston Globe, p. 1, p. 26, January 16, 1988.

STUDY QUESTIONS FOR EACH CHAPTER

(Part One) Chapter 1

1. Twenty-five years have passed since Vatican II. We have had sufficient time to "name" the council. What descriptive names would you give it?

2. Reflect on, and share with others, how Vatican II was implemented in your diocese and in your parish. If you do not remember, share an experience that reveals when you became conscious that Vatican II had happened in the church.

3. Imagine the kind of Catholic you would be today if Vatican II had not occurred. How do you feel about this identity? Do you regret that Vatican II happened? What do you miss from the church before the council?

4. Reflect on and share an experience you had, or someone you know had, of the effects of "mobility"—either moving to a different church setting or having a new priest or bishop replace one familiar to you.

5. Reflect on and share experiences you had in any of the following:

- associations or movements, i.e. cursillo, charismatic renewal, marriage encounter, etc.
- national conferences, i.e. Call to Action.
- signs of the times momentums, i.e. civil rights, resistance to Vietnam War, women's movement, etc.
- small support groups, i.e. separated and divorced, bereavement, RENEW, R.C.I.A., etc., alternate community, i.e. non-territorial parish.

Do you feel that you experienced a "conversion of identity" through this participation? If so, describe what that conversion was like.

6. "I'm just an ordinary layman." If you, at one time, felt passive and dependent within the church, share an experience that reveals those dynamics. How is your identity different today?

7. An image of a boat was used in this chapter to describe the migration of Catholics from the pre-conciliar culture of the church to the post-conciliar culture. As passengers who have migrated from one culture

to another, we are now supposed to disembark to engage in "mission in the terrifying, marvelously diverse cultures of our country and our world." The boat has reached the shore. Explain where you are and what that feels like.

—on land, engaged wholeheartedly in mission
—on the shore, considering how to engage in mission
—on the deck, waiting for those engaged in mission to return and tell me how to do it
—below the deck, not yet ready to leave ship

(Part One) Chapter 2

1. Reflect on the following settings and indicate those where you feel most like an adult and least like an adult. Share why you think this is so.

- Workplace
- Home
- Leisure activity
- Socializing with friends
- Visiting with parents and other relatives
- Church
- Shopping
- Going to the doctor

2. Why are both masculine and feminine qualities important when one defines adulthood?

3. Explain whether you agree or disagree with the following: For the exercise of authority and leadership within the church, (hierarchical gradations and titles) are necessary. How do you feel hierarchical gradations and titles affect lay women and lay men in a democratic society?

4. Describe someone who you would say has achieved Christian adulthood.

5. Do you feel that there is a lack of *positive* characteristics regarding lay identity in the church? If you do, how could that be changed?

6. How does belonging to your local church community enhance or lessen a sense of who you are as a person?

7. Explain why you agree or disagree with the premise that any human experience has the potential for being a spiritual experience.

(Part One) Chapter 3

1. Describe what happened in an event in which you experienced God.
What meaning does this event have for you?

How has this affected your life?

(If you wish, you may send your response to the National Association for Lay Ministry. See footnotes for address. Please indicate gender, age, and whether you are primarily engaged in ministry within the church or mission in the secular world.)

2. In an extended example "Jim O'Rourke" is described as a Catholic believer who no longer perceives himself as a good cop because he is a good Catholic. Rather, because Jim is a good cop he sees himself as a good Catholic. The author goes on to say that "his being Jim O'Rourke, his being a cop, his being a husband and father, a neighbor and citizen, his being part of a local church that truly is a community, come together and integrate in order to form his identity as a Catholic Christian."

Respond to the above. Discuss why you would or would not perceive yourself in a way similar to how the author has perceived Jim O'Rourke and Yvonne Gagnon.

(Part One) Chapter 4

1. The author suggests that we only come naked before God when we come as the *persons* we are (as Mark or Susan). If we come in a particular role (mother, priest, nurse), we might not hear all that God has to say to us, and we might inhibit God's formation of us. Respond to this from your own experience.

2. Putting away the things of a child is essential in the process of becoming an adult. The author contends that the best way "to put away" is to face and deal with whatever is there. Share from your own experience your process of putting away.

3. The author suggests that Jesus broke away (in the sense of maturing) from earthly parental figures in order to turn himself wholly over to the one he called Abba. Some lay adults have severed the apron strings with their natural parents but they like to think of the church as a parental figure. One person put it this way, "When the church is like a parent, I feel an umbrella over me, protecting me." How do you feel such an attitude helps or hinders spiritual maturity?

(Part Two) Chapter 1

1. Reflect on stories of ancestral figures you heard as a child. Select a story to share with others. Include in your sharing how you were influenced by this ancestral figure.

2. Let parental figures from your childhood emerge. Over a period of time reflect on them one by one. How did they help to form who you are today?

3. Remember a parental figure who engaged in activities *with* you. Select a story to share with others. Include in your story how the parental figure helped to form you through a dynamic of *cooperation.* How did you respond?

4. Remember a parental figure who expected obedience. How did you respond?

5. Sometimes intimacy, responsibility and authority are integrated. Sometimes they are separated out from one another. Can you find instances of both in your formation. Select a story to share that illustrates either.

6. In this chapter the author cites an "inheritance" from her father. Reflect on a parental figure who left you an inheritance that formed you.

7. As a parental figure what are your strengths and weaknesses in forming those of the younger generation?

8. In a family where there is a positive framework for intimacy parental figures gradually share responsibility and relinquish authority to the younger generation. This enables the younger generation to assume adulthood. How do you, or do you not, perceive a similar model in the church? Do you think such a model is workable for the church? Why? Why not?

(Part Two) Chapter 2

1. Over a period of time let friends from your past emerge in your consciousness. In addition to reflecting on them, you may want to contemplate them in prayer. Later select stories to share that reflect the following dynamics of friendship:

—interior turmoil
—privacy, confidentiality
—growing and changing through a friendship
—equality and mutuality

—respect and care
—being companions on the vessel to adulthood, midlife, old age
—revealing "who I am"
—betrayal
—fidelity

2. How has friendship been a school of Christian formation for you? Select a story to share that illustrates this.

3. How can God be both a parental figure and a friend?

4. Why is puppy love a significant formative factor in growing up? How does it differ from authentic contemplation?

5. Select a story to share about contemplating a spouse or friend. Reflect on the value of "receiving the reality" of the other.

6. If you have been part of a church community that operates as families of faith who worship together, select a community story that reveals the value of this form of church to marriage and family.

(Part Two) Chapter 3

1. How have intergenerational relationships been valuable in your family? How have they hindered family dynamics?

2. Discuss whether role expectations in marriage are inevitable. In what ways have parental figures or other "forces" outside of the relationship affected your relationship of marriage or friendship?

3. Describe a marriage and/or family you know in which responsibility and authority emerge from intimacy. Describe one that does not reveal this progression.

4. If intimacy is missing in a marriage is God impeded in trying to work with the two persons *as a couple*?

(Part Two) Chapter 4

1. The author claims that when we are pursuing *a calling* we experience a sense of freedom and zest for life, we feel a spiritual connection to what is beyond the here and now, we exercise gifts that come from our creator. Where in your life did you, and do you, experience callings?

2. The author distinguishes between callings and jobs. Do you agree that there can be a difference between a job and a calling? Have you had a job that was not a calling? Share your experience—describe it and tell how you felt about it. Have you had a job that was a calling? Share your experience—describe it and tell how you felt about it.

3. When Zap, the tennis player, first discovered the game, he claims he was "showed" something. Describe a time when you were "showed" something that led to your realizing you had a calling.

4. Avocations remove us from the world of *shoulds*. Avocations can encourage contemplation and intuitive thought rather than reasoning. Engaged in an avocation we get a different sense of ourselves—we touch the human rather than the functional side of ourselves. Share your experience with an avocation. Does it match what the author claims? (Passive activity like television watching is not considered an avocation.)

5. Lay people, in particular, live out call to discipleship, ministry and mission *through callings*. Share with others an experience from your own life that illustrates this.

6. If a lay believer is wholeheartedly living out a call through a calling, do you feel he or she should also be involved in "causes" not connected with the calling? If you feel it depends on the calling, please elaborate. Many adults eventually pursue a second career that aligns itself with a calling. Have you ever felt that desire? How did you respond to it? What in your life helps and what hinders you from doing this?

7. In the story from her husband's life, the author tells about a time when his job was a dead end and his sense of self-esteem came from pursuing an avocation beyond his work setting. If you have had that experience, share it with others.

8. Have you ever enabled someone who was working only for survival to have more choice about his or her work or to pursue a calling? Describe the experience. How could the church help in this regard?

9. Eileen loves her work and senses that it is a real calling. She was recently offered a position which she feels would enable her to do more for people in need. She does not feel any sense of calling or attraction for the actual work that she would have to do, but she feels she would be a better Christian if she accepted the job. What advice would you give her?

(Part Three) Chapter 1

1. Reflect on the issue of shunning in the church. Have you ever experienced shunning? What was that like? Have you ever witnessed others being shunned? How did you respond?

2. Do you agree with the author that reverse shunning is on the rise in the church? If you do, share instances you have seen of this, i.e. people drifting from the church.

3. Discuss the effects of shunning on mission.

4. How in your own life have you experienced the "best of times and the worst of times" in the church?

5. How do you envision the future of the church in the United States, considering the decline in priestly personnel? How do you envision the world church?

(Part Three) Chapter 2

1. Do you agree with the author that it is "not my mission . . . it's God's mission"? Share your reflections on why this is or is not an important distinction.

2. Reflect on your sense of destiny. Reflect on the goals you have set to help further your destiny. Share your reflections with others.

3. Think of a lay adult whom you feel is engaged in mission. Share with others how you perceive this as mission.

(Part Three) Chapters 3 and 4

1. The story of Rita exemplifies some of the points made in this chapter:

Rita came to me for spiritual direction regularly one winter. She wanted to "improve her prayer life and figure out how to live a more Christian life." For weeks Rita spent part of our hour together deprecating herself, particularly her contribution to the church. Because of her work schedule, Rita couldn't participate in the current RENEW segment in her parish. Many of her friends were able to be part of the entire RENEW program, making Rita feel even more guilty about her lack of involvement. Earlier she had tried volunteering in a local soup kitchen but she found that experience so emotionally draining that she finally stopped—"after I got up the courage to drop out . . . I felt like such a failure," as she put it. Rita was a eucharistic minister in her parish, but that service seemed to reinforce her feelings of guilt. "I don't feel as if I *deserve* to be one of the distributors because I don't serve in other ways."

We had to juggle our appointments around Rita's job schedule, but when I inquired about her work, Rita always made short shrift of it and returned to her need to engage in more parish service to believe she really was a good Catholic Christian. One week I suggested to Rita that we spend the hour talking only about her work. With a sigh she began to tell me how she traveled two weeks a month to different settings to talk with groups about the value of nursing as a career. She also served as a paid consultant to various hospitals to assist them in dealing with the shortage of nursing personnel. It was a rigorous, taxing job, calling for much attention to the immediacy of the nursing situation in the United States through reading reports and writing reports. At times, Rita testified before various civic bodies regarding nursing needs. A single woman, Rita found she had little time or energy to spare for parish activities. "When I'm honest, I know my job and being with friends and saving some time for prayer are about all I can handle!"

"And the only way you can see yourself as a good Christian is through parish service?" I asked.

"Well, that's how everybody else at St. Malachy's seems to size up themselves as Christians," she replied.

Rita has "sized up herself." How would you size up Rita? Where do you see mission in her life? What asceticisms is Rita carrying? What advice would you give to Rita?

2. Name an asceticism you have carried in your life. Can you also name a celebration at the end of an asceticism you've experienced similar to the one described by the author at the end of the burden of paying for college? Describe this. What asceticisms might you have to bear if you became more deeply involved in mission? How do you feel about that?

3. In the church today some people think that lay people who are involved in church ministries make other lay people feel like second class citizens. Has that been your experience? How could the church respond to this dilemma?

4. How, in your church "place," could lay mission efforts be more vigorously affirmed? Dream of some dynamics for enabling this.

5. What mission needs do you see in your region? in the country? in the world? Which ones seem to call to you? How could you respond?

6. The author infers that direct formation of offspring by urging a Christian "disposition" and responsibilities can intimidate or thwart their eventual need to "put away" and to "break away." The formation she discovered most effective in regard to her daughters was the passion for the world that the daughters saw in their parents. Respond to this from your own experience. What passions does the younger generation see in you?

(Part Four) Chapter 1

1. A reflective exercise on place—texture and flavor.

While doing this exercise it is important to take your time and let a response emerge from within you rather than off the "top of the head." The following are questions to stimulate response: Is the texture and flavor of the place where you live ethnic? Is the flavor racial? Macho? Feminist? Conservative? Traditionalist? How do you feel about the textures and flavors you are naming?

Is the texture diversity? Are there rich and poor with a sizable gap in between? Educated and those lacking in schooling, with a gap in between? Crime-ridden in sections and secure in others? Religiously diverse?

Or is the texture of place homogenous? All middle class? All stricken with poverty? All Yuppie? All families? All singles?

Is the flavor politics? How does your "place" compare with the place called Massachusetts 8th? Where is politics in your place? How does this affect you?

As you begin to distill the texture or the flavor of the place where you live, stay with this for a while. Let examples or images or stories emerge with color and life.

Then you might want to compare your present place with the flavor and texture of other places you have lived as an adult, and, lastly, with the flavor and texture of the place(s) where you spent your growing up years.

Or you may want to begin there and work your way up to the present. But it is important to *stay* with each image that comes into your consciousness for some time, enough time to let its details, color, sounds flesh it out. If you do that you may find the reflection revealing something about *yourself* in relationship to that place and its people.

2. If my own mores, akin to a second skin, are difficult to perceive, how can I discern *between my mores and my religious values?* The following suggestions may seem indirect but, if followed, they can result in greater clarity about one's own formative processes.

Make a list of the "shoulds" to which you feel your parents subscribed. Let it sit on your bureau for a week and add to it as you remember instances from your childhood that revealed particular mores. At the end of the week review the list and discern which "shoulds" are still part of your life. Spend some time in reflection or prayer on how you feel about this. Discern what action you want to take in regard to it.

Or you may want to make a list of the behaviors and attitudes that would have been considered outrageous in your home and/or neighborhood while you were growing up. The next day make a list of the behaviors and attitudes that would be considered outrageous among the people with whom you work, with whom you socialize, with whom you worship today. Notice how the lists differ. Culling from the lists, you may then want to make up a list that best reflects *your* mores. Compare it with your religious values.

Another way to get at the "shoulds" that are operative in one's life is to ask your children or students to reveal their "shoulds." Which ones relate to religious values? Which ones are like yours?

3. The following is an inventory related to ownership. After each per-

son in a group completes it individually, the group might want to use the responses as a basis for discussions.

Who owned your home-place when you were a child?

Who owns your home-place now?

Within your home-place are there places of shared ownership, i.e. areas, rooms, yard? Are there places you can call "your own" (private areas)? Does everyone who lives in the home-place have these?

Who owns your workplace? Are there places of "shared ownership" within this place, i.e. cafeteria? Of individual "ownership," i.e. office, file cabinet, lockers? Is there any space in your workplace that's your own?

Who owns the places where you enjoy leisure?

How do you feel about the above ownerships? Do you wish that you owned more? Less?

What places do you own?

What places do you own but could easily relinquish?

What would you do if you no longer owned your home?

What places do you inhabit that are under shared ownership? Would you like more or less of these? How could you bring this about?

How do you feel about multinational ownership? How do you feel about foreign countries owning factories and hotels and land in the United States? Is this shared ownership? What benefits does it enable? What risks?

(Part Four) Chapter 2

1. Fredrick Turner suggests that it is important to "participate emotionally in your place of living." Why do you agree or disagree?

2. How do you participate emotionally in the region where you live? Are there other places that have emotional meaning to you? Are they shared places or privately owned?

3. Bachelard claims that the house protects daydreaming yet the daydream helps us to leave home. Does this match your experience? Discuss whether homes today enable daydreaming and how dreams "animate the nerves of the future."

4. If we are always reacting to what is "outside" of us, competing may become compulsive. If we respond from our interior being, we are apt to be more contemplative about life. Reflect on how these statements match your own experience. Share your insights with others.

5. Why is thinking with images valuable? How do you respond to the images that emerge in your life?

6. Name places that change you interiorly.

(Part Four) Chapter 3

1. How is the world generative to us?
2. Share your feeling about and experiences of the following:

- Shared space
- Places that you own
- Places that you resist
- Places you have lost
- Places that are healing

3. Discuss what the author means when she says that the Christian adult eventually should come to see others and not self at the center of his or her daydreams.

4. Share your experience of praying with an image.

5. Respond to the three images described in this chapter:

- Grass and Jesus putting the bent-bending people on their feet
- The world as a lost sheep
- The world as a nest created from the "inside"

6. In your perception how is the world as shared home? or an object given to humans within limitless permission to alter?

7. Cite some examples from your city or town, region or country, of the world as a shared home. Cite some examples from your city or town, region or country, of treating the world as an object to be limitlessly altered.

8. Share with others an instance when you felt yourself "melting into the world."

9. The author has suggested that, in friendship and family, responsibility and authority emerge from intimacy. She also suggests this as a model for mission from our intimacy with the world as a shared home. Reflect on why you agree or disagree with this view. Share your insights.

(Part Four) Chapter 4

1. In an earlier chapter, we read Gaston Bachelard's insight about the house. The most important function of the house is to protect daydreaming, he claimed. But it is through daydreaming that we are eventually drawn from the house to enter the world because daydreams "animate the nerves of the future."

The analogy may be apropos of the church. The church is sometimes thought of as God's house. An important task for this house is to protect daydreaming about the kingdom of God. Eventually those who make this house a home for their faith are drawn from the house by their dreams and enter the rest of the world to engage in the mission of co-creating with God.

Respond to this analogy. Has this been your experience? How could it become a reality if it has not?

2. This chapter emphasized the *proclamation with the church* phase of mission. We find examples of this in the Acts of the Apostles and in the Pauline epistles. The author contends that only with the proclamation stage does the mission cycle reach its full spiritual potential.

Share with others the times you have been able to tell your mission stories in the church. Consider how more opportunities for this could become a reality.

3. Share your own mission stories. How could you proclaim them within the church?

BIBLIOGRAPHY

Books

Auer, Alphonse, ed.
The Christian and the World—Readings in Theology
P. J. Kenedy & Sons
Out of print but a classic. Articles written during Vatican Council II by
Auer, Rahner, Metz, Chenu et al.

Bachelard, Gaston
The Poetics of Space. Beacon Press 1969
The Poetics of Reverie. Beacon Press 1971

Barry, Joseph and Dereviany, John, ed.
Yuppies Invade My House at Dinnertime
Big River Publications 1987

Barry, William, S.J.
God and You.
Paulist Press 1987

Boyer, Ernest
Finding God at Home
Harper and Row 1987

Brooks, Rosalind and Christopher
Popular Religion in the Middle Ages
Thames and Hudson 1984

Caprio, Betsy and Hedberg, Thomas
Coming Home—A Handbook for Exploring the Sanctuary Within
Paulist Press 1986

Canonical Standards in Labor Management Relations
Canon Law Society of America
Catholic University of America Washington, D.C.

Carr, Anne
Transforming Grace—Christian Tradition and Women's Experience

Harper and Row 1988

Castelli, James, and Gallup, George Jr.
The American Catholic People
Doubleday 1987

*Christian Ecology: Building an Environmental Ethic for the Twenty-First
 Century*
PO Box 1405, San Francisco CA

Coleman, John, S.J.
An American Strategy
Paulist Press

Combs, Stephen
In the Church and in the World
Chicago Catholic Charities Research Services

Conner, Patrick
Looking at Art: People at Work
Atheneum 1982

Coordinating Parish Ministries 1988
Chicago Catholic (Diocesan Newspaper)
Excellent description of pastoral ministry and the kinds of pastoral min-
 istries that should be available to lay parishioners

Coughlan, Peter
The Hour of the Laity: Exploring Christifideles Laici
Bloomington: Meyer Stone Books

Daly, Gabriel, O.S.A.
*Transcendence and Immanence: A Study in Catholic Modernism and
 Integralism*
Clarenden Press 1980

Doohan, Leonard
John Paul II and the Laity Le Jacq Publishing Inc. 1984
The Laity: A Bibliography Michael Glazier Inc. 1987
The Lay Centered Church Winston Press 1984
Laity's Mission in the Local Church: Setting a New Direction Harper and
 Row 1986

Grass Roots Pastors Harper and Row 1989

Donders, Joseph
On the Path to Peace—Advent Scripture Reflections
Twenty-Third Publications 1988

Early Warning Manual Against Plant Closings
Midwest Center for Labor Research Chicago
(The Center also presents parish workshops on topic)

Ehrlich, Gretel
The Solace of Open Spaces
Viking 1986

Everett, Melissa
Breaking Ranks
Stories of men who have left careers in the military-industrial complex
New Society Publishers 1988

Fahey, Joseph and Armstrong, Richard, ed.
*The Peace Reader: Essential Readings on War, Justice, Non-Violence
    and World Order*
Paulist Press 1987

Fewell, Rebecca and Vadsay, Patricia
*Families of Handicapped Children; Needs and Supports Across the Life
    Span*
Pro-Ed 1986

Fiorenza, Elisabeth Schussler
In Memory of Her
Crossroad 1986

Fishman, Robert
Bourgeois Utopias—The Rise and Fall of Suburbia
Basic Books 1989

Foley, Nadine, O.P., ed.
Preaching and the Non-Ordained
Liturgical Press 1983

Fowler, James
Becoming Adult, Becoming Christian
Harper and Row 1987

Gallagher, Maureen
Spirituality of Parenting
Sheed and Ward 1988

Hayner, Don and McNamee, Tom
Streetwise Chicago
Loyola University Press 1987

Greeley, Andrew and McManus, William
Catholic Contributions
Thomas More Press 1987

Gremillion, Joseph and Leege, David
Notre Dame Study of Catholic Parish Life
University of Notre Dame

Haughton, Rosemary
The Passionate God
Paulist Press 1981

Hellwig, Monika
Christian Women in a Troubled World
Paulist Press 1985

Hoffman, Virginia
Birthing a Living Church
Crossroad 1988

Hoge, Dean
Future of Catholic Leadership Sheed & Ward 1987
Converts, Dropouts, Returnees The Pilgrim Press 1981

Holland, Joseph and Henriot, Peter, S.J.
Social Analysis
Dove Communications 1986
Holland, Joseph
Creative Communion—Toward a Spirituality of Work

Paulist Press 1989

Johnson, May Lee (with Ann Barsanti)
Coming Up on the Rough Side: A Black Catholic Story
Pillar Books 1988

Kennedy, Eugene
Tomorrow's Catholics/Yesterday's Church
Harper & Row 1988

Kornhaber, Arthur M.D. and Woodward, Kenneth L.
Grandparents/Grandchildren: The Vital Connection
Anchor Press–Doubleday 1985

Kritsberg, Wayne
The Adult Children of Alcoholics Syndrome
Health Communications, Inc. 1988

Lane, Belden
*Landscape of the Sacred—Geography and Narrative in American Spiritu-
    ality*
Paulist Press 1988

Larson, Jeanne and Micheels-Cyrus, Madge, ed.
Seeds of Peace: A Catalogue of Quotations
New Society Publications 1988

Leckey, Dolores
A Little Book: Practical Spirituality Sheed and Ward 1987
The Ordinary Way—A Family Spirituality Crossroad 1982

Lindemann, James E., and Lindemann, Sally J.
*Growing Up Proud: A Parent's Guide to the Psychological Care of Chil-
    dren with Disabilities*
Warner Books 1988

Lonergan, Anne and Richards, Caroline, ed.
Thomas Berry and the New Cosmology
Twenty-Third Publications 1987

Maurer, Daphne and Maurer, Charles
The World of the Newborn

Basic Books 1988

Mcgoldrick, Monica, Pearce, John K., Giordano, Joseph
Ethnicity and Family Therapy
The Guilford Press 1985

Mollat, Michael
The Poor in the Middle Ages
Yale University Press 1986
An excellent survey of attitudes toward the poor engendered by the
church and of lay efforts to assist those who were indigent.

Monette, Maurice, O.M.I.
Kindred Spirits: The Bonding of Religious and Laity
Sheed & Ward 1987

No Room in the Marketplace—The Health Care of the Poor
The Catholic Health Association of the U.S.
St. Louis, MO

Noble, Thomas and Contreni, John J.
Religion, Culture and Society in the Early Middle Ages
Medieval Institute Publications, 1987

O'Brien, David
Faith and Friendship Catholicism in the Diocese of Syracuse
Diocese of Syracuse 1987
A valuable and readable history of a diocese that reveals the history of a
people.

Occhiogrosso, Peter
Once a Catholic
Houghton Mifflin 1987

O'Collins, Gerald, S.J.
Fundamental Theology
Paulist Press 1981

O'Malley, John W., S.J.
Tradition and Transition: Historical Perspectives on Vatican II
Michael Glazier Inc. 1989

Ordinary Christians in a High Tech World Word Books 1986

Parks, Sharon
The Critical Years: The Young Adult and the Search for a Faith To Live By
Harper and Row 1986

Pobal: The Laity in Ireland
Columbia Press 1986

Powers, Mala
Follow the Year—A Celebration of Family Holidays
Harper and Row 1985

Rahner, Karl, S.J.
Christian in the Marketplace Sheed & Ward 1966
Mission and Grace, Vol. 1 Sheed and Ward 1963

Richard, Lucien, O.M.I., ed.
Vatican II: The Unfinished Agenda
Paulist Press 1987

Rifkin, Paul, ed.
The God Letters
Warner Books 1986

Rothberg, Dianne S. and Cook, Barbara Ensor
Part-time Professional
Acropolis Books, Ltd. 1985

Ruether, Rosemary Radford and McLaughlin, Eleanor, ed.
Women of Spirit—Female Leadership in Jewish and Christian Tradition
Simon and Schuster 1979

Rufo, Beth Ann and Rufo, Raymond
Called and Gifted—Lay Spirituality in Ordinary Life
Pillar Books 1988

Rybcynski, Witold
Home—A Short History of an Idea
Viking 1987

Traces historically the connection between the development of intimacy in the home and the design and increasing comfort of the home.

Sofield, Loughlin, S.T. and Hermann, Brenda, M.S.B.T.
Developing the Parish as a Community of Service
Human Development 1984

Strasser, Stephen
Phenomenology of Feeling
Duquesne University Press 1977

Swidler, Leonard and O'Brien, Herbert
A Catholic Bill of Rights
Sheed and Ward 1988

Swift, Helen, S.N.D. and Oppenheim, Frank, S.J.
The Mustard Seed Process
Paulist Press 1986

Thompson, Charlotte E., M.D.
Raising a Handicapped Child—A Helpful Guide for Parents of the Physically Disabled
Ballantine Books 1986

Ulanov, Ann
Picturing God
Cowley Publications 1987

Walesa, Lech
A Way of Hope—An Autobiography
Henry Holt 1987

Weaver, Mary-Jo
New Catholic Women
Harper and Row 1984

Westley, Dick
Redemptive Intimacy
Twenty-Third Publications 1985

Whelan, Joseph, S.J.
The Spirituality of Friedrich von Hugel

Newman Press 1971

Whitehead, Evelyn Eaton and Whitehead, James D.
Seasons of Strength: New Visions of Christian Maturing Doubleday 1984
The Emerging Laity: Returning Leadership to the Community of Faith
    Doubleday 1986
A Sense of Sexuality Doubleday 1989

Whyte, William and Kathleen
Making Mondragon: The Growth and Dynamics of the Worker Coopera-
    tive Couples
ILR Press 1988

Wolff, Pierre
May I Hate God?
Paulist Press 1979

Young Adult Ministry Resources
USCC 1988

*   *   *

FICTION AND AUTOBIOGRAPHY. The following books reveal in
    some way the impact of formation, particularly during early years.

Catholic Girls
Kit Reed
Ballantine Books 1987

Final Payments
The Company of Women
Mary Gordon

Holy Pictures
Clare Boylan
Penguin Books 1984

Household Saints
Francine Prose
St. Martin's Press 1981

An Interrupted Life: The Diaries of Etty Hillesum 1941–43
Washington Square Press 1985

Loving Kindness
Anne Roiphe
Warner Books 1987

Monkeys
Susan Minot
Washington Square Press 1986

Pastoral Letters, Articles, Newsletters and Videos

Between the Times. A musical theatre presentation on video that dramatizes the NCCB pastoral on the U.S. economy. By Chicago Call to Action. Credence Cassettes.

Breakthrough. Quarterly publication. Global Education Associates, New York, NY.

Centering. Newsletter. The Center for the Ministry of the Laity. Andover Newton Theological School, Newton, MA.

Chicago Studies. April 1989 issue: *Religion in the Marketplace* St. Mary of the Lake Seminary, Chicago, IL.

"City Kids—Three Boston Memoirs." *Boston College Magazine.* Summer 1988.

"Economic Justice for All: Catholic Social Teaching and the U.S. Economy." *Origins.* Vol. 16, No. 24, Nov. 27, 1986. NC Documentary Service.

"Episcopal Election: The Right of the Laity." Edward Kilmartin, S.J. *Concilium* 137, 1980.

Firmament: The Quarterly of Christian Ecology, The North American Conference on Christianity and Ecology, 309 E. Front St., Traverse City, MI 49684.

The Forest Letter. Newsletter. Ed Hays and the Community of Shanti-vanan. Easton, KS.

Formation of the Laity. Pontifical Council for the Laity. Vatican City 1987.

Gifts. Newsletter of the NCCB Secretariat for the Laity. NCCB Washington, DC.

"Hispanics in New York: An Archdiocesan Survey." Joseph P. Fitzpatrick, *America,* March 12, 1983.

Homeless and Housing. U.S.C.C. Publishing Service.

Initiatives: In support of the laity's vocation in and to the world. Newsletter. National Center for the Laity. Chicago, IL.

Inside Habitat World. Newsletter. Habitat for Humanity. Americus, GA.

Laity Exchange Ecumenical Newsletter. Laity Information Program of the Vesper Society. San Leandro, CA.

"Lay Participation in the Apostolate of the Hierarchy." Edward Kilmartin, S.J. *Jurist* 41, 1981, Catholic University of America.

Salt for justice-hungry Christians. Magazine with lay focus. Claretian Publications, Chicago, IL.

Segundo Encuentro Nacional de Pastoral: Conclusions on Evangelization. Committee on Evangelization, 3031 4th St., Washington, DC 20017.

THE WAY. January 1989 Issue: *Creation Centered Spirituality* Heythrop College London, England. "Why the Housing Scarcity: An Analysis." *RENEW UPDATE.* Religious Network for the Equality of Women. NY.

We Are God's Priestly People. Bishop Howard J. Hubbard. October 1988. The Evangelist (Diocesan Newspaper). Albany, NY.

Working Catholic. Newsletter. Center on Work and Christian Life. Genesco, IL.

Working for Economic Justice. Newsletter on the Pastoral Letter on the U.S. Economy. Office of Implementation, USCC.

"You are a royal priesthood." Archbishop William D. Borders. Pastoral

letter with a mission and lay focus. June 1988. The Catholic Review (Diocesan Newspaper), Baltimore, MD.

Programs

BOSTON LABOR GUILD
Quincy, MA 02170

Campion Renewal Center
Days of Reflection for Nurses
Weston, MA

CARING IN THE MARKETPLACE
Christian Laity of Chicago
Chicago, IL

CENTER FOR BUSINESS, RELIGION & PROFESSIONS
Pittsburgh Theological Seminary
Pittsburgh, PA

CENTER FOR CORPORATE PUBLIC INVESTMENT
Corporate Public Involvement
Washington, DC

CHRISTIAN VALUES IN THE WORKPLACE PROGRAM
Tom Caruso, Parish Social Ministry
2838 E. Burnside, Portland, OR 97214

THE CHRISTOPHERS
12 East 48th St., New York, NY 10017
Celebrating its 40th anniversary year of affirming the value of lay life and mission, The Christophers produce books, pamphlets and television programming of appeal to grass-roots laity.

The Community of St. Egidio
Piazza St. Egidio, 3/a 00153, ROMA, ITALIA

THE CROSSING COMMUNITY
St. Louis, MO

Crossroads Center for Faith & Work
Chicago, IL

DIOCESAN MINISTRIES INSTITUTE
Center for Adult Formation & Spirituality

Saginaw, MI

FINDING GOD IN DAILY WORK-PROGRAM FOR INTEGRATED SPIRITUALITY
Romero Center
4001 W. McNochols Rd. Detroit, MI 48221

HOLY NAME HOUSING CORP.
Omaha, NE

ITEST
Institute for Theological Encounter with Science & Technology
St. Louis, MO

JOB SEARCH SUPPORT GROUP
St. Thomas More Parish
San Antonio, TX

LAITY NETWORK TO HELP PEOPLE ENGAGED IN LAY MINISTRY
United Church of Christ Conference
Hartford, CT

LAWYERS ENCOUNTER CHRIST
The Cenacle
Chicago, IL

THE LAY ACADEMY
San Francisco, CA

LAY MINISTRY PROJECT
1309 Merchant Lane
McLean, VA 22101

LIFE AFTER FIVE
St. Mary's Church
Rochester, NY

NATIONAL ASSOCIATION FOR LAY MINISTRY
Mesa, AZ

NATIONAL CENTER FOR THE LAITY
Chicago, IL

NCCW
National Council of Catholic Women
Washington, DC 20005

Organize for Social Justice in the Workplace
AFL-CIO
Washington, DC

PARISH SOCIAL MINISTRY: AN EMPOWERMENT PROCESS
Catholic Charities/Social Concerns Office
Diocese of Joliet, IL

Parishes & Changing Neighborhoods
Parish Life Office
Diocese of Cleveland

Rainbows for All God's Children
Peer support group organization for single-parent family children
913 Margret St.
Des Plaines, IL 60010

SHED
Self Help Employ Development
Sponsored by Catholic Charities, Chicago

SUPPORT GROUP FOR BUSINESS & PROFESSIONAL WOMEN
The Cenacle
Chicago, IL

SUPPORT GROUP FOR PUBLIC SCHOOL TEACHERS
Maryknoll Procuro
745 W. Adams Blvd.
Los Angeles, CA 90007

TRINITY MINISTRIES CENTER
Stirling, NJ

UNION OF CONCERNED SCIENTISTS
Cambridge, MA

WORD
Parish-based program of adult formation and theological education
Institute of Pastoral Studies, Loyola University
Chicago, IL